Pre-Gay L.A.

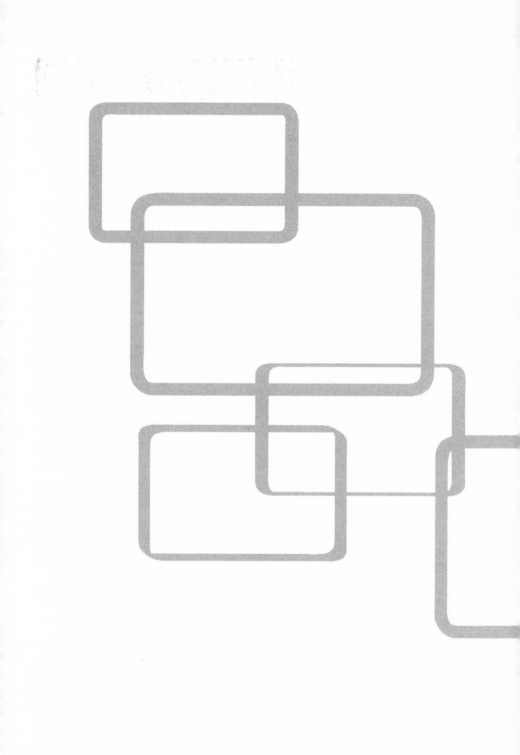

Pre-Gay
L.A.

A Social History of the
Movement for
Homosexual Rights

C. TODD WHITE

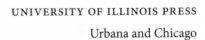

UNIVERSITY OF ILLINOIS PRESS

Urbana and Chicago

Library of Congress Cataloging-in-Publication Data
White, C. Todd
Pre-gay L.A. : a social history of the movement
for homosexual rights / by C. Todd White.
p. cm.
Includes bibliographical references and index.
ISBN 978-0-252-03441-1 (cloth : alk. paper) —
ISBN 978-0-252-07641-1 (pbk. : alk. paper)
1. Gay rights—California—Los Angeles—History.
2. Gay liberation movement—California—Los Angeles—History.
3. Gays—California—Los Angeles—History.
4. ONE Institute of Homophile Studies.
5. Los Angeles (Calif.)—History.
I. Title.
HQ76.8.U5W46   2009
323.3'2640979494—dc22   2008041146

Contents

To Mark Thompson,
who called me to the cause.

Preface

The anthropologist engages in peculiar work. He or she tries to understand a different culture to the point of finding it to be intelligible regardless of how strange it seems in comparison with one's own background. This is accomplished by attempting to experience the new culture from within, living in it for a time as a member, all the while maintaining sufficient detachment to observe and analyze it with some objectivity. This peculiar posture—being inside and outside at the same time—is called participant observation. It is a fruitful paradox, one that has allowed anthropologists to find sense and purpose within a society's seeming illogical and arbitrary customs and beliefs. . . . Working with one's own society, and more specifically with one's own ethnic and familial heritage, is perilous, and much more difficult. Yet it has a certain validity and value not available in other circumstances.
—Barbara Myerhoff, *Number Our Days,* p. 18

THIS BOOK, part ethnobiography and part social history, is the result of my eight-year exploration of the origins and history of the movement for homosexual rights, which originated in Los Angeles, California, in the late 1940s and continues today. My ambition was to construct a detailed and accurate accounting of the history of this movement as manifested through the emergence of four related organizations: Mattachine; ONE, Incorporated; the Homosexual Information Center (HIC); and the Institute for the Study of Human Resources (ISHR), which is currently doing business as ONE, Incorporated (the two organizations having legally merged in December 1995). As such, this is a chronicle of how one clandestine voluntary association emerged as a powerful political force that spawned several other organizations over a period of more than fifty years.

The story of the founding, ascension, and dissolution of the original Mattachine Foundation and of ONE, Incorporated, has been published several times, most famously by John D'Emilio (1983), Eric Marcus (1992, 2002), and Jonathan Ned Katz (1992). Although these histories have been properly lauded and deservedly serve as bedrocks for the study of the origins of the contemporary lesbian and gay movement, they suffer from two significant disadvantages. The first is a lack of proximity. None of these scholars spent substantial time perusing the original corporate records of the early Mattachine or ONE, Incorporated. Second, some of these scholars interviewed only one or two of the key people involved, thereby obtaining only a cursory understanding of the underlying complexities and nuances—the philosophical and emotional *convection*—rumbling beneath the fissures and fusions that repeatedly manifested in the California-based organizations during the first thirty years of the movement. Other scholars interviewed many of the movement's pioneers but were unable to spend the time necessary to cross-check and validate the perspectives they had heard. The biases of the subjects have thus often become the biases of the scholar, and slanted or fragmentary information—even falsehoods—are still being perpetuated, however unwittingly. For example, gay historian Charles Kaiser, in his widely read *The Gay Metropolis* (1997, 100–101), reports that the Mattachine Society published *ONE Magazine*, and this error is frequently repeated in the lesbian, gay, bisexual, and transgendered (LGBT) press. The ethnographic approach, with its emphasis on extended life-history interviews and years of participant observation, is highly effective in teasing out "reality"—not necessarily to prove one false and the other correct so much as to first reveal and then explicate the differing truths expressed in historical narratives and documents in an attempt to reconcile them.

This study emerged from two independent research projects. Soon after moving to Los Angeles in the fall of 1998, I set out to learn more about the life history of Jim Kepner. The result of that study, a short documentary film honoring Kepner that I directed and edited for a course in documentary filmmaking, was subsequently broadcasted by Trojan Vision in December 1999. The second project began when Dale Jennings died on May 11, 2000. HIC president Jim Schneider and University of Southern California (USC) professor Walter L. Williams recruited me to help distribute a press release and assist with Jennings's memorial service, the first public event hosted by ONE Institute and Archives in its newly acquired facility near the USC campus, at 909 West Adams Boulevard. I continued to learn more about Jennings and was surprised to discover that he was one of the original founders of Mattachine, the first successful homosexual organization in the United States. I had read of Mattachine but only in association with Harry Hay, who is frequently referred to as the "founder" or "father" of the gay rights movement (see esp. Bullough 2002b; Hay 1996; Roscoe 1996a; Thompson 1987; Timmons 1990). In the fall of 1952, Jennings helped to create the magazine

ONE, the nation's first periodical openly dedicated to homosexual issues, which began publication in January 1953. I continued to study Jennings in order to contribute a chapter for a book edited by Vern Bullough (2002a) and published by Harrington Park Press (Haworth) that profiled several of the pre-Stonewall pioneers, many of whom, I was surprised to find, had lived in my vicinity and also matriculated at USC.

Dale Jennings is commonly listed in the indices of gay history books such as those by D'Emilio (1983, 62–63, 70–71, 73, 80, 87), Katz (1992, 411–16), and Marcus (2002, 19, 24), but actual references to him are often pointed and brief. He is credited as one of the founders of the Mattachine Society and a follower of Harry Hay. After reading Stuart Timmons's biography *The Trouble with Harry Hay: Founder of the Modern Gay Movement* (1990), I concluded that Jennings was the black sheep of the Mattachine flock who otherwise gathered around the staff of Hay with the other glazed-eyed sheep. Although Hay is held aloft in the text as the founder of the movement, the lives and achievements of others, Jennings in particular, are unfairly distorted and usually diminished. There can hardly serve a better example of "great man" history than Timmons's book on Hay. Unfortunately, I used this text as a basis for my published profile on Jennings (White 2002a) and was dismayed to find out later that several "facts" I had repeated were problematic. Only late in my dissertation study (completed in May 2005) did I discover Jennings's letters to Slater regarding his frustration with Timmons's book. In this frank correspondence, Jennings complained of being the only Mattachine founder Timmons failed to interview and lamented the way he was represented. Jennings was hardly the Judas of Mattachines. Indeed, many have called him a hero. Sexologist Vern L. Bullough lauded Jennings as the "Rosa Parks of the Gay Rights Movement" for prevailing in the first court case in the United States where a man admitted in court to being a homosexual and still successfully fought charges of lewd conduct in a public place (2002a, 7). Riding the fame following the trial, Jennings next helped to launch *ONE* and to establish ONE, Incorporated.

As I learned more about Jennings and his accomplishments, I began to realize that the organizations he helped to establish significantly impacted legal policies not only in Los Angeles but also across the United States. The accomplishments of these organizations have affected the lives of most of us living in America today. Yet, despite their notable achievements, it seems that other events—most notably the famous Stonewall rebellion in Greenwich Village in June 1969—have overshadowed the history of these West Coast organizations, leaving many of those who fought and won significant battles for the movement on the historical sidelines, largely forgotten by the new generation of scholars of LGBT history that has emerged in the wake of the gay liberation movement. I hope that through this endeavor, Los Angeles pioneers such as Jennings will be more properly remembered.

Primary Consultants

Although I have conferred with many people through the construction of this history, two have served as my primary advisers and consultants throughout. The first is Jim Schneider, whom I first met at Jim Kepner's memorial service on May 22, 1998. Schneider and I developed an immediate rapport when we discovered that we both hailed from Nebraska. Soon after my move to Los Angeles later that year, I began to see him regularly as we labored with John O'Brien and Walter Williams to prepare the facility that was soon to house ONE Institute and Archives. Now in his seventies, Schneider is deaf in one ear and speaks in a slow, deliberate manner, so one needs patience when working with him. For those who do listen, Schneider's advice is sound, grounded in decades of experience in business and life. Although his collared shirts and polyester slacks may belie his agrarian past, Schneider still works from dawn to dusk, and his large, rugged hands—like those famously described by Sherwood Anderson—still seem ready-made for labor and prepared to brace anyone near who should fall.

My second primary consultant is Billy Glover, whom I first met over the Internet in 1999 soon after ONE Institute and Archives supporter Ernie Potvin died and I began answering ONE Institute's e-mail in his place. Initially I found Glover to be a strangely prolific man from Louisiana who sent out between six and twelve e-mails a day to numerous gay organizations and friends: he forwarded every single one to me, and I dutifully archived them. By the end of the year, I had received hundreds of messages (to date there are thousands) and through Glover's e-mails had made dozens of connections with fellow activists like Jeanne Barney, Wayne Dynes, Susan Howe, Aristide Laurent, and Tony Sanchez (a pseudonym). Glover was well-connected—and very much a team player. He became a dedicated soldier for *ONE Magazine* a few months after Schneider arrived on the scene in 1960. After Don Slater's death in 1997, Glover determined that none of the movement's pioneers would be forgotten by history. From his remote location in Bossier City, Louisiana, he still visits his local public library daily to send and receive e-mails and check on the progress of the movement. "Things sure have changed," he often muses in his deep southern drawl, with a slow, knowing nod and optimistic grin.

I have been privileged to hear Schneider and Glover share many fond memories of their adventures as participatory custodians of the homosexual rights movement. They are justly proud to have participated in meetings at all of ONE's locations. Glover recalls the excitement of picketing the *Los Angeles Times* and Fort MacArthur, and he played a key organizational role for the motorcade in 1966 about homosexuals and the military, appearing afterward on television shows hosted by Regis Philbin and Louis Lomax. Schneider often speaks of his attempt to reconcile the two factions of ONE after the 1965 division and of his role in helping to defend schoolteacher Don Odorrizi, his lover's colleague who was a victim of undue influence by the Bloomfield School District. Schneider and Glover have worked shoulder-to-shoulder with many of the great Los Angeles activists, most notably Vern and Bonnie Bullough, Joe and Jane Hansen, and Harry Hay and John Burnside. They both continue to support HIC today, working with Jeanne Barney, Susan Howe, John Richards, and others to keep Slater's Homosexual Information Center going.

Methods

When HIC's long-standing president, Don Slater, died on Valentine's Day 1997, Jim Schneider took his place and inherited over two hundred fifty boxes of papers, books, magazines, newspapers, bills, and thousands of old folders stuffed with fragments of the movement's ephemeral history. I had completed my initial research project on Jennings when Schneider and Billy Glover, HIC's vice president, asked me to help sort through these materials. I agreed to help, and this book is a result of what we discovered.

As we began sorting through HIC's history, I likened the process to my father's occupation, field archaeology. I found prior experience with the process of excavation helpful because it made the task ahead seem feasible: it could be tackled one piece, section, or "feature" at a time. The first trick was to sort boxes and compile an inventory, which meant that each box had to be opened and its contents listed on the side. Then Schneider and I, with a few volunteers, arranged the contents onto bookcases according to topic, the categories being roughly thus: books, magazines, newspapers yet to clip, files, and office supplies. Sometimes we had to shuffle the contents of the boxes to fit these categories, but this was often unnecessary since Slater had left the archives in good order.

We evaluated the books and, thanks to bookcases donated by HIC board member Joseph Hansen, were able to sort them into discrete sections: art, poetry, fiction, theater, history, social sciences, natural sciences, women's studies, psychology, anthropology, philosophy, and religion. Thanks to Slater's meticulous records, we were able to figure out which books were part of the original library of ONE, Incorporated, the nation's first archives dedicated to homosexuality, and we began to create an inventory of those materials and to set them aside, when discovered, for special archiving at California State University, Northridge (CSUN) and other collections. HIC's database manager, John Richards, created a FileMaker Pro database in which these titles are being cataloged and their provenance recorded. Through the assistance of other volunteers, the library is being virtually reconstructed and is now available on the Web at www.outhistory.org/wiki/Blanch_M._Baker_Memorial_Library.

As I discovered key historical records such as bylaws and other official government documents, I scanned them into a desktop computer and created and archived two files: a high-resolution graphic for purposes of reproduction and a second low-resolution image to post on the Internet. I created a Web site for HIC, *Tangents Online*, located at www.tangentgroup.org. Although this seems like a lot of work, having key documents on the Web frequently facilitated my research while at the same time made the materials accessible to others. Creating the Web site was also one way I could serve my consultants, giving them something of lasting value as they helped further my career as a cultural anthropologist interested in applying anthropological methods toward social and historical purposes. Recently, many of these materials have been posted on a Web site created by Jonathan Ned Katz and hosted by the Center for Lesbian and Gay Studies (CLAGS). These materials may be found at www.outhistory.org.

In deciding which documents were most significant for my endeavor, I kept a few research questions in mind: After over fifteen years of progress and significant victories, why did ONE, Incorporated, divide in the spring of 1965? What motivated Don Slater and his band of rebels to confiscate the entire office and move it to Cahuenga Boulevard, and why were Dorr Legg and his faction never able to regain control over those materials? The answer that I was first given, that it was simply a vitriolic conflict between two power-hungry and obstinate leaders, seemed unconvincing. I suspected there was more involved than a personality conflict: surely there must have been some deep-seated ideological conflict that pushed the organization toward fission. The answer, I was certain, would be found in the archives of the surviving aspects of the organization: ONE, Incorporated (now legally merged with ISHR), and HIC. But before I could start drawing conclusions, I had to begin by piecing together the sequence of events of this complicated and protracted social drama while getting a better idea of the life histories and motivations of the key players.

Acknowledgments

THIS HAS BEEN a collaborative—and thereby corroborative—endeavor, and so it is appropriate that I introduce with gratitude those who have made this work possible. I am grateful to Walter L. Williams, Ernie Potvin, Jim Schneider, Vern L. Bullough, Billy Glover, Joseph Hansen, Reid Rasmussen, John O'Brien, and Mark Thompson for recruiting me to the (local) cause and providing encouragement and support through the duration of the project. Paul D. Cain has been more than generous in providing transcripts of interviews that he conducted in Los Angeles and for the time he spent copyediting an early draft of this entire manuscript. I am grateful as well to my advisers in the Anthropology Department at USC who allowed me to change the original subject of my research when this opportunity presented itself. I could not have accomplished this study if not for the steadfast friendship, trust, and confidence of my dissertation chair, G. Alexander Moore. His textbook *Cultural Anthropology: The Field Study of Human Beings* (1998) has been of great value to this project, and it is from this text that I began to see the utility of casting historic events into the patterns of the social drama. Janet Hoskins has also been of great assistance. Her books *Biographical Objects* (1998) and *The Play of Time* (1993) have served as models and inspiration through their treatment of sacred objects and respect for the ephemeral. I would also like to thank Cheryl Mattingly, Nancy Lutkehaus, Andrei Simic, and Stephen O. Murray for their confidence and encouragement throughout the course of the dissertation process, and also Sarah Pratt, former dean of academic programs at USC, who lent a patient ear and provided generous support through difficult times. Dorothy Combs Hill assisted with the final copyediting of this book, for which every reader should be grateful. In these people I have indeed found a true community of scholars.

I could not have taken on the task without the assistance of many loyal and dedicated organizational volunteers, especially Stephen Allison, Megan Geier, Chuck Stewart, Sandi Meza, and Richard "Kitt" DeFatta for helping me sort through materials and organize HIC's books; Megan R. Geier for her many grueling and tedious hours of data entry; Joan Rivard for organizing the files and beautifying our office(s); and John Richards for creating and maintaining our database. A. J. Blythe and Andrew Madigan of Prime Crew Solutions in Rochester, New York, have done a great job of revamping the HIC Web site and helping to recast it in MediaWiki format. Tony Gardner, curator of special collections at Oviatt Library, CSUN, and Susan Curzon, dean of Oviatt Library, deserve special recognition for providing a safe and secure home for the HIC collection and for supporting the Vern and Bonnie Bullough Collection on Sex and Gender (http://library.csun.edu/spcoll/bullough). For the duration of this project, I was sustained through grants from ISHR, including four Hal Call Mattachine Scholar Awards (2000–2001 and again in 2006); two USC Lambda Alumni Association Research Awards (1999 and 2002); a Dissertation Research Fellowship Grant from the USC College of Letters, Arts, and Sciences (2003); and more than six years of teaching assistantships through the Department of Anthropology (1998–2003). More recently, undergraduate student workers at the State University of New York (SUNY) College at Brockport in New York have helped through transcriptions and data processing. My gratitude especially goes to Doug Feldman, Layla Arnold, Ben Levine, office secretary Jacquelyn Deats, and grants development director Colleen Donaldson. I am grateful as well to my partner, Ryan Reiss, for the love and music he has brought to my life.

No organization can survive for more than thirty years, as ONE and HIC have, without sound legal grounding. A corporation is as much a legal entity as it is a social phenomenon, making lawyers integral to the system. HIC owes a special thanks to past and present attorneys who have provided support and legal assistance: George Shibley, Eric Julber, Herb Selwyn, Edward Raiden, Stuart A. Simke, and Spencer Lugash have provided the legal advice necessary to navigate the organization through turbulent waters and difficult times. Most of these men have provided their assistance free of charge or at modest rates, providing support because they cared about the organization and wanted to see it survive. In F. G. Bailey's terms, this makes them part of the organization's core. I have repeatedly found that without the support of such white-knight lawyers, a small nonprofit organization will find it extremely difficult to survive, no matter how noble its cause.

Far more than I had anticipated, an applied approach to auto-ethnography required my familiarity with *the law*. Lawyers speak in a strange tongue; without a good legal interpreter, the novice anthropologist grasps for flotsam in a vast Latinate sea. It is through governments and laws that an organization obtains its fundamental structure: it is by no accident that politicians speak of "planks" and "platforms." Ship and sailing metaphors also lend themselves well to corporate vernacular, and I employ them often as "native" referents, borrowing from my sources and consultants themselves. While corporations truly float through the bureaucratic laws of finance and government policies, living people provide the forward motion and momentum necessary to keep sailing. Like any vessel, a corporation can founder: such factors as neglect, hostile action, and turbulent waters can sink it. Institutional renegades can still be forced to the plank with sabers pricking their backs. Minions can still mutiny, and corporate captains can still go down with their ships. The stakes are high in the corporate world, and the ultimate goal can often turn to short-term profit rather than long-term survival. Time is *always* of the essence.

Many of the first leaders of this movement passed away before I began my project, most notably my primary "protagonists" Don Slater, Dorr Legg, and Dale Jennings. Others, such as Harry Hay, Ernie Potvin, Fred Frisbie, Morris Kight, Joseph Hansen, and Vern Bullough have died during the course of the study. Many surviving consultants are past their seventieth birthdays. As I have seen my primary consultants age, the desire to finish this project has intensified, as has my sense of its value as a historical contribution. Through the writing process, they have since become my friends. In welcoming me into their friendship network—which I would call kindred—I have found a renewed sense of purpose and even a home away from home.

Abbreviations

Acronym	Full Name
ACLU	American Civil Liberties Union
CCOE	Citizens' Committee to Outlaw Entrapment
CRH	Council on Religion and the Homosexual
DOB	Daughters of Bilitis
EEF	Erickson Educational Foundation
GLF	Gay Liberation Front
GMMC	Gay Men's Medicine Circle
HIC	Homosexual Information Center
IGLA	International Gay and Lesbian Archives
ISHR	Institute for the Study of Human Resources
NACHO	North American Conference of Homophile Organizations
NPCHO	National Planning Conference of Homophile Organizations
OIQ	*ONE Institute Quarterly*
SOLGA	Society of Lesbian and Gay Anthropologists

Introduction

We believe that the homophile scholar can be the true eclectic, who by
the yardstick of his own different nature, and by the added objectivity of
his position as an outsider, discovers the boundaries of those philosophies
that naively try to measure all men by a single rule. He is therefore able to
find the good in each system, and the shortcomings of each. He is slave to
none of them—his initial bias is likely to release him from entrapment by
the smug and unnoticed conventional bias of many other students.

—Jim Kepner, *ONE Institute Quarterly*, Spring 1958

Some Key Influences on the
Homosexual Rights Movement

In an age where homosexuality is increasingly tolerated and discussed within North America's urban centers, it may be difficult to understand the apprehensions these men and women endured fifty years ago, fearful that the police or FBI might arrest them at any moment. The threat of a
raid, whether at a bar, a cruising ground, or even in one's home, was a very
real possibility. The police called the shots. Virtually no attorney would defend one accused of sexual perversion or subversion. The newspapers would
destroy one's reputation while the legal system sapped the accused of time
and resources. The police frequently used Mafia-like ruses and extortionary
tactics. It is no exaggeration to say that homosexuals legitimately feared the
very institutions that should have protected them.

"Lisa Ben" and Vice Versa

The first homosexual-themed publication on record to have been regularly
distributed in the United States was produced by "Lisa Ben," an anagram-
matic pseudonym for "Lesbian" that she adopted in the 1960s (Cain 2002,
13) in her office at RKO Studios in Los Angeles, beginning in June 1947.[1] This

was *Vice Versa*, subtitled *America's Gayest Magazine*, limited to ten copies distributed to a circle of friends who in turn were to pass it on to others (Cain 2002, 15; Licata 1978, 62–63; Marcus 2002, 9). Ben told historian Eric Marcus that she chose the title "because in those days our kind of life was considered a vice" (1992, 8). *Vice Versa* fluctuated from fourteen to twenty stapled pages consisting of play and film reviews, poetry, fiction, and pointed social commentary through a "Queer as It Seems" department. Ben stopped publishing *Vice Versa* in February 1948 after nine issues. She has attributed its demise to the lack of privacy in the office (Cain 2002, 15), to the sale of RKO to Howard Hughes (Marcus 2002, 12), and to her desire to pursue a more active social life, to "live [a lesbian lifestyle] rather than write about it" (Streitmatter 1995, 5).

Although copies of the "magazine" were scarce, their influence proved significant. "She and some of her readers gained confidence and identity through *Vice Versa* and went on to become active in the homophile organizations of the fifties," wrote Licata (1978, 63). Dorr Legg (writing as Marvin Cutler) noted, "There is little doubt that this truly remarkable earlier effort prepared the way for feminine participation in what has been called America's first successful homosexual magazine, and so has had a very considerable influence on publishing history in the United States" (1956, 91).

The Kinsey Report

The 1948 publication of Kinsey, Pomeroy, and Martin's *Sexual Behavior in the Human Male* is heralded as the dawn of the sexual revolution. It was comprehensive in scope, didactic, data rich, seemingly objective, and scientific. Kinsey was an entomologist at Indiana University. His study was grounded both in the social and biological sciences, being strongly influenced by biologists such as Frank Beach and anthropologists such as Ruth Benedict and Clellen Ford. One must appreciate these combined influences to understand Kinsey's approach and conclusions and why his work inspired hope and confidence in so many homosexual people. He believed that differences in human behavior should be attributed to heredity and biological factors, including the environment, psychological conditioning, and social pressures. Kinsey referred to Benedict's 1934 book *Patterns of Culture* and other anthropologists' works to evoke the notion of cultural relativism and to imply that such an approach could explain the great diversity of sexual behavior in human societies (1948, 202). He challenged psychologists to consider not only social deviance but also what psychological mechanisms are at play in those who more readily conform to social expectations. In other words, the normal deserved study as much as the peculiar.

Kinsey was not afraid to advocate on behalf of his research. This passage from his chapter on "Psychosexual Development in Health and Disease" is bold and daring. Kinsey does not hesitate to point his blaming finger toward the institutions of morality and the social treatment of sexual deviants. It merits citing at length because it well summarizes the pertinent issues around which the homosexual movement would concentrate during the next two decades:

> The enforcement of these fundamentally religious codes against the so-called sexual perversions has been accomplished, throughout the centuries, by attaching considerable emotional significance to them. This has been effected, in part, by synonymizing the terms clean, natural, normal, moral, and right, and the terms unclean, unnatural, abnormal, immoral, and wrong. Modern philosophers have added concepts of mental degeneracy and psychosexual immaturity to the synonymy. The emotions evoked by these classifications have been responsible for some of the most sordid chapters in human history. Rarely has man been more cruel against man than in the condemnation and punishment of those accused of the so-called sexual perversions. The punishment for sexual acts which are crimes against persons has never been more severe. The penalties have included imprisonment, torture, the loss of life or limb, banishment, blackmail, social ostracism, the loss of social prestige, renunciation by friends and families, the loss of position in school or in business, severe penalties meted out for convictions of men serving in the armed forces, public condemnation by emotionally insecure and vindictive judges on the bench, and the torture endured by those who live in perpetual fear that their non-conformant sexual behavior will be exposed to public view. These are the penalties which have been imposed on and against persons who have failed to adhere to the mandated custom. Such cruelties have not often been matched, except in religious and racial persecutions. (1948, 16–17)

The Kinsey report sold more than 200,000 copies within two months of its publication on January 5, 1948. In March of that year, a reviewer for *Time* magazine wrote that booksellers had not seen such a success since *Gone with the Wind*, and the *New York Times Book Review* dubbed it one of the most important works of the century (Archer 2002, 118). Homosexual people sensed they had a champion in Kinsey. Based on their own personal experiences, many were not surprised by his findings.

Ford, Beach, and Benedict: Patterns of Sexual Behavior

In 1951, Yale professors Clellen Ford and Frank Beach published *Patterns of Sexual Behavior*, which broke new ground in fields first sown by the Boasian anthropologists and largely left fallow since the maelstrom of the Second World War. Ford and Beach combined Benedict's philosophies of diverse cultural patterns with knowledge of American sexuality as articulated by Kinsey, using the discursive space his study had opened to explore the question of homosexuality from a cross-cultural and even cross-species perspective. In contrasting one hundred and ninety different societies, Ford and Beach found evidence of homosexual behavior in seventy-six of them. This was considered somewhat below actual levels of incidence because of severe sanctions against homosexuality in several of the cultures. In twenty-eight of the societies surveyed, homosexual encounters were frowned upon, occurrences being infrequent and best not discussed. However, in the majority, forty-nine societies, such activity was considered normal. In such societies, "the most common form of institutionalized homosexuality is that of the berdache or transvestite. The berdache is a male who dresses like a woman, performs women's tasks, and adopts some aspects of the feminine role in sexual behavior with male partners. Less frequently a woman dresses like a man and seeks to adopt the male sex role" (1951, 130).

Ford's training in anthropology and Beach's background in psychology combined to make *Patterns* an educated, thoughtful, and engaging book for a broad and intelligent audience. It showed what many homosexuals had suspected: that homosexual behavior was pervasive in all cultures and populations, yet homosexuals had been forgotten by history and silenced within most modern nations. Homosexuals lived isolated from one another and in such small numbers that they had been totally unaware of the potential magnitude of their cumulative influence. After World War II, though, the thought occurred to some, especially in port cities like Los Angeles, San Francisco, and New York, that if they could organize homosexuals into an *underground* social movement—as the Communists had—they could mobilize on behalf of homosexual rights while still protecting the privacy of their groups' members. This unifying act could be a source of great social power, giving hope to the downtrodden and inspiring pride where shame had been. In the early 1950s, the talk turned to action, and the first homosexual rights organizations were formed in Los Angeles in order, as D'Emilio put it, "to forge a unified movement of homosexuals ready to fight against their oppression" (1983, 64–66).

The Homosexual in America

In 1951, Greenberg published *The Homosexual in America: A Subjective Approach* by Donald Webster Cory (a pseudonym for Edward Sagarin chosen in homage to André Gide's Corydon). True to its title, the book was written from a homosexual's perspective. The book was a great success, published several times in the 1950s and translated into Spanish and French. It described what it was like to be a member of a persecuted and stigmatized group and argued for the rights of homosexual people. Cory did not dispute that homosexuality was a psychological malady, but he did ask for compassion and understanding from the greater community. He wrote in a personable style free from scientific jargon and statistics, although he did evoke the Kinsey report to support his conclusions. All told, *The Homosexual in America* provided a beacon of hope for many of the nation's homosexuals by suggesting that they were not alone and that, collectively, they formed a significant sociological minority on par with other ethnic groups (Cory, 1953, 4). It appealed to women as well as men. Barbara Gittings was so impressed with it that in 1955 she traveled from her home in Philadelphia to New York to meet the author. He referred her to ONE, so she traveled to Los Angeles the following year. There she was introduced to the San Francisco–based Daughters of Bilitis (DOB), and a decade later she was one of the most prominent lesbian activists in the nation and editor of the DOB magazine, *The Ladder* (Gallo 2006, 13). In a review of Cory's book published in the April 1952 edition of the *American Journal of Psychotherapy,* Dr. Harry Benjamin went so far as to suggest that it was society rather than the homosexual that was in need of treatment: "If adjustment is necessary, it should be made primarily with regard to the position the homosexual occupies in present-day society and society should more often be the patient to be treated rather than the invert" (Benjamin 1952, 357).

Cory was listed as contributing editor for *ONE* magazine from its first issue through the April–May issue of 1956 (vol. 4, no. 4). Although he contributed on occasion, his moniker was listed primarily for prestige, and he continued to live and work in New York during this time. He remained peripheral to the movement until he lost a bid to become president of the Mattachine Society of New York. From then on, he turned against the movement he had inspired, publishing such works as *Structure and Ideology in an Association of Deviants* (1966) and *Odd Man In: Societies of Deviants in America* (1969) in which, writing by his real name of Edward Sagarin, he promoted the notion that homosexuality was indeed a pathological illness, and the best homosexuals could do was to form self-help organizations similar to Alcoholics Anonymous (see esp. Murray 2002).

A Side Note: Why L.A.?

According to gay historian/journalist Jim Kepner, Los Angeles had not only a rich gay history, but also a rich prehistory. He noted that when a band of Mexican settlers called *pobladores* arrived in the Los Angeles area, they found the "berdache" role prevalent among the local Gabrielino Indians. Kepner noted that these people "wore clothing of the opposite gender and often took on a variety of magic social roles" (1998, 1). He had also heard of one strapping young *Californio* from Rancho San Antonio who appeared with an entourage of handsome men at the plaza area famously known as Olvera Street who "weren't interested" when the local "*señioritas* got the flutters" (Kepner 1998, 1). In the 1950s, the intrepid pioneers of the movement frequently met in the taverns of Olvera Street where Slater's Hispanic partner, Antonio Sanchez, was a star performer.

As for which gay bar first emerged in the Los Angeles area, Kepner wrote, "Each gay or lesbian I've talked to recalled a different bar in different years." In the downtown area, bars such as Maxwell's, the Biltmore, Numbers, the Crown Jewel, the Waldorf, and Jolie's were known homosexual hangouts for years. Bunker Hill had been a "gay neighborhood for decades, from at least the time when Stockton's sailors started building a fortification there in 1848" (Kepner 1998, 2). Other such neighborhoods were Echo Park, Silver Lake, Boyle Heights, and Westlake. West Hollywood, originally called Sherman, was "outside of the homophobic LAPD's reach," so it became a safe haven for many gays. Kepner reports that in 1943 there were "dozens of gay bars" in the vicinity of Hollywood and Cherokee, such as Bradley's. Hollywood itself "was our promenade," he wrote, "and there was still a good chance of seeing movie stars on the street—or in the cruising spots, where many big names got into trouble which the studio publicity departments had to hush up" (1998, 4).

None of this, however, explains why Los Angeles should have been the birthplace of Mattachine, ONE, and the movement for homosexual rights. Once, during an interview, Joseph Hansen admitted that he was perplexed as to why things began there. After all, New York was the cultural capital of the United States, and most of the large publishing houses resided there. But "Don Slater was *here*," Hansen stated, "and the rest of these guys—Harry

Hay and other, let us say, eccentric people—were here and were willing to bet their all on an impossible long shot."[2]

Wayne Dynes noted that there were both positive and negative factors involved. Positive factors included tolerance for various faiths and interracial relationships, "Bohemian" neighborhoods and the film colony, and a general "hedonistic" atmosphere. Negative factors included the ruthless vice squad and the prevalent psychotherapy movement that promulgated the belief that homosexuality was a psychosis that could be cured.[3]

The late sexologist and historian Vern L. Bullough played an important consulting role for this study. After the 1965 split of ONE, he became one of the few activists who stayed neutral and maintained positive relations with both factions. Bullough and his wife, Bonnie, were heterosexual outsiders who were accepted as allies by many in the movement, but not by all. Bullough agreed with Hansen that what happened in Los Angeles was a result of the confluence of the right people gathered together at the right time to fight for a common cause. At the same time, many more discreet homosexuals were affluent or could at least make a living relatively easily. California was a wealthy state in the 1950s and a giddy optimism wafted in the air, a hangover from victory in World War II. While Europe struggled to regain its ground, America moved forward, a land of renewed opportunity where nearly anything could happen with a little hard work, determination, and ingenuity. Bullough repeatedly emphasized economic factors and also pointed out that many of the full-time activists, such as Slater, Legg, Wolf, and Corbin, could not have dedicated so much time to the cause if not for loving partners who supported them financially.

Of course, there were many homosexuals in Los Angeles, especially in the movie industry. Bullough pointed out that many of those who migrated to Los Angeles, or stayed here after the war, had no families. They were free, in a sense, to make their own identity and begin to reform traditional bonds of friendship and kinship. "There is always some moving, but there was a massive number of people moving here then, as there is now again," he commented during what was to be my final interview with him at his home in Westlake Village,[4] and many of these newcomers sought partners. Those looking for a different social venue than the bar scene followed the address in ONE's masthead directly to ONE's doorstep. Like intrepid pilgrims, budding activists like Schneider, Bullough, Glover, and Hansen came from distant places to pay their respects to the staff of ONE and to contribute however they could to the magazine, the organization, and the movement. They were willing to take a stand.

In his book *Homosexuals Today: A Handbook of Organizations and Publications*, published in 1956, ONE's business manager Dorr Legg (writing as Marvin Cutler) likewise had a difficult time precisely articulating why Los Angeles should have been the birthplace for the movement: "The stage was set. The time had come in America for the appearance of organizations avowedly dedicated to the problems of the homosexual, and to the welfare of the homosexual. Why this idea, still apparently of shocking novelty to many, should have first found permanent expression in Los Angeles is something social historians may one day explain. Perhaps the brutalities of some police officials and the periodic 'clean up drives' fostered by an administration said to be much indebted to certain church groups had something to do with goading action. Perhaps the teeming intellectual ferment characterizing the city played its part. Perhaps a realization of the injustices suffered by minority groups in a city of so many minority groups . . . was unusually vivid" (1956, 2–3). At any rate, in Los Angeles, so far as is known, the first large-scale movement still in existence by or for homosexuals was started in 1950.

Many forces, then, convened to make Los Angeles the birthplace of the modern homosexual rights movement, but it seems that in several cities in North America the time was right for homosexuals to begin working together to fight to decriminalize homosexuality and to obtain equal rights for those who lived a homosexual lifestyle. A few brave and talented people needed to stand up, stop complaining among themselves about their situation, and start taking action for change. Although there were several factors involved, I believe that had it not started in Los Angeles, the movement surely could have originated in other cities with large immigrant homosexual populations at this time, most probably San Francisco or New York.

Overview

In some ways, this study follows from a dissertation in USC's history department that was published in 1978, Salvatore J. Licata's *Gay Power: A History of the American Gay Movement, 1908–1974*. Licata divided the movement into three historical periods: the period of the pioneers characterized the 1950s; the period of civil rights activism comprised the 1960s; and the "modern Stonewall gay liberation period" began in 1969. Gay rights historians often espouse this progressive and tri-episodic time line as if the pre–gay libbers had gone the way of the dinosaur. While I agree that the Stonewall rebellion marked an important milestone in the movement's history and undoubtedly marked a significant change in social attitudes both within and outside the movement, I will shift the traditional emphasis and consider the split of ONE, Incorporated, as the most significant pivotal event in the movement.

For present purposes, the pre-split era in Los Angeles may be segmented into three distinct periods, each marked by who was actively leading ONE, Incorporated. First came the era of Dale Jennings, one of the five original members of Mattachine and the first editor of *ONE* magazine. This is the subject of chapters 2 and 3. After Jennings resigned from ONE in the fall of 1953, Jim Kepner's recruitment to the editorial board marked the second era of ONE, as is discussed in chapter 5. The third era, marked by Kepner's resignation, is characterized by rising tension between those with Dorr Legg, who felt ONE was foremost an education organization, and those with Don Slater, who felt the magazine should remain its first priority. This is the subject of chapter 6, which concludes with the infamous split. Chapter 7 details the fallout, the two years of legal wrangling after the schism that left both factions decimated. Chapter 8 covers the founding of the Institute for the Study of Human Resources (ISHR) and the Homosexual Information Center (HIC) and touches on the origination of Christopher Street West. The final chapter discusses the deaths of several of the movement's pioneers and brings the history up to the present.

I should note that I would never have set out with the ambition of record-ing the fifty-year history of this movement for my doctoral research study. The scope of the project would have been overwhelming, and there were too many conflicting stories circulating and too many personalities involved—it would take years to sort things out. Engaging the process through a person-centered approach, however, allowed me to get a grasp on this elusive history, and moving from the personal to the political made the task manageable. After years of research and active participation in the HIC, I have been able to perceive patterns of organizational change and growth that are not only interesting in their own right but also yield insight as to the causes of fission/fusion politics in voluntary associations and similar institutions.

In a way, this project is an attempt at what some have called "salvage anthropology," an attempt to capture the history of ONE before it vanishes entirely into the past. The project itself began as an attempt on my part to "salvage" for history the life histories of three of those recently passed; namely, Kepner, Jennings, and Slater. Rather than a lament, this is a story of friend-ship and camaraderie, of how a common interest transcended the needs of its original purpose to form lasting relationships that the survivors themselves refer to as a kinship network that anthropologist Kath Weston would call a kindred of choice, men and women "brought together in a family of their own making" (1991, xviii). It is a tale not only of separation and division and fissions and fusions, but it is also a tale of continuity, longevity, victory, hope, and triumph. Homosexual, heterosexual, lesbian, transgendered, gay—all of these identities are herein represented as individuals united in purpose and ambition as articulated in the mission statement of HIC's articles of incorporation, ratified in 1968: "To conduct a continuing examination into the nature, circumstances and social issues of homosexuality, and to generate, gather, organize, make available and broadcast the best current thought on sexual questions generally."

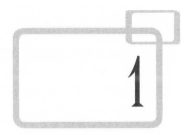

Mattachine
(1948–52)

It would not be too much of a stretch to see the Mattachine's Harry Hay as a visionary, perhaps even a prophet.
—Bert Archer, *The End of Gay (and the Death of Heterosexuality)*

The Harry Hay of the '50s had all the humor of Moses striding down the mountain with that dratted Decalogue.
—Dale Jennings (as quoted in Hansen, *A Few Doors West of Hope*)

IT WOULD SEEM that today's lesbian and gay rights movement, commonly referred to as the LGBT or LGBTQ movement since it came to include the rights of bisexual, transgendered, and queer people, began in 1950 largely through the efforts of one man, Harry Hay. More has been written about Hay, often lauded as the "father" of the gay rights movement, than about any other pioneer of the Los Angeles homosexual movement.

Henry "Harry" Hay was born on April 7, 1912, in Sussex, England, and raised in an upper-middle-class neighborhood in Los Angeles. His first sexual encounter was with a sailor named Matt, whom he met on a steamship bound for Los Angeles, when he was fourteen. After their encounter, the sailor gave Hay a bit of prophetic advice that Hay later claimed was "the most beautiful gift that any older man ever gave a younger man": "Someday you're going to come to a port, and you won't understand a word that's said around you, and you won't see a face, you won't get a smell that's familiar to you at all and you'll be frightened, and terrified, and afraid. And all of the sudden across this room, because you're a tall boy, you'll see a pair of eyes open and glow, at you, as you lift your eyes open and glowing at him. At that moment of eye lock you are home, and you are safe, and you are free. This is my gift."[1]

From this experience, Hay came to believe that homosexual men comprised a secret, sacred brotherhood, with an imperative to "protect each other's anonymity with [their] lives": "Over the centuries, this is how we have managed to stay alive and this is how we have managed to prevail: we have always guarded each other's anonymity as if it were our own, because if I guard you, you in turn will guard me and that's the only safety we've got. I've never forgotten this; it is something that was embedded in my very young mind and I've remembered this many, many times."[2]

An active and articulate scholar through high school, Hay graduated with honors in 1929 and then spent the next year working for an attorney in a downtown office (Licata 1978, 105). During this time, he discovered "cruising" in nearby Pershing Square and had a sexual encounter there with an older man called "Champ," who was probably in his early thirties (Licata 1978, 106). In 1931, Hay left Los Angeles to matriculate at Stanford University, but he did not complete a degree. In the fall of 1932, after having an affair with James Broughton and coming out to his classmates as "temperamental," he moved back to Los Angeles. The next February, Hay became an actor for the Antonio Pastor Theatre, performing character and comedy roles. He soon began dating Will Geer, the theater's lead actor, who would later become famous as Grandpa Walton (Hay 1996, 356; Slade 2001).

Hay was first drawn to social activism in 1934 when he witnessed a V-shaped wedge of mounted police force their way through a crowd of people gathered before the Los Angeles City Hall, demonstrating for milk. As described by Licata, Hay "grew furious" with what he saw. "Hay hurled a rock, which hit the lead policeman, knocking him from his horse. He was saved from arrest when a friendly Mexican-American pulled him into a maze of humble dwellings that scaled the nearby hill" (1978, 107). Hay later told Will Roscoe that a well-known drag queen named Clarabelle helped usher him to safety as he escaped into Bunker Hill (Hay 1996, 356; Roscoe 1996b, 37). Later that year, a second event was to make a life-changing impression on him. He had traveled with Geer to San Francisco to participate in the longshoremen's strike of 1934. When the National Guard opened fire on the crowd, Hay heard bullets whizzing past his ear. Two people were killed and many others wounded. A funeral march followed with a procession of 100,000 people that snaked its way through the streets of the city. Here, Hay first glimpsed the "power of the people" and knew that it was mobilizing the masses where real power lay—the power to change and to improve society (Slade 2001).

Hay had been attending Communist Party meetings since February 1933. Under directives from Moscow, the party at that time attempted to form coalitions with all other groups opposed to fascism, even if ideologically they opposed socialism. This "Popular Front" policy "called on artists to foster social consciousness and mobilize the masses through art" (Roscoe 1996b, 38). Such tactics proved somewhat successful in Los Angeles, where "many of the writers, actors, and crafts people in the burgeoning film industry joined Popular Front organizations." Hay was hooked—he had certainly found his place. "He signed up for nearly every progressive cause and organization that arose in the 1930s" (Roscoe 1996b, 38) and remained an active party member for the next eighteen years (Katz 1992, 412).

From 1939 to 1942, Hay lived in New York where he studied the lives and works of Karl Marx and Friedrich Engels and intended to become a Communist Party teacher (Roscoe 1996b, 39). According to Licata, "Hay introduced folk singing into the progressive left, putting on Hootenannies with talent such as Pete Seeger, Burl Ives, Leadbelly, and Woody Guthrie" (1978, 107). He learned at this time the efficacy of music, pageantry, theater, and ritual in social movements. If those cultural elements were focused on a social cause, one could build a formidable movement around a core of common values through which common objectives could be thoughtfully determined and attained.

Hay returned to Los Angeles in the winter of 1942 where he continued to teach Marxist courses on political economy. After Hay staged a successful "Big Sing Fest" in October 1945, local leftist organizations invited him to conduct "a ten-week educational program of people's songs." His first course, taught at Oleson Studios, was successful enough that Hay was soon teaching such courses in workshops all around Los Angeles (Licata 1978, 108). In 1946, he joined forces with his folk-music associates to form Los Angeles People's Songs, later affiliated with Seeger's People's Songs, Inc., in New York. Later that year, Hay developed a course called "Music, Barometer of the Class Struggle" for the Peoples' Education Center (PEC). The course was offered in 1947 through the Southern California Labor School, a successor to the PEC that in fact was actually the Hollywood Communist Party (Licata 1978, 108; Roscoe 1996b, 45). It was partially through the success of these and subsequent courses that Hay began to research homosexuality and to conceive of homosexuals as a repressed cultural minority. He began pondering ways by which homosexuals, such as the dozens he met on beaches and in bars or closer to home in Pershing Square, could be stimulated toward social action.

One summer night in August 1948, having been invited by a man he met while cruising Westlake Park, thirty-six-year-old Hay attended a party of "gay" students (as he later called them) somewhere near the USC campus (Timmons 1990, 134). Hay proposed to the partygoers that they set about to organize homosexuals within some sort of club or society, and several seemed enthusiastic about the idea. In an afterglow, Hay wrote a proposal the following night calling for the formation of a homosexual organization named Bachelors Anonymous, but future meetings never took place (Roscoe 1996a, 4). Writing under the pseudonym "Eann MacDonald," Hay posed three primary questions whose answers he would pursue for the rest of his life: Who are the homosexuals? What is their purpose in life? And how can they negotiate within the parent society to make significant contributions as a group? (Licata 1978, 108–9). No copies of this original document survive, and nothing came of it for two years—that is, until he shared a later version with his new lover, fashion designer Rudi Gernreich.

Hay's account of the influences and inspirations behind this now-famous prospectus calling for homosexual rights has been recorded in *Radically Gay: Gay Liberation in the Words of Its Founder*, edited by Will Roscoe (Hay 1996). Roscoe, who became an intimate friend of Hay's, traced these influences to several sources, some organizational and some cultural. While I will later elaborate on the structural and organizational aspects of Mattachine and some of its subsequent manifestations, it is also important to point to the cultural and literary influences that impacted the "Mattachinos," as they called themselves in the early days,[3] for it is from these that Hay drew his conception of homophiles (and, later, gays) as a repressed cultural minority.

Hay's first cultural model was the Native American tradition of the berdache, now often referred to as "two-spirit" in the anthropological literature.[4] Hay first learned of the berdache in the early 1930s through reading a Modern Library compilation titled *The Making of Man: An Outline of Anthropology*, edited by V. F. Calverton (1931), which included articles by Edward Carpenter and Edward Westermarck (Roscoe 1996b, 47). Later, by the mid-1940s, Hay discovered the works of Marxist anthropologist Gordon Childe and the Boasian cultural anthropologists, especially Margaret Mead and Ruth Benedict (Roscoe 1996b, 39). Hay was particularly inspired by the berdache described in Ruth Benedict's *Patterns of Culture* (1934). From Benedict, Hay envisioned the berdache as having "a reputation not only for excellence in crafts and domestic work, but in many tribes they were religious specialists as well" (Roscoe 1996b, 47).

Hay was also inspired by the Kinsey report, which provided scientific proof that as many as 10 percent of the world's population regularly or occasionally engage in homosexual acts. A percentage of those were considered to be exclusively homosexual, and Hay believed they should be allowed the right to that existence: "Rather than a few isolated misfits lurking about the red-light districts of the largest cities, there were, in fact, millions of homosexuals— everywhere" (Hay 1996, 60). The trick was to organize them and focus their latent resources and energies on improving their status in society. A 1949 version of Hay's prospectus "described how we would set up the guilds, how we would keep them underground and separated so that no one group could ever know who all the other members were and their anonymity would be secured" (Katz 1992, 411).

Through his studies, Hay came to believe in a primitive or primal matriarchy, a theory he publicly advocated as early as 1953 (Hay 1996). He believed that matriarchal societies had existed in Europe in the not-too-distant past, and these "folk" societies had their own form of ritualized berdache, which often manifested as the jester or ritual fool. Hay referred to this hypothetical personage as the "Folk Berdache" (Hay 1996, 110) and lamented that the homosexual's role in society had diminished considerably since "the whole Matriarchal cultural structure—known as the folk—was transformed and, thus, disappeared as a social force in history" (Hay 1996, 113). He began to envision organizing homosexuals into a revitalization movement, a call to arms for a people silenced and divided for millennia. He thought that, through teaching the history of such people, the homosexual minority could use the archetype of the folk berdache to hearken back to a time and place where it "was an accepted institution" and, "having no household and children to care for, could devote most of their time—aside from filling their own . . . bellies—with the social, economic, and educational need of their communities generally" (Hay 1996, 114).

Historian John D'Emilio wrote extensively on what life was like for homosexuals in the 1950s in his book *Sexual Politics, Sexual Communities: The Making of a Homosexual Minority in the United States, 1940–1970* (1983). D'Emilio's book focuses on the active and relentless pursuit that police departments across the country carried out against homosexual persons and behavior. In 1950, President Eisenhower signed Executive Order 10450, which equated homosexuality with sexual perversion and barred all homosexuals from working in the federal government. During the next several years in Washington, D.C., more than 1,000 people were arrested per year for homosexual conduct. Other cites in which homosexuals were especially targeted in the 1950s include Baltimore, Philadelphia, Wichita, Dallas, Memphis, Seattle, Boise, Ann Arbor, and Los Angeles (D'Emilio 1983, 49–50).

Since the 1950s, Harry Hay's philosophies have appealed to many, and after Mattachine he proceeded to found or inspire so many homosexual and gay associations that Vern Bullough dubbed him "the Johnny Appleseed of the American gay movement" (2002a, 73). Because of the magnitude of his influence on the homophile, homosexual, gay, and modern LGBT movements, one might consider Hay to have been a true prophet, one who influenced and was admired by many and who grounded his authority in a spiritual calling (Moore 1998, 146). At the outset, of course, Hay had to build his following one person at a time, and the inevitability of success was far from assured.[5]

The Founding of Mattachine

After years of planning and forethought, Hay's project finally got under way when he met Rudi Gernreich, who for years was identified by historians only as "X" (Katz 1992, 409; Licata 1978, 108). The two met on Saturday morning, July 6, 1950, at a rehearsal at the Lester Horton Dance Theater, and according to Hay they fell in love almost immediately (Hay 1996, 314). Gernreich had survived the Auschwitz concentration camp. As Hay told Katz, "he and his family had come through some horrible experiences" (Katz 1992, 409). Gernreich became a talented and controversial fashion designer, most famously known for designing the women's topless swimsuit in 1964, and is also credited with the thong, circa 1979. His styles were as avant-garde as his ideas, and he is known in science-fiction circles for having designed the costumes for *Space, 1999*. At the time he met Hay, Gernreich tended to be socially aloof: "He wasn't a practicing member of anything" (Katz 1992). However, Gernreich thrilled to Hay's idea of a homosexual organization, and he prompted his clandestine lover to revive it yet again.

Together, Gernreich and Hay visited homosexual beaches to circulate the Stockholm Peace Petition in protest of the Korean War. Between August and October 1950, they secured 500 signatures. At the same time, they asked beachgoers if they had heard of the Kinsey report. If so, would they mind attending discussion groups focused on Kinsey's data? As Hay told Katz, "We also used this petition activity as a way of talking about our prospectus

. . . some of the guys gave us their names and addresses—in case we ever got a Gay organization going. They were some of the people we eventually contacted for our discussion groups" (1992, 411).

In November, prompted by Gernreich, Hay gave a copy of his prospectus, "Preliminary Concepts," calling for the unification of the "androgynes of the world" to Bob Hull, a student in his music class at the Labor School whom Hay suspected might be homosexual[6] (Hay 1996, 315; Katz 1992, 411). Hull was a slender man, soft-spoken with a "chipper" attitude.[7] He was a very talented organist, described by Jim Kepner as a "brilliant" musician who also composed his own music.[8] Hay's hunch was right, and Hull was thrilled with the document. He called to ask Hay if he could bring two friends over to discuss the matter. These were Hull's roommate and ex-lover, Chuck Rowland, and Hull's current boyfriend, Dale Jennings.

On November 11, 1950, the five met to discuss the matter at Hay's residence at 2328 Cove Avenue, in the Silver Lake district of Los Angeles (Hay 1996: 63–75, 358; Center for Preservation Education and Planning, 2000). As Hay remembers it, "Bob Hull, Chuck Rowland, and Dale Jennings come flying into my yard waving the prospectus, saying, "We could have written this ourselves—when do we begin?" (Katz 1992, 411).

Chuck Rowland once announced to his cohorts that he would willingly devote his life to the organization, provided they develop some "sound theory or philosophy" from which they could unify and proceed.[9] Hay replied instantly, "We are an oppressed cultural minority." This comment profoundly impacted Rowland, who wholeheartedly agreed and continued to advocate on behalf of that minority for years to come. "To me, the gay culture idea was the cornerstone of the Mattachine," he later wrote in an October 1990 letter to Jennings. "You say we wanted to change the laws, and that was and is a worthy objective. But changing laws is almost meaningless unless one changes the hearts of men, both homosexual and heterosexual, and the heart change is, to me, what the Mattachine was all about." Gay journalist Jim Kepner would later refer to Rowland as "the founders' best organizer" (1994, 11).

Through the end of 1950 and into 1951, the five men met weekly to plan their organization. Between meetings, they approached others, hoping to expand their circle. But no one showed any interest until April 1951, when two strangers showed up for a meeting.[10] These were Konrad Stevens, commonly known as Steve, and James (Jim) Gruber. As lovers, Steve and Jim were so often in full agreement with each other that Jennings christened them collectively as "Stim."[11] With the addition of this pair, the five founders became a magical seven, and things began to happen. These seven became known as the "fifth order," or chief administrators of the growing association. They had tentatively called themselves the Society of Fools (Timmons 1990, 150), but now a better name seemed desirable. They had collectively tossed around monikers "derived from the itinerant entertainers of the Middle Ages: Robin Goodfellows, Le matchin, Los Matachines." Stevens stated that he liked "matachine" best, and Rowland suggested they Americanize the word to Mattachine. As Rowland later recalled, "Everyone instantly agreed," and the group had its name.[12]

Dale Jennings had a different recollection of this evening's events. According to him, the meeting was arduous and far from somber: "When he [Hay] pressed the historical analogy between us and the medieval fools and jesters, we were torn between indignation and laughter. I suspect it was our loudly vocal scorn that made Harry stick to his guns and finally wear us down to occasion. We voted to accept because the meetings were always too long and we wanted to go home and get in a little loving. But the vote was provisional and neither unanimous nor enthusiastic."[13] Of course it is likely that both Jennings and Rowland are correct in their assessment of the evening. The two different perspectives of the event, though, are telling, and well illustrate the differences between the two men that would perpetuate and intensify over the next few years.

On July 20, 1951, Mattachine formally adopted its mission and purposes (Katz 1992, 412). The group's primary purpose was to unify homosexuals "isolated from their own kind." The second purpose was to educate both homosexuals and the general heterosexual populace. The third purpose was to "provide leadership to the whole mass of social deviates" (Katz 1992). With a name and a clear purpose, the Mattachine fellowship set out to make a positive difference in the lives of homosexual people in Los Angeles and in America at large.

For the first two years of Mattachine, each time members gathered in private homes, they did so fearfully. Shades were always drawn when they couldn't meet in a basement, and someone always kept a sharp lookout for the police or FBI. Nevertheless, discussion groups proliferated throughout southern California and San Francisco, and anonymity was protected at all costs. The meetings usually took place in private homes, but they "were conducted in such a way that most of those attending had no idea who was in charge. The identities of the Mattachine leaders . . . were kept secret from all but a handful of Mattachine members at the top of the organization's hierarchy" (Marcus 1992, 26). Jennings suspected that the group had probably been infiltrated, but police found the group's activities "too innocuous to bother with" (Alwood 1996, 26). He told journalist Edward Alwood in a 1994 interview, "There were meetings, meetings, meetings every night of the week. When the police realized we were a bunch of commies debating legal questions, they must have realized there wasn't any reason to arrest us" (1996, 27–28).

While fear and a common stigma were cohesive factors in unifying the first "Mattachinos," in order for the organization to gain staying power it needed to develop and perpetuate rituals. Such rituals first occur as definitional ceremonies, or "performances of identity, sanctified at the level of myth" (Myerhoff 1979, 32). The fifth-order founders formulated rituals and their ceremonies deriving from three primary sources: the Communists, fraternal organizations such as the Masons, and Alcoholics Anonymous. Inspired by the structure of the Communist Party and from self-help groups such as Alcoholics Anonymous, Hay devised a cell-like structure that would guarantee its members anonymity. While teaching music history for the Labor School, he learned of "the Guild System and the Freemasonry movement" (Katz 1992, 411). From the Masons came secret oaths, rituals by candlelight, the solemnity of a brotherhood, and a profound respect for "ancestors," the many who had gone before. Of all the operational metaphors embraced by the early Mattachine, none resonated stronger than that of a brotherhood. Even naysayers such as Jennings agreed that there was something special about this agnatic clan, something bordering on the transcendental or sacred. Not only talks of politics and planning drew this group together; equally cohesive was the palpable energy of their collective presence, a force anthropologist Victor Turner (1974) termed "communitas" and the Mattachinos often referred to as "magic."

Not all of Mattachine's founders, however, agreed with Hay's notion that homosexuals were a latent cultural minority. Dale Jennings in particular resisted the notion that homosexuals comprised a people. How could they possibly hope to unify "a people" around what they did in bed? The idea to him was laughable.

Considering how much he craved privacy and desired a career as a Hollywood filmmaker, it is ironic that Dale Jennings should be the one to galvanize Mattachine and bring it to the attention of the American public. The precipitating event was his arrest in the spring of 1952 for allegedly soliciting a police officer in a bathroom in Westlake Park, now MacArthur Park, near downtown Los Angeles. Before that part of the story should be told, however, I want to provide a more detailed introduction to this recalcitrant Mattachino.

Introducing Dale Jennings

The following biographical sketch of Dale Jennings is the most extensive profile in this book for several reasons. First, it was largely through learning about Jennings that I became interested in researching the Los Angeles movement for homosexual rights—or even became aware such a movement existed. I first learned of his history and philosophies in the summer of 2000 when Jim Schneider approached me to broadcast an obituary/press release for Jennings that he had written with Walter Williams. Through distributing the release, I became fascinated by Jennings and desired to learn more about his life history in order to better appreciate his accomplishments as an author and activist. I revisited the histories I had found of Mattachine members and began to reconsider what had been written about Jennings in contrast to the person I was coming to know through reading his journals and sorting through his personal archives, bequeathed to HIC and archived within the Vern and Bonnie Bullough Collection on Sex and Gender at Oviatt Library at California State University, Northridge (CSUN). When Vern Bullough invited me to write a profile on Jennings to include in an upcoming collection of biographical sketches of early activists in the history of the movement, I jumped at the opportunity. The result of that study has been published (White 2002a), and this is an updated version of that history.

William Dale Jennings was born on October 21, 1917, in Amarillo, Texas. His father, William Arthur Jennings, was a salesman and his mother, Charlotte Sophie [Knebel] Jennings, was a housewife.[14] All the men in Jennings's family shared the first name William; accordingly, each was known by his middle name. This suited young Jennings fine; he later wrote to a fan that his grandfather once called him "Willy" and in so doing "both turned my stomach and alienated the two of us."[15] He later came to admire this granddad after learning that he had been an early railroad engineer and a pioneer settler in Colorado.[16] Also, Jennings shared his grandfather's passion for travel. As a youth, he sold the *Saturday Evening Post* door to door and began to collect the paper's illustrations of windjammers by Anton Otto Fischer. "Oddly," he later wrote in an unpublished essay (1992), "the tall ships thrilled me right down to the toes." His family pondered the strange fascination as his collection of ship pictures continued to grow.

Jennings was a child prodigy of sorts, a ballet dancer.[17] His artistic endeavors were encouraged by his parents, and according to his nephew Patrick, he was "given music lessons while the rest of the family carried him along."

His sister Elaine, older by two years, also wanted to take lessons, but there was not enough money to send them both to private classes. Young Dale was always considered "the talented one," and "if he was rude or obnoxious, well, he was 'special' and it just had to be forgiven."[18] He graduated from South Senior High School in Denver, Colorado, in 1935 and then enrolled at Denver University, where he studied speech and rhetoric for eighteen months.

Jennings then decided to move to Los Angeles, where he rented an old stable from which he ran a theater company, Theatre Caravan, at the corner of Olympic and Alvarado in the Westlake district, from January 1939 until January 1941. He reportedly wrote and produced sixty plays for Caravan[19] but earned little in the process. As the troupe's producer, he designed sets, composed music, and performed on stage with his fellow actors, whom he hired and directed. I discovered old negatives in a crisp, faded envelope with "Dale Dancing" printed on the front. Once developed, these provided a rare glimpse of the young man: a slender Jennings, probably in his early twenties, leaping about someone's patio, feet off the ground in poses that seemed part jazz and part ballet, part raw and part sophisticated.[20] I later learned from his correspondence with Slater that Jennings had studied dance in Los Angeles under modern dance pioneer Lester Horton,[21] and, according to Tony Sanchez, he had also danced for the legendary Martha Graham.[22]

Jennings's days of dancing and theater came to an end with the start of World War II. He entered into active service at Fort MacArthur on November 13, 1942, one month after his twenty-fifth birthday. After three months of training as a private in basic training and antiaircraft technology, he was promoted to technical sergeant, a noncommissioned intelligence officer. He received two weeks of training in cryptography at Camp Hulen, Texas, where he was trained in air and ground liaison and operation of the M-209 converter and other cryptographic devices. Then, on December 10, 1943, Jennings shipped out to join the 356th Searchlight Battalion in the Asiatic-Pacific Theater. He spent the next two years stationed in the southern Philippines and spent some time on Guadalcanal after the bloody winter battle of 1942–43. While there, he presented lectures to the battalion on orientation censorship, information, and education. He taught instructional courses on scouting and patrolling, drew up reconnaissance maps and charts as assigned and also served as the editor of the battalion's newspaper.

While in the Philippines, Sergeant Jennings kept a fascinating journal, perhaps as much fiction as diary, which interestingly enough has the word "ONE" etched in tall letters on both front and back covers, in red crayon. Jennings recorded nothing truly personal or intimate in the diary even though he kept it locked in a safe; he knew his bunkmates and others would jump on the chance to read it. The diary occasionally refers to his wife back home, named "Tuck,"[23] but it also speaks openly of an appreciation for masculine beauty and homosexual angst. "I looked at him today and knew that our friendship is a nighttime thing. More than him being brusque and me militarily respectful— for by day, with all his features sharp and clear, I do not know him." Many passages also exemplify Jennings's talents as a writer. I found this passage particularly striking: "There is a delicate tropic fern, of finely balanced proportions, that closes up when touched. A design of rich, green living changed in the moment of touching into a withered, brown, dead-seeming wisp of rubble. Then don't touch it; look, enjoy (love) and pass by." A few pages later, Jennings mentions the plant again: "He and Captain Abbey were looking at the little folding fern; they had stopped on the way from chow, were touching frond after frond, watching them wither. Lt. R. hobbled up on his crutches as the Captain in his final way, labeled them 'cannibal plants.' R. said flatly and at once, 'They're a homosexual plant. Use their pollen on themselves,' and hobbled off without a smile or goodbye. Somehow, I was very angry."

Jennings returned to Fort MacArthur on Christmas Eve of 1945 after two years and fifteen days of foreign duty. In addition to a medal for good conduct, he also received a World War II victory medal, an American campaign medal, an Asiatic-Pacific campaign medal, and a Philippine liberation ribbon with one Bronze Star. Jennings received an honorable discharge on January 2, 1946. Six months later, on June 10, a court granted Jennings a divorce from Esther Slayton Jennings, the "Tuck" of his journal.[24] The marriage's brevity suggests that, indeed, much of the talk of "the girl back home" was to deflect charges of homosexuality—or to assure a real or potential sexual partner that one's eggs really were in the right basket and that any hanky-panky in the meantime was no more than a release of pent-up (and properly masculine) tension.

After the war, Jennings worked for a traveling ice show (Jennings 1992). Sometime in the latter half of the 1940s, he studied filmmaking for two years at USC through the benefits of the G.I. Bill. During this time his attraction to other men continued, but he was hardly open about it. A queer-hating boss told him, "I understand you only wear red socks, Jennings. Has it anything to do with why Rock Hudson wears them?" He described his reaction to such intimidation: "I wasn't about to be tagged as fag and so leaned over backwards playing it straight" (Jennings 1992). The attempt was ultimately unsuccessful, however, and on September 27, 1950, his third attempt at heterosexual partnership ended as another brief marriage, this time to Jacqueline Carney Jennings, was annulled.

Two months after the annulment, Dale Jennings's life was to take a dramatic turn when he began dating Bob Hull and was introduced to Hull's Communist mentor and music teacher, Harry Hay. His life was to change even more drastically in the spring of 1952 when he was arrested for lewd conduct in a public place and his homosexuality was made public, his career and his reputation left in a shambles.

The Arrest of Dale Jennings

As the story goes, Jennings left his Echo Park home one spring evening and began the mile-long walk toward the Westlake district, hoping to take in a good movie. Once there, he decided against the first two shows and then stepped into a public restroom on his way to another theater. He didn't dally and left about 9 p.m. "having done nothing that the city architect didn't have in mind when he designed the place." Only now, a "big, rough looking character who appeared out of nowhere" began following him. Jennings proceeded to the theater only to discover that he'd seen that show already, so he turned back for home—still followed by the burly stranger (Jennings 1953a, 12).

Jennings grew afraid that the man intended to rob him, so he "walked fast, took detours and said goodbye at each street corner." Once Jennings arrived at his own front door, the stranger pushed past him and entered the house. Jennings describes what happened then in an article later printed in the first issue of *ONE* magazine:

> What followed would have been a nightmare even if he hadn't turned out to be vice squad. Sure now that this big character was a thug, I—as the prosecutor described it—"flitted wildly" from room to room wondering how to get rid of this person sprawled on the divan making sexual gestures and proposals. I was almost relieved when he strolled into the back bedroom because now I could call the police. . . . Then he called twice, "Come in here!" His voice was loud and commanding. He'd taken his jacket off, was sprawled on the bed and his shirt was unbuttoned half way down. . . . [H]e insisted that I was homosexual and urged me to "let down my hair." He'd been in the navy and "all us guys played around." I told him repeatedly that he had the wrong guy; he got angrier each time I said it. At last he grabbed my hand and tried to force it down the front of his trousers. I jumped up and away. Then there was the badge and he was snapping the handcuffs on with the remark, "Maybe you'll talk better with my partner outside." (Jennings 1953a, 12)

The partner, Jennings wrote, was nowhere to be found when they left the house. The vice officer paraded Jennings all the way back to the park, then ushered him into the waiting patrol car. The arresting officer sat in the back seat beside him, and he and two others in the front seat asked a barrage of baited questions, such as "How long have you been this way?" The officers "repeatedly made jokes about police brutality, laughingly asked . . . if they'd been brutal and each of the three instructed me to plead guilty and everything would be alright." Jennings feared "the usual beating," probably out in the country somewhere, but eventually they all arrived at the police station. Although the cops booked Jennings at 11:30 p.m., they would not allow him to make his phone call until after 3:00 a.m. the next morning (Jennings 1953a, 12–13).

Jennings called Harry Hay to ask for the $50 bail. Hay later stated that the only reason Jennings called him was because Hay was the only one known to have a checkbook (Slade 2001). Hay posted bail by 6:30 a.m., and he and Jennings went for breakfast at the Brown Derby, where they decided that Mattachine would help contest the charge. According to Jennings, contesting the charges was Hay's idea. Jennings wrote in an unpublished article titled "The Trouble with Fairies" (1990) that while most tall people shrank from using their height, Hay was "the only tall person I ever met who used it with the imperial self-confidence of the chosen. . . . From his great height, [Hay] laid heavy hands on my shoulders, stared intensely down at me in his best S.A.G.[25] style, and made his great and solemn pitch." When this happened, Jennings's spirits sank: he had seen Hay do this "to so many squirming people" before. Hay told Jennings not to fear, that he and Mattachine would stand behind him through the fight. "The Great Man pointed out that I, in my miserable way, would be somewhat Chosen, too, if I stood up to the Establishment. I had nothing to lose but my chains. After all, working in a family business, I couldn't get fired. Being recently divorced, it would not hurt my wife and I could continue at USC as something of a hero if the straights on campus didn't go to work on me as they did all the fairies. He himself would be honored to do such a thing, but of course, he had too many familial responsibilities. Oh, I was lucky" (Jennings 1990, 2).

After breakfast, Hay called an emergency meeting, and the Mattachine clan convened in Jennings's house later than night to hear the news and discuss a strategy. However, Hay's recollection of the arrest somewhat differs from Jennings's version: "Dale had just broken off with Bob Hull and was not, I know, feeling very great. He told me that he had met someone in the can at Westlake Park. The man had his hand on his crotch, but Dale wasn't interested. He said the man insisted on following him home, and almost pushed his way through the door. He asked for coffee, and when Dale went to get it, he saw the man moving the window blind, as if signaling to someone else. He got scared and started to say something, when there was a sudden pounding on the door, and Dale was arrested" (Timmons 1990, 164).

Of course, no one will ever know what really happened that night, except for Jennings and the arresting officer. Jennings admitted later that the man had indeed been quite handsome (Slade 2001), and he knew some of his fellow Mattachinos did not entirely believe his story. He wrote in the first issue of *ONE* magazine: "To be innocent and yet not be able to convince even your own firm constituents, carries a peculiar agony" (1953a, 11). He later wrote of his cohorts, "They were unanimously willing to support my supposed perjury to defy a statute as unjust as 288a."[26]

Hay persuaded Long Beach defense lawyer George E. Shibley to take the case. Under Shibley's advisement, Mattachine organized the Citizens' Committee to Outlaw Entrapment (CCOE), a nonprofit organization that raised funds and promoted Jennings's pending trial through use of leaflets and flyers. According to one of these flyers, reprinted in Dorr Legg's *Homosexuals Today*, the committee primarily intended to stand against police brutality toward homosexuals: "[Goaded by recent] scientific research and statistics by such eminent authorities as Donald Webster Cory, Dr. Alfred Kinsey, Dr. William Kroger, Dr. Clara Thompson, and others, [homosexuals have become aware] of themselves as a social Minority with the group-culture characteristics (patterns, problems, and oppressions) that are common to all Minorities similarly persecuted by baseless myths and vulgar prejudices" (Legg 1956, 22).

The CCOE intended "to expose to all eyes an injudicial [*sic*] and unconstitutional police conspiracy which, under the cloak of protecting public morals, threatens not only all Minorities but civil rights and privileges generally." The organization claimed the odds were "six-to-one that the victim will offer to pay during the two hours it takes the prowl car to get to the nearest district station three miles away, a time-lapse known as the 'sweat-out' period." Should a person decide to plead his innocence, he faced a "nine-to-one chance of a GUILTY verdict" because of five fundamental facts:

(1) The literal impossibility of a person, presumed guilty, proving innocence in a prejudiced court-room;

(2) The perjured evidence of a plain-clothes "decoy" . . . ;

(3) The prejudice of both jury and press automatically equating every Homosexual with a fabricated lewd and dissolute "stereotype";

(4) The Roman-holiday sport of forcing a defendant to testify against himself in order to prove innocence against perjured and false testimony;

(5) The well-established pattern of denying the Homosexual the capacity of innocence by negating his testimony even though the evidence is overwhelmingly against his giving trespass as charged. (Legg 1956, 22–23)

The committee added that all people should be treated as innocent until proven guilty beyond any shadow of a doubt and followed with this call for a libertarian-based code of ethics:

> Every American Citizen is guaranteed the right to hold his own opinions. If he wishes to hug to his bosom the vipers of hate for Jews, for Negroes, or for South Sicilian Catholics, he is at liberty to do so. The right of every individual to transform his personal opinions into personal emotions is likewise tolerated though not encouraged since such agitations conceivably can become infections. As citizens we all have these rights. BUT AS CITIZENS WE ALSO HAVE THE DUTY TO SEE THAT SUCH OPINIONS AND EMOTIONS DO NOT TRANSGRESS THE CIVIL RIGHTS OF OTHERS. The areas of personally held opinions and of civil safeguards are carefully separated by the causeways of the Law. When emotions impinge upon civil privilege we call it Anarchy. The moment a jury, or a newspaper, or a community, convicts an accused as guilty because (convicted in their own minds that every Homosexual is automatically a lewd and dissolute stereotype) they deem him capable of having committed the charge even though in the given instance he may be innocent. . . . It is commonplace for the Los Angeles City Vice Squad to telephone the employer of a victim, who chooses to fight to maintain his integrity—BEFORE THE TRIAL IS EVEN CALLED. To be sure this should be labelled as employing undue influence to obstruct the established patterns of justice. (Legg 1956, 23–24)

The much-publicized trial began on June 23, 1952. Jennings admitted his homosexuality in court but adamantly denied any wrongdoing. After ten days, the jury deadlocked eleven to one in Jennings's favor. Although the arresting officer had been caught in a lie, one person stymied the jury. The judge then dismissed the charges, and a stunned Jennings left the courthouse a free man. He later said, "Walking out of the courtroom free was a liberation that I'd never anticipated. It didn't happen in our society. You went to jail for this sort of thing. And so I was numb for some time, and it began to dawn on me that we did have a victory" (Slade 2001).

The newspapers did little to cover the trial, so the Mattachine distributed a flyer through Los Angeles that proclaimed victory. The flyer (reprinted in Legg 1956, 25) gave Jennings and Shibley credit for their aggressive fight and for their stance that being a homosexual did not necessarily make one prone to or guilty of "lewd nor dissolute" behavior. The flyer pointed out that this was a victory for everyone, heterosexuals as well as homosexuals, since both were "potential victims of entrapment." The CCOE asked for donations to continue the legal fight and asked that checks be made payable to "Miss Romayne Cox, Treasurer" and sent in care of the Mattachine Foundation, Inc., in Los Angeles.

The controversial case drew local and eventually national attention to Mattachine, and through the summer following the trial, organizational membership ballooned. Mattachine-like discussion groups immediately sprang up in Long Beach, Laguna Beach, and Fresno. By early 1953, groups had formed as far away as San Diego, San Francisco, Oakland, Berkeley, and Chicago. Emboldened by the triumph, men and women of the Mattachine brought the days of fear, silence, and secrecy to an end.

2

The Launch of *ONE* (1952–53)

Socially disdained groups have to find their own standards, generating internal codes for taking each other's measure. Only by doing so can they avoid the devastating consequences of judging themselves in the terms used by people who disdain them, in whose system they will always amount to nothing.
—Barbara Myerhoff, *Number Our Days*

We were young and tired of whispering to each other. We were tired of locking the doors and pulling down the shades whenever we wanted to talk about who we were. So we just decided, "What the hell?" and decided to take a different course of action.
—Dale Jennings

AS MATTACHINE'S POPULARITY grew after Jennings's trial in the summer of 1952, Hay felt his authority within Mattachine—the organization that he had created and nurtured—begin to diminish. Hay became increasingly annoyed by Jennings, who was becoming disdainful and seemed to oppose anything Hay favored (Timmons 1990, 178). Although Hay insisted that gays were a unique and especially talented people who had formerly played an integral role within "folk" and tribal societies and needed to unify in order to reclaim those sacred traditional roles, Jennings insisted that there was no essential difference between males who preferred sex with women and those who preferred men—one might as well try to unify coffee drinkers. Hay wanted to call forth a separate class of people that Jennings felt should remain integrated. Where Hay desired visibility, Jennings wanted privacy. Hay craved publicity whereas Jennings wanted to be left alone.

After he had been publicly outed as a homosexual and humiliated through the trial, his right to privacy was out of the question. Jennings grew restless. Neither he nor the Mattachine could retreat back into oblivion, nor would they want to. But the next move was far from clear. How could Jennings channel Mattachine's collective energy into a productive endeavor on behalf of homosexuals? The answer came later in the fall in the form of an offhand idea tossed around at a party near downtown Los Angeles.

A Heck of an Idea . . .

One day in early October 1952, a Los Angeles engineer by the name of Fred Frisbie brought home a young black man he met while cruising. After a brief but intimate tryst, the stranger began talking about this amazing organization he was in called Mattachine. Not knowing what to expect but full of curiosity, Frisbie followed a hunch and invited his new friend to bring Mattachine to his house and offered to provide a keg of beer. Ten days later, seven cars pulled up to Frisbie's capacious home near USC, and twenty-six revelers poured onto the premises. Frisbie recalled several young women present and four younger men who were barely over eighteen. The rest were adult males of thirty years or older, with a stately and erudite man named Bill Lambert the senior elder. One man began playing the parlor grand. Some gathered around the piano to sing while others danced, mingled, or joined in a game of cards dealt by a handsome man with an eye patch. Frisbie was especially entertained by a stout young man named Martin Block, who began "camping it up" with a cocktail umbrella. Frisbie felt right at home with this rebellious band of revelers. It was a surprisingly festive occasion he would recall fondly for the rest of his life.[1]

About ten days later, on Wednesday, October 15, Frisbie and the others met for another Mattachine discussion group at Bill Lambert's home at the corner of Twenty-seventh and Dalton. Early in the meeting, Lambert invited Frisbie and his "wife," a cross-dressed and effeminate man, to become official members of Mattachine, and they heartily accepted.[2] According to corporate minutes published in the fall 1958 issue of *ONE Confidential*, Jennings,[3] Block, Lambert, Rowland, and "John B."[4] attended that meeting. It was here that the idea to create a publication dedicated to homosexuals was first put forth.

Bill Lambert, later and most famously known as W. Dorr Legg, was proud that the idea for *ONE* first emerged in his house. He often credited this event as ONE, Incorporated's, first organizational meeting, but that is not really so, as we will see. Nevertheless, ONE would hereafter celebrate the anniversary of its founding on October 15, and Lambert was indeed crucial in its establishment, acting as business manager for the entire duration of the corporation's history. Often described as imperious and domineering, Lambert was accorded tacit deference on account of his age—he was forty-seven at the time of ONE's founding—and in recognition of the fact that he was the most educated among them.

However significant his role in the organization's history, no one ever really knew much about Lambert's backstory or his personal life. According to Kepner,[5] Lambert's full name was William Dorr Lambert Legg.[6] Born in Michigan on December 15, 1904, he was orphaned at an early age and brought up by relatives. As a youth, he practiced Christian Science. In college, he studied piano as an undergraduate and then proceeded to earn two master's degrees, in landscape design and urban planning, from the University of Michigan. After graduating in 1928, he moved to New York, where he worked as an urban planner for an architectural agency. After leaving Manhattan, Lambert moved to Florida and then Oregon before settling in Los Angeles in 1949 (Cain 2002; Dynes 2002). He worked as an urban planner for most of that time, resigning from what he called "that provincial life" to work exclusively for ONE about 1958.[7]

According to Wayne Dynes, Lambert first "began to explore the link between gay social life and the almost equally taboo world of black-white friendships" through Broadway plays, speakeasies, and drag balls in Harlem (2002, 97). His first homosexual encounter happened in Florida when he was nineteen years old. Dynes recalled how Lambert once told him of his arrival in Los Angeles with his African American lover, Marvin Edwards. "They took a long slow drive down Wilshire Boulevard to the beach. That was when they knew that 'this was the place.'"[8]

The first homosexual organization Lambert participated in was Knights of the Clock,[9] founded by African American Merton L. Bird in June 1951[10] (Dynes 2002, 98). The Knights held monthly business meetings, sponsored two to three social events per year, and offered employment and housing services to mixed-race homosexual partners (Legg 1956, 93). They never had more than a dozen active members but, according to Lambert, the Knights planned on creating a newsletter or magazine. Thus, when the idea for the magazine arose at that October 15 Mattachine discussion meeting in Lambert's home, three of the Knights immediately expressed an interest in the project (Legg 1956).

The week following the seminal gathering at Lambert's, on October 22 (the day after Dale Jennings's thirty-fifth birthday), those interested gathered in the home of "John B." [11] in order "to explore the possibility of a publication devoted to homosexuality and [its] attendant problems." They originally conceived of the magazine as an inexpensive mimeograph. Along with Jennings, Rowland, Block, Lambert, and the host, a puckish and energetic young man was there by invitation of Jennings: Don Slater, a recent USC graduate with a bachelor's degree in English. Slater had known of the Mattachine for some time but had avoided it, calling it a "stitch-and bitch club." But the idea of starting a magazine for homosexuals intrigued him, so, fortified with a passion for literature and writing, he enthusiastically dedicated himself to this new cause.

Of all of the editors destined to work for *ONE* in the years ahead, none would last as long nor have more influence on the magazine than Don Slater. Slater had lived in the Los Angeles area all of his life, having been born in Pasadena on August 21, 1923, the firstborn of identical twins. His father, Warren Steven Slater, was athletic director of the Pasadena YMCA. Students in Pasadena and later in Glendale, Los Angeles, and Oceanside affectionately called the elder Slater "Coach." Coach Slater spent many years as a president of the Pasadena and Glendale YMCAs or the Los Angeles–area Boys Clubs, and in 1956 the Oceanside club elected him "Dad of the Year" (Hansen 2002, 103–4).

The Slater family moved often during the 1920s and '30s, although they remained in the greater Los Angeles area. Still, the constant upheaval meant that young Slater could not form long-term friendships in his childhood: each time he made new friends, his family soon moved. Although it would thus be difficult to track Slater's academic history, he spent some time at John Marshall Junior High in Glendale and graduated from Chaffey High in Capistrano Beach in 1942. The U.S. Army drafted Slater soon afterward, in February 1943 (Hansen 1998, 2002).

Slater was a short, spirited man as well as a sensitive intellectual, not nearly as athletic as his father but just as likable. He did not take to competitive sports and was not interested in discussions of local or national teams. However, he had a great passion for nature and the outdoors, and he loved to swim and ski. Once inducted, the army sent him to Camp Hale, Colorado, to train as a ski trooper. Although short-lived, his stint in the military was an important phase in Slater's life. In October 1943, he was confined to the infirmary, "his heart beating double time" (Hansen 2002, 104). A few weeks later, Slater accepted an honorable discharge and headed back home to Los Angeles.

One spring night in 1945, when he was twenty-one years old, Slater went cruising in the brambles of nearby Pershing Square, where he met a slender Hispanic boy of sixteen, Antonio Sanchez.[12] As Slater later described the meeting to Joseph Hansen, the two repeatedly bumped into each other while prowling. "What! You again?" they laughed. The two joked that they must have been meant for each other, and indeed, they would remain partners until Slater's death nearly fifty-two years later.

With the assistance of the army's rehabilitation program, Slater enrolled at USC in February 1944 to work toward a bachelor's degree in English. USC's campus was situated in a neighborhood surrounded by old Victorian houses like those he loved at Bunker Hill. He and Sanchez were poor in those days and frequently moved from apartment to apartment. After living together for a while in a ski lodge belonging to Slater's parents, the couple moved into an apartment at 221 South Bunker Hill Avenue, where they occupied a section of a refurbished Victorian mansion. The house on Bunker Hill was "a few doors west of Hope Street,"[13] thus the title of Hansen's biography of Slater.

Hansen reports that Slater "didn't pay a lot of attention to his studies" at USC, but having seen some of his notebooks, I would add that when a class caught his fancy, such as one pertaining to literature or American history, he kept meticulous notes and often jotted thoughtful commentary in the margins. During his first few years at USC, Slater studied French, organic evolution, and anatomy. He took especially detailed notes for his English courses, including grammar and the history of the novel. Slater became known as a bit of a rebel on campus. He had "collected traffic tickets like trophies, then decided to act like Thoreau, refuse to pay the fines, and go to jail for civil disobedience. His position was that the state had no business telling him where he could park" (Hansen 2002, 104). Slater worked in USC's Doheny Memorial Library by day as a stack supervisor. At night, he would hang out with his friend "Hal Bargelt and other members of the University's 'gay underground' boozing in the bars on sleazy Main Street." Bargelt told Hansen that Slater especially "'enjoyed the transvestites' and was as friendly with them and the other lost souls adrift in the gritty shadows of Main Street's gaudy neon as he was with his fellow students by day" (Hansen 2002, 104).

In 1948, Slater fell ill with rheumatic fever. By this time he was a senior at USC, but, as a result of extended absence on account of illness, he withdrew from classes and asked for a fresh start the following term. He made good use of the free time allotted him once he recovered: "Don had his *Wanderjahr* in the best Eugene O'Neill style, going ashore to explore the waterfronts of Oslo, Stockholm, Bremen, Le Havre, Marseilles, and other fabled ports of call" (Hansen 2002, 106). After his extended adventure, he returned to Los Angeles and his studies at USC. Now approaching twenty-nine years old, he received his B.A. in English literature in 1952 with an emphasis on the Victorian novel. After graduating, Slater donned a tie and began working for Vroman's bookstore in Pasadena, making fifty cents an hour while Sanchez earned a better income through his musical performances on Olvera Street. Slater tended to put principles before his own needs, and he made little money working for the bookstore. Sanchez found this situation uncomfortable, having once described Slater to me as "very bright, but not too practical."

Crafting a Magazine

The group reached no great conclusions for the magazine that first night of planning, but they prudently decided to seek legal counsel before proceeding. One week later, on October 29, Block, Slater, Jennings, Lambert, and an African American schoolteacher named Bailey Whitaker met at the home of Mattachine's attorney, a man named Fred Snider.[14] Apart from the legal questions of publishing, the group discussed mail permits, city licensing, and what legal form the corporation should take. They began fishing for a name, but nothing really caught on. The determined but daunted crew met again on November 5 in the home of someone called "Cliff." Here, the group considered and rejected twenty-five names, with *BRIDGE* or *WEDGE* surviving as possibilities—an interesting juxtaposition, with one name implying unity and the other separation. At last they resolved that the magazine would be professionally printed, not mimeographed.

The group reconvened at Jennings's house on Wednesday, November 12, 1952, with Bock, Slater, Lambert, and Sanchez in attendance. Their first act was to approve Jennings's idea of publishing a pocket-sized monthly dedicated to homosexual issues. They discussed practical and production factors such as the number of pages and method of printing, then decided to use offset printing. Jennings would ask his sister Elaine for help. She owned a small printing company with her husband and lived next door to Jennings in Echo Park. But how would they raise the necessary funds?

Block, Whitaker, Lambert, Jennings, Slater, and Merton Bird met back at Lambert's house the following Sunday. Bird came to offer as a potential model the charters of two existing corporations (one probably from the Knights of the Clock), but that offer was rejected. They next discussed a possible merger with the Knights, an offer that was likewise declined. Someone then presented a proposed structure for an editorial board and advisory council, but after consideration, the group took no action.

During a meeting held in the home of Slater and Sanchez[15] on Wednesday, November 19, 1952, officials from the Mattachine Foundation offered $100 toward publication costs, but that offer met with some suspicion and was tabled. The group then resolved that in the future, "all gifts must come without stipulations or conditions" (although it is unclear precisely what stipulations Mattachine had proffered). Next, Slater, Sanchez, Jennings, Whitaker, and Lambert discussed and edited copy for their first promotional sheet.

The next meeting convened on Sunday, November 23, at Whitaker's home at 3916 Lomitas Drive. Whitaker proposed calling the magazine *ONE*, from a passage he had read in a Thomas Carlyle essay on the works of Goethe: "Of a truth, men are mystically united: a mystic bond of brotherhood makes all men one." The name immediately caught on.[16] Those assembled discussed and enthusiastically accepted the title, and then they reviewed the first manuscripts for the magazine. They decided to submit their ideas for the magazine's credo at the next meeting. Whitaker, Block, Jennings, Slater, and Lambert continued a discussion of the corporate structure in preparation for a formal meeting of incorporation.

On Saturday, November 29, 1952, the founders met in Martin Block's Studio Bookshop, 6661½ Hollywood Boulevard, for the ultimate definitional ritual: the meeting of incorporation for ONE, Incorporated. In compliance with state law, the founders chose three officers: Block as president, Slater as vice president, and Jennings as the corporation's first secretary. These three also comprised *ONE*'s editorial board. Whitaker, Bird, Sanchez, and Lambert were also voted onto the board, making a total of seven voting members (though a motion had been adopted to set corporate membership at nine). In preliminary discussions, three of these nine members, called "trustees," were to be women. In keeping with the theme of unity-in-diversity, the founders decided that at least one board member should be a Negro, one Asian, and another should be a member of another racial or ethnic group. Whitaker was put in charge of circulation, and Joan Corbin, as "Eve Elloree," was recruited as the magazine's primary artist. Fred Frisbie (as "George Mortenson") and Corbin's lover Irma "Corky" Wolf (as "Ann Carll Reid") would also contribute artwork as needed. Those in attendance again discussed a credo for the magazine but reached no resolution. Finally, the trustees appointed Bill Lambert as business manager for the corporation and, with this action, ONE, Incorporated, was in business.

The second corporate meeting occurred a few days later, on December 2, where they discussed the contents of the first issue. Slater took the minutes, penned in the same USC spiral notebook in which he and Sanchez had written their notes from Glen Lukens's ceramics class that they had taken together in the spring of 1952. (Lukens had taken a liking to Sanchez and had decided to let him audit the class at Slater's request.) Lambert and Whitaker also attended. After discussing some of the initial content, they adopted ONE's first editorial policy, determining to discuss each manuscript at the meeting immediately following its receipt and resolving to take some action one way or another, thus taming the "slush pile" before its anticipated accumulation. Once again, they briefly discussed a credo. Whitaker proposed one possibility that all agreed captured the magazine's essence, but it still needed editing because "it wandered a bit." The participants deemed Jennings's proposed credo "somewhat chatty," adding, "It needs to be more impersonal. Should be a discussion rather than a statement." They decided to leave the title of the credo column undetermined at that time, though discussion would continue. The editorial board decided to refrain from attacking the philosophical content of the articles submitted, focusing instead on "form and diction." They also decided on pseudonyms. Jennings was listed "Jeff Winters," Slater was "Gregory James," and Whitaker became "René." Bill Lambert was listed by his "real" name, which was considered a brave thing for him to do (he was not yet known as Dorr Legg). With this settled, they decided to meet the following week at Jennings's home in Echo Park.

On December 8, 1952, Lambert, Whitaker, Slater, and Jennings convened in Jennings's house for another editorial board meeting. Whitaker became ONE's promotional manager, and Rowland was assigned to circulation. The board accepted Jennings's article, "To Be Accused, Is to Be Guilty," as revised. One resolution prohibited the editorial board from discussing the magazine's content with outsiders, and a second stated that each member of the corporation would bring two pertinent news items, a letter and a proposed credo, to the next meeting. Whitaker agreed to contact Donald Webster Cory, famous for his 1951 publication of The Homosexual in America, to see if he would consider contributing.

On December 12, Jennings, Slater, and Whitaker met to discuss mailing and circulation issues. First, Jennings offered to contribute a two-column article describing the Mattachine Foundation and its work. Next, they agreed that although the printing and folding of the magazine had to be done by an outside source, they would do the stapling. They decided to use mailing sleeves instead of envelopes, and the addresses would be typed on stickers four months in advance. They hoped it would cost no more than 1½ cents to send each magazine via the post office.

The trustees held three more board meetings before the end of 1952, on December 16, 21, and 26, to decide on the content of the magazine and codify the policies of the corporation. On December 16, 1953, a credo was finally adopted by combining paragraphs from articles submitted by Jennings, Whitaker, and Slater. On the meeting on December 21, with Slater, Jennings, and Lambert present, a suggestion that *ONE* be published as a quarterly was promptly overruled. An article dealing with bisexuality, by Betty Perdue as "Geraldine Jackson," was accepted for publication pending revision. Jennings's article on his entrapment ordeal was accepted, and the title of the essay, "To Be Accused, Is To Be Guilty," would provide the teaser for the cover of the first issue. His Mattachine article was also accepted, under the bizarre pseudonym "Hieronymous K.," with the title to be determined. The board resolved that, in the future, all factual articles would be submitted to an attorney for review.

Lambert, as business manager, reported that the magazine had garnered $28.40 in cash contributions and $37 in checks since October 22, 1952.[17] One subscription had been sold during the November 19 meeting. Those present authorized Lambert to open a bank account for the organization and to write a letter to Mattachine's officers to see if it they wanted to purchase a full-page advertisement. After a bout of copyediting, *ONE*'s progenitors adjourned with plans to meet again at 7:30 on Thursday evening, New Year's Day, 1953.

It was during this meeting that the magazine really came together. Slater, Lambert, and Jennings proofread the remaining articles and letters. The cover format was accepted as designed by Lambert, who also contributed a letter. An editorial "To *ONE*'s Readers" was accepted as revised by the board, and it was decided that the Carlyle quotation that inspired the magazine's name would be used above the contents listing in connection with the title. Further discussion of the credo was tabled and, after discussing additions to a new column, the editorial board adjourned with the next meeting scheduled for January 4 at Whitaker's house.

There are no surviving records of a meeting on that day. However, at 9:30 on Friday night, January 9, 1953, Bird, Lambert, Jennings, and Slater met at an unspecified location. Slater brought a friend with him, Jack Gibson, who adopted the pseudonym "Les Colfax." Gibson was to become a shadowy figure in the history of ONE. He and Slater met while working together at USC's Doheny Memorial Library, and Gibson was the organization's first (and only) trained librarian. Gibson was a reclusive man who did not want to be known for his association with *ONE* and, although he and Slater became close friends who would frequently travel together, wanted little to do with the movement.

For the first item of business, Jennings presented a bill for $30 for the plates from Abbey Lithograph. Nonglossy paper would run from $5 to $7 per 1,000 sheets, and the cover would cost $9. There would be a $24 charge for printing and another $7 for folding. It would be up to the editorial board to fold and staple in the subscription blanks. Based on these estimates, a bill of $77.77 was approved. A motion was passed to pay the typesetting bill of $22.77. Lambert gave this amount to Jennings, who would pass it on to his sister Elaine, the owner of the press. Lambert would send ONE's attorney, Fred Snider, the $50 needed to cover the cost of incorporating the organization. It was further agreed that Martin Block's Studio Bookshop would serve as the undercover distribution center for the magazine. A motion was made and seconded that "Mrs. H. Nicolis" would "be received as one of the owners and the owners be included as part of the body," but the motion did not pass. Discussion of the matter followed, but nothing was resolved. It was decided that attorneys Snider and Shibley would receive complimentary copies, as would Dr. Karl M. Bowman and Donald Webster Cory. A final motion was made and seconded that a letter be sent to the directors of Mattachine thanking them for the $100 check for subscriptions and advertising.

The following day, Saturday the 10th, Jennings, Slater, and Lambert met at Slater's home for a business meeting. Lambert presented Slater with $50.25 to cover attorney's fees and gave Jennings $.23 in stamps for mailing. A financial report followed that showed a petty cash balance as of January 1 to be $11.56 after all expenditures to date had been paid. As of the 10th, the directors had sold seventy-two one-year, three six-month, and three single-issue subscriptions. Donations from discussion group meetings yielded $25, including $5 donations from Fred Frisbie and Betty Purdue. The Knights of the Clock had contributed $34.54 through their fund-raising party. These funds added to their cash on hand, which totaled just under $275, less printing costs, taxes, mailbox rental, and pending attorneys' fees. Annual subscriptions had sold for $2, so they set aside $132.05 for future reserves.

An article and letter from Donald Webster Cory were received and filed for future publication. Motions were made and passed that "Harriet Nicholos," "Mrs. Jennings," and Slater's lover Antonio Sanchez be elected to membership and be authorized to sign the papers of incorporation. This is the first time Sanchez is noted as being active in ONE, but I have been unable to learn anything about Nicholos (spelled "Nicholis" in Slater's minutes from

January 9th) or what Mrs. Jennings, presumably Dale's mother, had to do with anything. Aside from Jennings's articles, the first issue would include a translation from *Die Insel*, a mission statement from the World Federation for the Rights of Man reprinted from the July 1952 issue of the German magazine. With these actions, the planning phase was done. In a matter of days, *ONE* was born at last.

A Shout in the Wind

The first issue of *ONE* looked decidedly odd, nearly square at six by seven inches, with a drab gray cover and the logo and stripes in purple ink. As planned, this debut issue was printed in the basement of Jennings's sister and brother-in-law's house, on a press they owned through their business, California Market Sketch and Press.[18] The editorial board of that first issue included Block, Jennings, and Slater—with no pseudonyms used—with Donald Webster Cory listed as contributing editor, William Lambert as business manager, and Guy Rousseau as circulation manager. Its creators peddled the initial issue "from bar stool to bar stool" in the local bars of Los Angeles (Hansen 1998, 28). The price was twenty cents—the price of a beer—and according to Sanchez, "the amateur peddlers all came home with pockets jingling" (Hansen 1998, 28). The magazine, if not a smash hit, proved a success.

As *ONE* was the heart of ONE, Incorporated, so Dale Jennings was the heart of *ONE*, at least during its first year of production. A seasoned playwright and budding author, he had at last found (or created) his own niche in the homosexual rights movement as *ONE*'s editor-in-chief and a primary contributor. Fred Frisbie, who later served as president of ONE, recalled, "Dale Jennings was the only one who had been exposed to the process of pamphleteering in the process of helping his sister issue broadsides and advertising matter in her sewing business. So Dale Jennings was busy from morning till night coaching we [*sic*] novices, in this and that nicety from scribbled notes to properly formed 'Dummies' ready for the printer—to be set in type, how to indicate the position of artwork relative to text, etc."[19]

Jennings often wrote pointed and angry essays in those early issues, and the personas under which he wrote invited lively debate. For example, in the second issue of *ONE*, Jennings, as Jeff Winters,[20] scathingly chastised Christine Jorgensen, equating her much-discussed sex-change operation with cosmetic surgery and calling her a self-imposed eunuch: "You're not a woman you know . . . those expensive scalpels only gave you the legal right

to transvestitism." He continued, "Homosexuals are not a third sex, personalities in the body of the wrong sex, biological confusions of nature. Most
neurotic symptoms they display—and there are plenty—can just as easily
have been caused by society refusing to adjust to them as the reverse. Their
vast number in both history and present makes it impossible to label them
freaks and so unusual as to be called abnormal" (13).

Clearly, Jennings often used the Winters pseudonym to stir up controversy.
However, I believe that many of these ideas accurately reflect his opinion at
the time he wrote them. Jennings lacked the respect for "swishes" conveyed
by Kepner, Slater, and Hay. Jennings seemed to think their nelly behavior
was a bizarre affectation, not a legitimate and natural signifier of an innately
felt identity. Jennings had learned how to be a man through his service in the
war. Perhaps with a little like coaching, effeminate men such as Jorgensen
could be remodeled. Stubborn and opinionated, Jennings held to this belief
until very late in his life.

In the May 1953 issue of *ONE*, Rowland responded to Jennings's earlier
assertion that homosexuals did not comprise a cultural minority.[21] Rowland
based his argument on Webster Dictionary's primary definition of *culture*:
"The complex distinctive attainments, beliefs, traditions, etc., constituting
the background of a racial, religious, or social group." Rowland stated that
ONE's very existence proved such a culture existed. Not all homosexuals
actively participated in this culture, though; he estimated that "only a few
of the 1,500,000 'absolute' American homosexuals participate." This "small
minority within a small minority" could be distinguished as those "homosexuals who visit the homosexual bars, who walk or talk or gesticulate in the
universally recognized, homosexual manner." These few realized that they
were on the cutting edge of "an emergent homosexual culture" and sought to
develop a homosexual code of ethics that differed from that of heterosexuals. Rowland pointed out that many participated in the homosexual culture,
some part time and others more exclusively, but many also participated in
other cultures as well. Homosexuality was but one aspect of their cultural
awareness. Rowland also encouraged consideration of religious and ethnic
factors as well: "Most homosexuals in this country as a matter of fact, do
participate in homosexual culture and also in the dominant, heterosexual
culture and in any other culture from which they sprang or in which their
lives involve them." In the pages of *ONE*, Jennings and Rowland continued
the "Are we a people?" debate, a carryover from their Mattachine discussions.
Although in part the "culture wars" may have been a gimmick designed to
ignite controversy and stimulate sales, it also signified a genuine division

within the homosexual rights movement, one present from the very first meeting. At this stage of *ONE's* history, the controversy was harnessed for the betterment of the organization. "Culturalists,"[22] such as Rowland, Legg, and Hay, and Libertarians, namely Slater and Jennings, needed each other to further their cause and fight a common adversary. Ultimately, however, the divisive issue was to threaten the organization's future and vitality.

In the summer of 1953, Jennings sent complimentary issues of *ONE* to more than a hundred scholars, journalists, authors, and intellectuals, with a letter requesting submissions for "one of the first publications in the English language to offer space to the literature of deviation." He encouraged them to submit any essays, stories, or poems to *ONE* that remained unpublished. Jennings stated they would receive no remuneration for the work because ONE, Incorporated, was a nonprofit corporation. Among those contacted were Jean Cocteau, Noel Coward, Lillian Hellman, Gilbert Highet, Aldous Huxley, Christopher Isherwood, Norman Mailer, Thomas Mann, Margaret Mead, Dorothy Parker, Jean Paul Sartre, Tennessee Williams, and Evelyn Waugh. The plea met with minimal response: Mailer contributed an article titled "The Homosexual Villain," which appeared in *ONE's* January 1955 issue. But the list also reflects the editors' high-reaching ambitions and widely diverse interests. "*ONE* is a new magazine which concerns itself with the many aspects of homosexuality. Its purposes are to inform the heterosexual majority about deviation, the homosexuals about themselves and to criticize as well as attempt to bridge a gap. . . . It aims to be read in every home." With Jennings at the helm, *ONE* proceeded at full speed ahead. He seemed certain that word of this little magazine would spread around the world.

When we recall that, in the first years of *ONE's* publication, homosexual acts were illegal in every state in America, then we can better appreciate the courageous act of these writers and editors. Through thought-provoking essays, daring social commentary, and a sharp contemporary design, *ONE* prevailed against dire odds. On the cover of the November 1953 issue, *ONE* proclaimed itself "The Homosexual Magazine," and from this point on, the full title changed from *ONE* to *ONE Magazine*. Through the editorial prowess of Wolf and Slater and the artistic contributions of Corbin and Sanchez, *ONE* soon became the first official voice of America's homosexual movement, which surprised even the core officers of the origination. As one of *ONE's* first regular contributors, Stella Rush, put it, "We only expected *ONE* to be information and education. It didn't occur to us that people would be hanging on to us like a lifeline" (Soule 2006, 17).

Cleaning House
(1953–54)

Dale's life revolved around the court case. . . . It was a huge focus of his life, defined him and his path for the remainder of his days. He could never escape it, could never forget it when it became a burden. He did not easily carry that enormous weight of the icon that had landed on his shoulders, but it was his destiny.

—Patrick Dale Porter (May 26, 2000, letter to Jim Schneider)

I am aware of my almost total preoccupation with the male and male sexuality. It is life-long. I prefer to think that I'd not have accomplished my bit without it instead of the depressing possibility that I'd have done more.

—Dale Jennings (October 19, 1990, letter to Don Slater)

THIS CHAPTER DOCUMENTS a paradoxical time of prosperity and growth on the one hand, internal strife and ultimatums on the other. When it became clear in 1953 that they were on to something, the men of ONE began jockeying for power. Who would be the first to reap the financial reward? As the organization became solvent—the distribution for *ONE Magazine* rose from 500 to 6,000 copies—many started looking at the dollars. All of a sudden, ONE's integrative ideals went right out the window and, over the course of the year, African American members fell by the wayside and the women of ONE became marginalized and unsung. This was a time of purging for both ONE and Mattachine. Despite the copious metaphors of inclusion bantered about in the formative days, white (non-Communist) men would control both organizations by the year's end.

Many of the facts, dates, and political wrangling presented in this chapter have been reconstructed almost entirely from historic documents, especially minutes of business and editorial meetings. Although I have tried to identify and present salient passages and citations pertaining most directly to the institutional history of ONE and the evolution of the Los Angeles–based movement, there are as many different ways of presenting and interpreting this information as there are thoughtful minds interested in this story. Needless to say, there is far more information available than is presented here, as any narrative history is an act of asyndeton, of necessity omitting more than it can possibly include. Readers who want more details of these meetings and events are encouraged to visit the history section of the HIC Web site where the minutes and other documents referred to herein are available for public perusal (www.tangentgroup.org). Readers will also find posted several "who's-on-first" time lines to help the reader and other researchers to keep track of ONE's board members, editors, and corporate correspondence.

In its early days, *ONE* was distributed throughout the Los Angeles area in a variety of ways. At first, many newsstands refused to distribute the magazine. Martin Block recalls distributing *ONE* in the Los Angeles bars: "Only after the bar sales proved that the magazines could make a profit did a few newsstand owners agree to stock copies. As soon as they did, 90 percent of sales were by single copies, rather than subscription. By the end of the decade, the three magazines [*ONE*, *The Ladder*, and *Mattachine Review*] were selling at dozens of newsstands and adult bookstores across the country, with *ONE* boasting that it was selling copies in every state" (Streitmatter 1995, 28–29).

Increasingly, local subscribers helped to bolster *ONE's* sales, and the editors relied increasingly on the post office to distribute the magazine. Of course, via post or newsstand, it usually came discreetly wrapped in a plain brown wrapper. The editorial board was listed on the masthead of the first six issues as Block, Jennings, and Slater, with William Lambert noted as business manager and Donald Webster Cory as contributing editor.

Jennings, Block, and Antonio Sanchez signed ONE's articles of incorporation on February 7, 1953, and the State of California granted ONE's charter on May 27. This document established the primary and ancillary missions of ONE, Incorporated, which were first and foremost to publish *ONE Magazine*: "The specific and primary purposes for which this corporation was formed are to publish and disseminate a magazine dealing primarily with homosexuality from the scientific, historical and critical point of view, and to aid in the social integration and rehabilitation of the sexual variant."

The articles also established six more general purposes. First, ONE would publish books and papers "concerned with medical, social, pathological, psychological and therapeutic research of every kind and description pertaining to socio-sexual behavior." ONE would also seek "to sponsor, supervise, and conduct educational programs . . . to promote among the general public an interest, knowledge and understanding of the problems" of "all social and emotional variants." The next purpose, accordingly, was to "stimulate, sponsor, aid, supervise and conduct research" on homosexuality and said "variants."

The fourth purpose proved the most controversial and divisive within the homosexual rights movement: to "promote the integration into society of such persons whose behavior varies from the current moral and social standards and to aid the development of the social and moral responsibility of all such persons." This goal contradicted many of the central tenets of the more radical post-Stonewall gay rights movement, which championed the right to be *different*. Hay wrote those in favor of integration as assimilationists, and, although he granted—and even fought for—their right to privacy, he criticized them for being cowards and felt that they were in denial of their true essence or being. Most important, these twin goals of integration and the establishment of a moral code of ethics provided cornerstones of the homosexual/homophile rights movement and subsequently helped to define it against the later gay movement where, rather than blending in, the universal rite of passage involved the process of "coming out." ONE's remaining goals, involving research, scholarship, and education, are essential to homosexuals, homophiles, and gays—and probably all social movements pertaining to promoting equal rights.

The final two purposes expressed in the articles of incorporation allowed ONE to hold and/or trade property and to expand on its missions, as stated above, in ways deemed appropriate "to promote the interests of the corporation." The corporation asserted its nonprofit status pursuant to part 1 of division 1 of title 1 of the corporate code of the State of California, with its principal office located in Los Angeles County. Block, Jennings, and Sanchez served as ONE's first directors. Membership classifications would be set forth in the corporation's bylaws, to be adopted by said first directors.

ONE's founders had intended from the beginning that theirs would become a nonprofit corporation. Indeed, in the first issue, ONE prematurely declared itself "a nonprofit corporation dedicated to the service of humanity." Attorney Fred Snider had been processing the paperwork but, in a letter dated

February 24, 1953,[1] California's franchise tax board rejected ONE's application for tax exemption. In the words of John J. Campbell, executive officer of the franchise tax board, "In order to be exempt under Section 23701d, an organization must be organized and operated exclusively for educational and scientific purposes. Because the above corporation will publish and sell a magazine relating to such purposes, it will not be operated exclusively for educational and scientific purposes." This response baffled ONE's directors, who continued to tell members that their donations were tax deductible. This declaration would create problems in the future, as will be seen, and, despite its pedagogic and humanistic intentions, ONE would never operate as a legitimate nonprofit corporation.

ONE's business manager certainly wasn't troubled by this turn of events, however. As ONE was now a decidedly capitalistic venture, an egalitarian ethos began to seem out of place in the corporation. There would no longer be much use for the Communists among them either.

The Red Menace

In January 1953, the month *ONE* was first published, Jim Kepner attended his first meeting of the Mattachine Foundation, by invitation of his neighbor Betty Perdue, who wrote for *ONE* (and later *Tangents*) as "Geraldine Jackson." There were more than a few people present, he recalled, and no one thought to pull the shades out of fear in this Hollywood home. Similarly, German filmmaker Rosa von Praunheim wrote of his extended visit to Los Angeles, "There has been a lot of talk about how clandestine, how fearful the early Mattachine meetings were. I'm sure some of them were that, but I did not see the evidence of it" (1979, 37). This vignette illustrates the brevity of the "secret society" phase of the Los Angeles movement (less than eighteen months passed between the establishment of Mattachine and the Jennings trial). As has been seen, the clandestine period ended abruptly: only so much could be done under cover. With Mattachine out in the open, Kepner and dozens if not hundreds of homosexuals like him could finally find a home, a "people," and a mission.

As Kepner and others would soon find, however, this was hardly a halcyon time for the Los Angeles movement. In the spring of 1953, the Mattachine Foundation "began to rip itself apart," as Kepner later put it. Although the original five founders of Mattachine had "taken their analysis of homosexual conditions from Marxist social theory," newcomers to the organization were "horrified [by the Communist] radicals in their midst." So "Hay imperiously resigned in the founders' name" and the "new leaders adopted an apologetic assimilationist course" (Kepner 1998, 3).

The interim committee of the administrative council of the Mattachine Foundation, Inc., issued an "Official Statement of Policy on Political Questions and Related Matters" in which the purposes of the organizations were succinctly put: "The Mattachine Foundation, Inc., is a nonprofit corporation organized in conformity with the corporate laws of the State of California to study the questions of sexual deviation and their relation to American society as a whole." This was the organization's sole purpose, as distinct from taking any political or religious stand unrelated to the topic of homosexuality and "the problems of sexual deviation." To clarify, the policy's framers added, "The Foundation has never been, is not now and must never be identified with any 'ism'—political, religious or otherwise. The Foundation has never solicited and does not welcome the endorsement or assistance of individuals or groups wishing to further the goals of those individuals or groups to the detriment of the missions of the Foundation."

According to Will Roscoe, after the original leaders were expunged from Mattachine in May 1953, "the broad grass-roots base of Mattachine vanished, never to reach its pre-1953 levels again" (1996a, 4). The San Francisco Area Council soon became the most active aspect of Mattachine, headed by Hal Call, editor of the region's newsletter and of Pan Graphic Press, which published several books and the *Mattachine Review* (see esp. Sears 2006). As Mattachine in Los Angeles languished, ONE, Incorporated, began to grow.

On a side note, it should be stated that Kepner and Hay's assertion that those who hijacked the Mattachine Foundation "adopted an apologetic assimilationist course" is not entirely fair. Many of those who stayed active in Mattachine, be it in Los Angeles or San Francisco, were not entirely apologetic, nor were they assimilationists. Many on the other side of the culture wars, such as Jennings and Slater, were beginning to live openly as homosexuals. In a way, Hay's discounting of these second-wave Mattachinos as "assimilationists" is just as wrong as their branding him a Communist. Such synecdochic name-calling only serves to reduce a person to one stigmatized label, written off as insignificant at best and, at worst, a betrayer of the cause. Many a valuable activist has been exiled from the movement for just this reason, and the movement has repeatedly suffered for it.

Although business was improving, ONE was not immune from the kind of turmoil that had rattled Mattachine, and 1953 became a year rife with political struggles and power plays. In early June, Lambert proposed that he try to eke a living out of his work with ONE. During a meeting on June 7—with Lambert, Slater, Jennings, and Merton Bird in attendance—a lengthy discussion ensued in which it was decided that "if Mr. Lambert were going to try such a thing it should be on the basis that he set his own commission on Advertisement and from Subscription to the amount commensurate with his needs but at no time detrimental to the financial status of ONE." Lambert was to report back to the board the following month to assess the feasibility of his proposal.

During a corporate meeting on June 28, former Mattachinos Chuck Rowland and Jim Gruber were added to *ONE*'s editorial board, and Rowland was elected to corporate membership. Jennings formally announced that his "primary interest [was] to become either a contributing editor or Editor-in-Chief," but no motion was proposed on this matter. Because of the prolonged absences of Bird and Block, the board decided to prompt them to action. Accordingly, Jennings sent each a letter on July 3. Block was advised that he had been retained on the editorial board of *ONE* as a contributing editor, which excused him from editorial meetings. Jennings urged Block to attend the next corporate meeting at 7:00 p.m. on Sunday, July 19, at the home of Slater and Sanchez. Jennings's letter addressed to "Dear Byrd" was far less cordial: "You are instructed to attend the next corporate meeting to show just cause why your name should not be dropped as a member of the corporation. . . . Failure to appear will result in your name being automatically dropped without appeal." It is unclear to me as to why Bird and Block had lost interest in the organization or why they would receive such different treatment on behalf of Jennings. Although I would not go so far as to brand Jennings as racist, his actions clearly served to marginalize the African Americans who had served ONE from the start.

Other significant changes occurred in the summer of 1953. First, because of *ONE*'s rapid growth and early successes, the price of the magazine rose to fifty cents in June. Joan Corbin and Corky Wolf were appointed members of the circulation department, and in July they were listed as assistants to the editorial board. (It should be noted that at this time, despite early talk of equality and inclusion, all editorial board members were men.)

Jennings achieved his goal of becoming editor-in-chief during an editorial board meeting on Wednesday, July 15, 1953, under the stipulation that he would only have the power to arrange the layout and make minor space changes. He could also select the magazine's fillers, designs, and type styles. Slater, however, did not respond well to Jennings's new authority, and he tendered his resignation from the board unless it would promote him to contributing editor. That motion was tabled "to be taken up at the next editorial meeting if he persists."

On Sunday, July 19, the corporation experienced its first significant shake-up. Because neither Block nor Bird attended, the board dropped Bird from membership. Block's membership status was "tabled indefinitely," and the board elected Corbin and Wolf to fill the vacancies. Although the minutes make no mention of his bid for salary, Lambert was elected the new chairman. Jennings became ONE's new vice-chairman, and Rowland was elected the new secretary-treasurer. Bailey Whitaker became the magazine's official proofreader.

Eve Elloree's (Joan Corbin's) bold cover on the September 1953 issue poses the question "Homosexual Marriage?" as a teaser for an article therein titled "Reformer's Choice: Marriage License or Just License," supposedly submitted by reader "E. B. Saunders." This article poses the hypothetical assumption that the goals of social acceptance espoused by the Mattachine Society will come about by the year 2053. But would society then allow homosexuals to continue in their promiscuous ways? Saunders says that this would ultimately be like "legalizing promiscuity for a special section of the population," and this freedom, in turn, would make the bonds of heterosexual unions even less tenable. "Heterosexual marriage must be protected. The acceptance of homosexuality without homosexual marriage ties would be an attack upon it." Saunders asserts that with homosexual marriage would come the problem of homosexual adultery: "To those living adulterous lives since discovering themselves to be deviates, this comes as a ludicrous suggestion. Yet to heterosexuals it is of great moment and quite to the point. Equal rights mean equal responsibility: equal freedoms mean equal limitations." Saunders concludes by restating the original problem, that Mattachine was hitting the ground running before selecting a proper destination: "When one digs, it must be to make a ditch, a well, a trench: something! Otherwise all of this energetic work merely produces a hole. Any bomb can do that."[2]

The next editorial in this issue, "The Fey and Free Will" by "Walter B.," ponders whether one becomes a homosexual or is born gay. This is in response to a letter from "Donald Ferrar" of Oakland that ran in the May issue that stated in surprisingly contemporary terms: "It looks like you're fighting not just for rights but for *special* rights." Ferrar noted that many of his "gay" friends felt no different from anyone else, nor did they want to "stand up and be counted." In fact, he says, "They wanted the counting stopped." Ferrar said he felt betrayed by those who insisted that "gays" were different: "I thought you wanted to be accepted—not honored." He concluded: "I strongly suggest you decide soon whether you want civil rights or a legal cult." Walter B.'s article, contrary to Ferrar's comment regarding whether one was born or made gay, asserts that it actually matters a lot. "Becoming gay" was an act of choice or will, whereas being "born gay" made it an "incurable . . . mental illness." Society had cast homosexuals into this "dualistic and absurd thinking," not a place where they necessarily wanted to find themselves. Nevertheless, provided this dichotomy, most gays preferred the "born gay" scenario, to combat the implications of the Christian concepts of sinning versus free will. "This is the only way of turning aside the legal and social persecution that would otherwise be the homosexual's part." Walter B. then states that people should consider the causes of homosexuality on more "deterministic" grounds, where "everyone in the environment of the perpetrator is responsible for the latter's antisocial acts—and, *a fortiori*, in greater or lesser degree, for the latter's being gay— which makes the idea of punishment absurd."

Two pages later, almost as an afterthought to the above article, Jennings published a quote from Margaret Mead's *Coming of Age in Samoa.* Clearly, Jennings's little magazine contained several cutting-edge thoughts and con-trasting points of view; there remained a lot of original, creative material here for the 1950s reader—and the contemporary audience—to ponder.

Indeed, many of the debates first breached in *ONE's* pages continue today, and the subjects remain just as controversial. When this "Homosexual Mar-riage?" issue was delivered to the post office on August 27, the Los Angeles postal service confiscated it and withheld *ONE* from distribution until postal officials in Washington, D.C., could decide whether the magazine crossed the line into obscenity. Whether the postmaster truly felt that the magazine was obscene or whether he was rattled by the idea that two people of the same gender could form long-term and healthy relationships is unclear. It seems to me that the authorities at this time were not as offended by a frank discussion of sex as they were by the idea that homosexual relationships could be based on love and might prove enduring. The postmaster held the issues from September 2nd through the 18th.

According to ONE's minutes dated Sunday, September 6, 1953, ONE's directors seem to have considered the postmaster's actions to be more an inconvenience than a major setback. Lambert's first report as ONE's chairman lauded the August issue of *ONE Magazine* as "the most important landmark" in the organization's brief history. He congratulated Corbin and Wolf for their contributions to the subscriptions, mailing, art, and editorial depart-ments. He noted their inaugural appearance on the magazine's masthead.

Lambert further noted that only one thousand copies of the first issue had been printed, and six hundred of those were by direct order of the Mattachine Foundation. There were only six hundred issues printed in February, and half of those were damaged through "printing difficulties." In March, another thousand were printed, and, for the first time, the magazine was cut and stapled commercially. In April, fifteen hundred copies came off the press, and in May, June, and July, the volume reached two thousand. That proved too many, as hundreds of copies remained at summer's end. Readers were unenthusiastic about *ONE's* May issue, which deadened sales in June. Sales increased somewhat in July, which Lambert credited to a "lively June issue." In July, the editors printed their first short story, "But They'll Outgrow It," a pastoral romance contributed by Rowland about two boys who lived near a prairie lake. With renewed sales, three thousand issues of *ONE* were printed in August. Soon after, New York distribution centers took an interest in the little homosexual magazine from Los Angeles, and their orders justified September's increase to five thousand copies.

Fortunately, ONE had retained the services of a bright young attorney named Eric Julber early in August. With Julber's help, the September issue was ultimately released. The editors of *ONE* responded indignantly by printing "ONE is NOT GRATEFUL" across the front cover of the October 1953 issue, with this on the back: "ONE thanks no one for this reluctant acceptance. It is true that this decision is historic. Never before has a governmental agency of this size admitted that homosexuals not only have legal rights but might have respectable motives as well. The admission is welcome, but it's tardy and far from enough. As we sit around quietly like nice little ladies and gentlemen gradually educating the public and the courts at our leisure, thousands of homosexuals are being unjustly arrested, blackmailed, fined, jailed, intimidated, beaten, ruined, and murdered. . . . [T]he deviate hearing of our late August issue through mail bars will not be overly impressed."

Beside the recent board upheavals and the small but significant victory over the post office, Jennings had other matters on his mind. On October 12, he sent a letter to Whitaker and other board members that called for a corporate meeting to convene at his home on Lemoyne Street at 7:00 p.m. on October 18, 1953, in order to discuss "past and present remuneration for all of ONE's employees, and to set up a scale for the future." Article 6 of ONE's bylaws clearly gave the directors authority to "fix all rates of compensation and salaries to be paid to Directors, officers, members, or others." As Lambert had pointed out during his September 9 presentation, ONE needed to pay down the debt to its workers and clear the slate for the future.

Rules and Regulations

On October 16, 1953, ONE, Incorporated, filed its bylaws with California's secretary of state—a full year after the organization's inception. These bylaws established positions of directors, officers, and members, with directors and officers being one and the same: the chairman, vice-chairman, and secretary-treasurer. The founding directors would be replaced at the first annual meeting, in January 1954. Directors would be elected at the 1954 annual meeting and every third year thereafter. Officers would be elected by the directors annually. In case of a vacancy, someone would be appointed to the office during the next monthly directors' meeting. Should a director resign, the remaining members would appoint a member to serve until the next annual meeting when a new election would be held to determine who would complete the remainder of the unexpired term.

ONE's bylaws established two categories of membership: voting and nonvoting. The corporation would consist of nine voting members, or directors, of the corporation, including the three officers (president, vice president, and secretary-treasurer). In case of resignation or vacancy, the directors would appoint a stand-in to serve until the next annual meeting. A nominee required two-thirds majority of the voting members present to become a director. If the candidate failed the vote, then the vacancy would remain until the following annual meeting. A person could be removed from membership by a unanimous vote of the directors present and voting at any of the monthly director's meetings, provided that person had been notified of the pending action prior to the meeting and had been invited to defend his or her position by addressing the board. Directors were empowered to form departments or committees and appoint project managers to coordinate with the board and provide the annual reports on that department's behalf. This person would act as the department or committee's board adviser. A class of nonvoting members was also created, commonly referred to as the "Friends of ONE." Typically, each Friend received a subscription to *ONE*, a wallet-sized membership card, and other ancillary publications such as *ONE Confidential* and occasional newsletters. The bylaws further stipulated that meetings would be "conducted in accordance with *Robert's Rules of Order.*"

A good understanding of these bylaws and of *Robert's Rules* is essential if one is to comprehend the bedlam that ensued in the 1960s, a decade after ONE's founding. Anyone involved in small corporations, nonprofit agencies, or special-interest associations would likewise do well to consider the merits of this corporate design.[3] While framing the bylaws, the founders assumed that the board would always be comprised of amenable leaders. The two-thirds majority rule guarded against a renegade newcomer coming aboard who might stage a mutiny or change the corporate course. However, this same rule made it difficult to recruit new blood and fresh perspectives when needed. Reliance on *Robert's Rules* provided a ready-made structure for the business meetings; however, these rules suffer from significant shortcomings. *Robert's Rules* delegates significant power to the chairperson, who sets the meeting's agenda and facilitates discussion. The chairperson has the power to waylay arguments he or she deems insignificant and can silence a speaker by declaring the person "out of order." While in spirit *Robert's Rules* strives to protect dissenting or minority voices, in practice it is up to a judicious chair to ensure that such voices are respected and heard. An unsupportive or agenda-ridden chairperson can thus stifle discussion and enforce a tyrannical majority, and even a slight majority can, with the chairperson's support, rule over and even hijack a corporation, as will be seen in the chapters that follow.

What Jennings failed to anticipate for the October 18 meeting was a rebellion brewing under his leadership. Chuck Rowland and Jim Gruber did not attend this meeting. In their place came a letter of resignation that complained of Jennings's tyrannical hold over the magazine. "We have always felt that the operations of the magazine are too much dominated by the personal philosophy and subjective attitudes of one individual," they wrote. "Through circumstance and manipulation he maintains his omnipotence to the point of ineffectuality of other members and impotence of the magazine." Rowland and Gruber felt that any gesture toward collective decision making regarding the magazine's content was illusory. They claimed that, although they were on the editorial board, every time they received a new issue of the magazine, they were "nearly as unfamiliar with its content as subscribers." It seems that Jennings had rejected most of their contributions and had "forgotten" to inform them of meetings in which policy was discussed and *ONE*'s content selected. With this said, and with apologies addressed to their readers, Rowland and Gruber resigned from the editorial board. They would be dropped from corporate membership later, on December 1, 1953.

Jennings wrote the minutes for this October meeting. Like a nervous upbraided child, he doodled arrows and figures in the notebook and sketched only a crude skeleton of a very important meeting. Eric Julber had apparently approved a "lobby fund," but the purpose for this is not stated. The new bylaws were read, but no action could be taken on them because there was no quorum.[4] Rowland and Gruber's letter was read and accepted, and Slater requested an editorial report from Jennings to clarify their assertions. A new size for the magazine was proposed—it is unknown by whom—to be taken up in the November meeting. Any discussion for writers' pay was tabled, and it seems that the organization was to move into a room at 232 South Hill Street the following month. Such news! Yet all that survives of this important meeting are ten stark lines sketched on lined paper covered with Jennings's doodles.

On November 1, the organization moved its records from Slater's home on Bunker Hill to its new office at 232 South Hill Street. This office was described by *ONE* contributor Ross Ingersoll as "two dismal rooms in a shabby gray building in a decaying section of downtown L.A., furnished with scrappy second-hand desks and chairs, shelving and file cabinets, gifts of the 'friends of one'" (as quoted in Hansen 1998, 29–30). Hansen later used the dismal office setting in one of his David Brandstetter mystery novels. Historians Joyce Murdoch and Deb Price provide a deft description of the office: "In the dingy third-floor hallway, the dull whir of sewing machines was jarringly punctuated by a soprano singing teacher, whose voice wandered around on every note. . . . That undistinguished location [seemed] straight out of a film noir set, a white-on-black hand-lettered sign on a frosted glass door read simply ONE" (2001, 27–28).

On that same evening, in their new environment, the board of directors convened to declare the first directors of the corporation: Martin Block, Eve Elloree, David Freeman, Dale Jennings, William Lambert, Donald Slater, Ann Carll Reid, Tony Sanchez, and Guy Rousseau. It was acknowledged that each had served informally since ONE's date of incorporation, May 27, 1953. With this action, and with little to no fanfare, the board secured the legal status of the corporation.

From Platform to Plank: Eliminating Dale Jennings

On November 15, 1953, the Mattachine Society honored *ONE*'s editor-in-chief with an achievement award, recognizing his work on *ONE* magazine and steadfast dedication to ONE, Incorporated.[5] The tone and style of the narrative of the acceptance speech are typical Dale Jennings, his narrative persona shifting from bashful to braggart, sounding first the winds and then the brass. But a political message toward the end of the speech may provide a key for understanding Jennings's fate within ONE. Jennings began his speech with rousing and relevant tones: "Each of us here tonight is a hero, each has a place in history," he began. "We are that little band that the Future will celebrate. . . . We are despised, yet we sit here tonight in courageous defiance of a society given to lynching." He declared that his opinion was that of an "immoderate man . . . wholly unrestrained, more than a little vulgar and shockingly belligerent" and added that moderation was a form of fear. "When we avoid action by pleading its imprudence, we in our fear forget those most imprudent men at Valley Forge. . . . The Jew Moses did not say, 'Thou shalt commit less adultery.' Yet the established order against which he revolted was no more primitive than the identical bigotry which we face." He continued, "Before smiling away these grand comparisons, think for a moment how gigantic is the oppression under which we live. None has ever equaled it in completeness. We are dictated to in every facet of human behavior. Where we live, whom we shall have for friends, how we shall express that friendship, the color of our friends, their number: we shall not have physical satisfaction of any kind not approved by courts of law, what we wear, how we wear it, how we move, our facial expressions, gestures, vocabularies and what we say with them, our very tones of voice—and even the way we think! We know well the punishments for non-conformity. This is a tyranny beyond any tyranny ever known! Then is it immoderate to say tonight that those who fight this tyranny deserve the highest praise?"

But Jennings did not flatter his audience for long. His lecture turned on the observation that "[w]hile moderation is a form of fear, fear takes the form of many immoderate acts." He pointed out that in more reasonable times people would laud these acts as just means to overthrow unfair or tyrannical laws. He cautioned that the freedom of speech necessary to engage such laws in a public forum was being mitigated; one could silence an activist simply by calling him or her by "a certain name pre-filled with odium." Nevertheless, one particular "*Readers' Digest* version of a four letter word is thrown about like rice at a wedding. Take a handful and let go; you're sure to hit someone." One might expect that many in the audience would anticipate the dreaded word as having something to do with homosexuality, like "queer," "homo," or "faggot." But in the era of Senator Joe McCarthy, the Red Scare also occupied their collective minds.

By the end of 1953, ONE, Incorporated, had earned $4,779.70 from magazine sales and another $507.33 in gifts and memberships. According to the 1953 annual report, they had averaged 929 subscriptions each month with 1,515 more issues distributed via the newsstands. ONE had printed 36,867 total copies of *ONE* and produced twelve issues, distributing 29,311. Annual nonvoting membership fees to ONE, which included a year's subscription to the magazine, cost $10. One could also become a contributing member for $25, associate for $50, or a life member for $100.

In January of 1954, *ONE* changed to a larger format of 8½ by 5½ inches. The cover of this issue featured a black-and-white photo of a man silhouetted against the surf, his right hand reaching up as if to grasp the sun, which was rising (or setting) beside the caption "Miami Junks the Constitution." Joan Corbin contributed illustrations, as she had in the past, and other sketches were provided by Jennings.[6]

The theme of this issue consists of the legal hassles homosexuals continually suffered. A short story titled "Anyway, They Asked for It," warns of the dangers of entrapment and the corruption of the legal system. This is followed by an article titled "The Law" that reminds *ONE*'s readers that sodomy at this time was a crime in every state, and per California Penal Code Section 288a, "[A]ny person participating in the act of copulation with the mouth of one person with the sexual organ of another is punishable by imprisonment in the state prison for not exceeding 15 years." Also included is a fourteen-point statement, "Your Rights in Case of Arrest," compiled by one of ONE's attorneys.[7] This was crucial information for any homosexual person because this was years before the Supreme Court was to determine that police officers had to notify a suspect of his or her Miranda rights when making an arrest.

An article by Jennings entitled "A Frank Look at the Mattachine" (published under the Winters pseudonym) contrasts the original Mattachine Foundation with the new Mattachine Society. Jennings asserts that the new Mattachine was a failure, run by cowards with no mission or purpose. He challenged Mattachine's leaders to "initiate a series of projects concretely beneficial to both society and the homosexual" or else face "gradual dissolution or spontaneous combustion." Of course, few of *ONE*'s readers would know that this angry article was written by one of Mattachine's original founders—one who was also a Communist.

The February 1954 issue was markedly different but just as important. This was the first dedicated to "The Feminine Viewpoint," and this issue was progressive in many ways. An essay by "D. M. Woods" entitled "The Human Hybrid" is one of the most concise articles to articulate the integrationist approach ever to be published in *ONE*. The author begins by stating, "Since neither natural selection, legislation nor prejudice has significantly affected [the incidence of homosexuality], it is perhaps logical and necessary to presume a purpose in its persistent existence." It follows that because homosexuals had always and would always be present in society, then they should be integrated within it rather than cast aside as anomalies. Further, "any real integration of the homosexual will emancipate not only him but the heterosexual as well." The article concludes, "Homosexuals do not desire an especial place in society but merely the assurance that they too belong and may function within its just laws and make their contributions as human beings to that society." Clearly, the idea is not to disappear nor to blend in but to be open and honest about one's sexuality while continuing to contribute to and function within a tolerant and accepting society. This would allow people to stop living double lives, "paying lip service to one type of sexuality while in practice indulging in quite another sort."

A letter from "M. F." in this issue marks the second essay where the word "gay" appears in ONE Magazine. In this letter, the word is always bracketed in quotes, as when the writer asks, "What place does the 'gay girl' hold within the covers of your magazine?" and complains that prior to this issue, "[the gay girl] would seem to have been pretty much ignored." The writer stresses that "the 'gay girl' is neither in temperament nor in action much like the gay fellow" and asks that these differences be acknowledged and explored, while of course keeping in mind "the existing close similarities." Although the writer once refers to a "gay population" (also in quotes), it is important to note that the term is not used in its modern idiom of representing a people—the word is always used as an adjective and never as a noun.

At this time in Los Angles, the word "gay" is most often used as an insider's parlance, an indexical trope that never, in the entire run of ONE Magazine, takes on the personal and political ramifications it would to develop in the mid- to late 1960s. For this reason, I often find it awkward and anachronistic to apply the term "gay" to periods prior to the Stonewall riots that famously began in Greenwich Village early on Saturday morning, June 28, 1969.[8]

Of course, many times it is the pioneers themselves who blur this distinction. When Harry Hay, for instance, described to Jonathan Ned Katz the pre-Mattachine gathering near the USC campus where he first proposed the idea of a homosexual organization, he referred to it as a "Gay party" although this event was in character and composition probably nothing like a gay party by today's standards. When Katz asked whether "[t]his was to be an openly Gay group?" Hay replied, "Yes. We didn't have the words in those years, but that was what we were going to be" (Katz 1992, 613). Indeed, as is also seen in chapter 9, Hay publicly used and defended the word "homophile" as late as 1966. Although Hay might be forgiven for his Whiggish use of the term—his "homosexuals are a people" argument (and his conception of what it meant to be a "homophile") certainly anticipates the later gay rights movement—historians who project the term "gay" onto the pre-Stonewall homosexual/homophile movement blur some important historical distinctions.

Although I do not wish to belabor the point, I feel this error is frequently perpetrated in contemporary LGBT history, and I certainly want to address it. Am I wrong to cringe when reading how Hollywood was full of "gay and lesbian actors" in the 1930s, although these people were not "gay" in any way a contemporary gay or lesbian would recognize? Or when I read how silent screen stars Lilyan Tashman and Edmund Lowe "accepted the fact that their Hollywood careers demanded they play the movie game by appearing to be heterosexual, regardless of where they fell on the Kinsey scale," even though that scale would not be conceived of for anther two and a half decades (Faderman and Timmons 2006, 63–64)? If one can play such historical sleight of hand, we might as well imagine Tashman and Lowe Rollerblading hand in hand along Venice Beach during off hours while listening to the Village People on their iPods.

As Franz Boas once stated, "In order to understand history it is necessary to know not only how things are, but how they have come to be" (1920, 314). If we retroactively treat "gay" as a social and cultural inevitability, we impose a contemporary sensibility onto a prior time and/or place with no regard for social or historical context. We also diminish the courage and bravery of these pre-Stonewall pioneers, who spoke out at a time when homosexuals were actively persecuted and treated as though psychotic. LGBT historians who retrofit the past do so in order to glorify the present, even though nuances in social and cultural context are often blurred or ignored. When the means are rewoven to fit the ends, innumerable—and important—historical and cultural distinctions are often brushed under the carpet with the excuse of "well, it was bound to happen anyway." As Boas also pointed out, "[T]here is a close parallelism between the history of language and the history of general cultural development" (1920, 317). It follows that if we pay close attention to how words such as *homosexual, homophile, lesbian,* and *gay* are used, we can gain better insight as to the evolutionary process of the movement, now and in the future. If we ignore such historic context, then we are bound to misread letters such as this one from M. F. and underestimate or misunderstand their significance.

A third article in this first feminine viewpoint issue that deserves mention is the inaugural article by a woman who was to become an important lesbian activist: Stella Rush, who wrote under the pseudonym Sten Russell. Rush, then twenty-eight years old, met Corky Wolf and Joan Corbin at a party in Los Angeles soon after ONE's formation. She had written an essay early in 1953 regarding her feelings about L.A.'s homosexual bar scene, and when she showed it to Corbin and Wolf, they asked if they could print it (Gallo 2006, xxxvi–xxxviii). In her "Letter to a Newcomer," Rush laments the fact that neophytes to the homosexual lifestyle had to initiate their rite of passage in bars: "We are sorry we do not have a more honorable, nor a more equitable society, to launch you in." She compares the bars to sewers, the plague, and to hell: "I would like to see a better meeting place for those who wish more from life than a nightmare of whisky and sex, brutality and vanity, self-pity and despair."

Despite *ONE*'s amazing success, we have seen that some underlying problems troubled the leadership of ONE, Incorporated, during this time. Stubborn and temporarily triumphant, Jennings became ONE's official secretary-treasurer at the annual meeting in January 1954 when Lambert was officially elected chairman and Wolf vice-chairman. According to the minutes of business meetings held through February of that year, Jennings, perhaps having learned from the resignation of Rowland and Gruber, made several overtures to indicate his willingness to share power and authority. For instance, during a special meeting on January 22, 1954, Ben Tabor was elected to the editorial board as news and letter editor, and Corky Wolf became *ONE*'s women's editor and bibliographer. It was further resolved that the editor would only vote to resolve ties in manuscript judging. This should have ensured that the complaint previously levied by Rowland and Gruber, that the editor had "omnipotent" rule in what was or was not printed in the magazine, would never recur.

The underlying tensions within ONE's staff were clearly expressed in a letter written and distributed by Jennings requesting a corporate meeting convene on Monday, February 1, at which the directors would more clearly define a few of ONE's core policies—namely those pertaining to finances, artistic style of the magazine, and the editorship. There were three primary complaints laid forth. Lambert complained of "the amount of cooperation he is getting." Corbin felt that there was too much "interference with her artwork," and Jennings felt that he bore "the criticism but not the authority of the editor." It was also said that "those . . . who don't get paid don't work as hard as those that do." He further suggested that many of these complaints had been aired in private but needed to be brought out in the open: "Playing such things 'cool' and using Machiavelli as a practical business pattern does not tend to satisfy all of our constituents all of the time." The letter requested that corporate members devise formal proposals dealing with the aforesaid policies, to be discussed at the forthcoming corporate meeting.

The only surviving record of this meeting is a five-page handwritten speech by Lambert, who seemed to believe that the only real problem was that ONE was experiencing growing pains. Whereas in the early days the corporation operated under a "spirit of improvisation," it had more recently taken the necessary steps toward becoming "more orderly and systematized." Apart from this, the principal problem was the lack of communication between the departments; there was too much "going ahead and asking later." Lambert's primary example of this impudence was Jennings's discussion at the Mattachine Society. Lambert felt that Jennings had no right to say what he said that night: it was "not a literary question but one of policy." Another problem was too much verbiage by ONE's editors and not enough creative editorializing and other work. Lambert complained that the December issue, comprised of one poem and five short stories, "was [such] a betrayal of the minority as well as of myself that I seriously considered resigning and retiring to more lucrative, easier work." While everyone at ONE had made sacrifices, Lambert said that he "did not contract to give up a profitable professional career and go through endless humiliating financial sacrifices [only] to make possible the publications of article after article by one or two writers."

Clearly, despite his overtures in 1954 toward inclusion and cooperation, Jennings's behavior as *ONE*'s editor-in-chief during the first year of publication was not going to be forgotten. Although he had worked hard for the organization, arguably the driving force behind the magazine's success, Jennings would not last much longer at the magazine's helm. He had been constantly bossy and headstrong around ONE's offices in 1953, and although he seems to have softened a bit during the magazine's second year, this did not appease his colleagues. While he had not expressly admitted his affiliation with the Communist movement, his circuitous denial upon receiving the Mattachine Society achievement award may have served to breed suspicion. Perhaps, as with Mattachine, many feared that ONE had been equally infested with reds. Whatever the case, according to the minutes of a special meeting convened on March 22, 1954, with "Bill, Dale, Joan, Corky, Ed, Ben, and Chuck" present, Dale Jennings resigned.[9] The minutes of this meeting state that those present also discussed other business, but no details are recorded. In the March 1954 issue of *ONE*, the masthead from February was copied verbatim—only where the former issue had read "Editor: Dale Jennings," this issue had a long empty space.

Shipshape (The Corporate Vessel)

Throughout this history, I have often utilized nautical metaphors as "native referents" to convey the process by which ONE, Incorporated, was founded.

I first began to ponder the metaphor of a ship as a reference for ONE's corporate ethos when Jim Schneider told me that Slater preferred to think of his actions in the spring of 1965 as a mutiny rather than a heist. In putting the needs of the magazine before the needs of the corporation, the ship had been constructed mast and sails first, so to speak. The launch of the second issue relied entirely on the success of the first. The third issue finally caught on in the newsstands, facilitating local distribution that in turn led to more subscribers. After several months, ONE magazine became ONE, Incorporated, and the vessel now had a hull. Jennings knew this, and Slater would never let Lambert forget it: ONE, Incorporated, did not create ONE magazine. To the contrary, ONE Magazine created ONE, Incorporated. If, under the masthead of ONE, the pages of the magazine could be considered the sails of the corporation and the artists and editors thought of as crew, then the corporation itself would comprise the vessel's hull, its protective (legal) casing. Because ONE generated most of its revenue through magazine subscriptions and sales, it would need no office, editor, or business manager should the magazine fail. Thus, ONE magazine's readers provided the wind, granting through their feedback and subscriptions the momentum necessary to keep the information flowing, thus facilitating a frank and open discussion on homosexual rights and issues.

The metaphor of the ship, of course, evokes feelings of instability, of being wave-tossed and vulnerable to lurking beasts and tempestuous weather. Slater and Jennings had become accustomed to such situations through their life experiences. Nothing was ever truly predictable; no matter how one might desire stability, change proved as inevitable as income tax, and nearly as routine. In the view of editors Slater and Jennings, the corporation's success relied entirely on the support of ONE's readers and subscribers, although, for the most part, they remained an invisible and usually silent resource. As business manager, Bill Lambert preferred a different metaphor regarding how to manage a corporation. Although the ship analogy may have fit in ONE's early years, it had been a mere stage in its evolution, and clearly ONE's participants needed to move on. In order for the corporation to grow, Lambert began to conceive of ONE as an *institution*—a different model altogether.

I turn again to Lambert's first report as chair, delivered on September 6, 1953, where he lauded the editors for their landmark August issue and welcomed Corky Wolf to the editorial board. These remarks were a brief overture. After three paragraphs of kind words, Lambert turned to "more general matters," his euphemism for the more particular subject of business. He reminded the crew that their advances were in no way due to their forethought and planning, "We have blundered along, leaping a bit precariously from position to position, certain procedures have gradually emerged not by any special vision or foresight on our parts, but because the logic of events has demanded them." He continued that they needed to learn from their past in order to plot a better future: "It is important that we all review some of these procedures, in order that we may more effectively go about the colossal task of doing what has never before been done in our country: providing a public forum for the frank and fearless consideration of homosexuality."

Lambert seems to have envisioned ONE, Incorporated, as more of a forum, an ancient Roman assembly where judicial and other public business was discussed and carried out. A forum provides for open discussion of public policies, a place where politics converge with the marketplace. This forum, in Lambert's estimation, was the core of ONE. To him, the organization produced the magazine, not the other way around, so that *ONE*'s editors had no real say in corporate policy. "The corporation . . . is comprised of the three directors, whose names appear on the charter, and six other members. These nine persons are the owners and publishers, and it is they [who] determine ALL of the policies of the corporation, including, of course, editorial policies."

Lambert continued by stating that the corporation had to employ various people to achieve its goals. Although many had worked as volunteers, these workers deserved payment for their time and those who worked the most should get paid the most. He asked each employee to keep a record of his or her time and work invested in preparation for future remuneration by the company. As for content, he reminded *ONE*'s editors that selecting and printing content was but the first step. From there, the magazine went into production and circulation phases. Advertising sales was also an important consideration, and all of these departments answered to the business office itself—and thus to Mr. Lambert. He suggested that those corporate members who had used their true names bore a greater burden than those who did not: "In any legal action, the corporation members are required to state their correct names and addresses, whatever else they may choose not to state, under constitutional privileges."

Although it would be fruitless to try to discern the more correct structural metaphor, it is worthwhile to note that there were not only contrasting philosophies but also contrasting business models operating within the organization. Jennings always put the magazine's needs before those of the corporation and may have perceived his role as editor-in-chief to be analogous to a captain of a ship surrounded by a crew of worthy assistants and advisers; Lambert's corporate conception put the magazine on the bottom, more the effect of their labor than the driving cause. His model was that of a pyramidal power structure where the business administrators kept things in order; ultimately, he, as ONE's business manager, should have the last word. Clearly, the two business models were operating at cross purposes, and the directors of ONE would have to either bring their conceptions into alignment or else some of them would have to go—as Jennings had.

Despite these conflicting conceptions of the organization's purpose and intent, ONE, Incorporated, managed to survive, with Lambert now its undisputed leader. The eldest of the crew and others seem to have naturally deferred to Lambert for leadership. He had sacrificed his career in city planning for the benefit of the corporation—a brave if not foolish act, but one that endeared him to his cohorts, who looked up to him for guidance. Although he was the first full-time employee of the homosexual movement, Lambert's salary was never guaranteed. His commitment to ONE committed him to a meager existence and, although he tallied every penny the corporation owed him, he did not seem to hold a grudge when his salary could not be paid. Lambert dedicated himself to the organization one hundred percent. Perhaps, if the corporation continued to grow and the magazine continued to gain readers, then others, such as the magazine's editor and art director, would eventually receive compensation for their contributions. For the time being, though, that was not possible, and ONE continued to resemble a common-interest association more than it did a legitimate corporation. Much work remained before ONE would be financially stable enough to pay its workers. But with a determined Lambert in charge of the dedicated volunteers, there was great hope for the corporation. ONE would continue to grow and, in time, perhaps, all would prosper.

The Establishment of
ONE Institute
(1955–60)

> Realizing that our own ways are not humanly inevitable nor God-
> ordained, but are the fruit of long and turbulent history, we may well
> examine all of our institutions, thrown into strong relief against the
> history of other civilizations, and weighing them in the balance, be not
> afraid to find them wanting.
> —Margaret Mead (from *Coming of Age in Samoa,* quoted in the
> September 1953 issue of *ONE Magazine*)

OUSTING DALE JENNINGS did not solve any of the problems sim-
mering within ONE, Incorporated. But it did significantly shift the balance
of power from the editor-in-chief to the senior bureaucratic administrator,
Bill Lambert. Indeed, as will be seen, Jennings's resignation seems to have
shocked many into silence and deference. No one really knew precisely what
transpired during the special meeting with Jennings on March 22, 1954. Although several board members were present, none seem to have discussed
the occasion afterward, and this pivotal moment in the history of the organization haunted those remaining. Newcomers to the organization became
especially cautious about what they said, although they felt optimistic that
the corporation would endure.

The March 22 meeting was a peculiar and rare occurrence in ONE, Incorporated's, history. Although it was a definitive moment, it produced a strange silence—no letter of resignation or discussion of the details survive in the corporate minutes, and the usually vociferous editors of *ONE* remained totally quiet regarding the matter. It was almost as if Jennings had never existed. Because of this, and given the means by which Jennings's resignation was achieved, I consider this event a closed-door coup. As such, it is worth further elaboration because such events occur again in the future with some regularity—frequently enough to consider them a form of corporate ritual.

A closed-door coup has several distinct features. Often, despite significant repercussions within the organization, only a few directors participate. Minimally, this would include a protagonist, an antagonist, and one key witness who is implicit in the action yet likely to remain silent or else support the event afterward. The antagonist may or may not stand to gain by the expulsion, or he or she may feel that the protagonist should leave for the corporation's ultimate good. In any case, of those who enter the room, one will leave bereft of all stations and duties held within the corporation. Thus, the event qualifies as a coup—a change in governance.

The closed-door coup serves as a kind of definitional ritual for an organization. Although the ousted individual will probably experience the event as a crisis or tragedy, his or her expulsion surmounts some impasse and may prevent or delay more severe factionalizing. As for whether such an event promotes the corporation's welfare or acts to its detriment is probably a question subject to history and perspective; however, the regularity of such events suggests their crucial role in the history of some organizations. In this case, two other pivotal closed-door coup attempts followed, both in 1965, when the corporation physically and permanently divided. These events are taken up in chapter 8.

As the dust settled around the office, ONE's directors began trying on different hats. After Corky Wolf held the position pro tem for a week, Don Slater settled in as corporate secretary. On March 31, 1954, Lambert and Wolf met for a special meeting of the directors to decide who should fill Jennings's vacated position as secretary. First, they appointed Wolf as secretary pro tem. According to ONE's bylaws, only those who had been members of the corporation at the January 3, 1954, annual meeting would be eligible, which meant they could only consider Corbin, Sanchez, and Slater. Ben Tabor— who, according to the minutes of this March 31 meeting, had been elected as a director the prior February 21—was removed from corporate membership when the vote in which he was elected was now declared "out of order, hence invalid." Tabor would have to wait until the annual meeting in January to be renominated. Lambert and Wolf further decided that Sanchez should not be considered because he had served a full term as director. Corbin, serving as art editor, was also declared ineligible; thus, through the process of elimination, they appointed Don Slater to fill the vacancy.[1] During a special meeting held a few days later on March 24, the directors decided that "the girls," Corky and Joan, "assume duties of editor-in-chief until the April meeting." The directors further resolved to finalize and accept Jennings's resignation.

When Wolf, Slater, and Lambert met on Thursday, April 1, they officially elected Slater ONE's secretary-treasurer to succeed Jennings. Slater's mark was added to the signature card, below Lambert's, at California Bank's branch at Sixth and Western. Undated minutes from about this time indicate that discussion as to who would be appointed editor continued among the voting members. They agreed that the responsibilities for the position were in flux because of the "rapid growth and expansion of the magazine." They also agreed that the editor should be more concerned with the shaping of policy than in writing for the magazine, and should "be at all times capable of, and in position to represent, the magazine publicly." Because no one person present seemed to hold all of these qualities, discussion of who would be ONE's next editor was tabled, although it was decided Wolf would be appointed managing editor for the magazine to coordinate the work of the editorial board and help keep the magazine on schedule. It was also decided that each of ONE's editors and the company bookkeeper would receive a meager salary of five dollars per week.

Chuck Rowland was brought back into the fold during this meeting and was appointed to the position of circulation manager. During an editorial board meeting on April 7, Rowland was nominated to become ONE's new editor-in-chief, but for some reason Eric Julber nixed the idea, "because of the high probability of future problems." Perhaps they feared some sort of retaliation from Jennings? Julber also advised those present that they should be especially careful as to what they published because they were in the process of applying for a second-class mailing permit. Absolutely no physique ads, he warned, and fiction should be carefully screened. There should be no provocative scenes and no physical contact between characters. Whereas poetry could be permitted, there could be "no love lyrics," and descriptions of people should be kept to a subtle minimum. Any photos of real people could be dangerous and, if printed, should only depict people in social situations.

There was a new name added to the company roster for this meeting: Jim Kepner. Kepner was also listed as present for an editorial meeting a week later, on April 14, where it was decided that more articles would be printed because of the high quality of unsolicited manuscripts received. No more letters commenting on the E. B. Saunders article would run—apparently Jennings's article on homosexual marriage published the prior September had created quite a stir. *ONE's* editors could reprint more excerpts of classic works, though, and thus begin to lay claim to the role of homosexuals and of homophile love in history.

Jim Kepner was appointed ONE's editorial secretary and science editor during a board meeting held on June 11, 1954. This was to begin Kepner's long career with the magazine. The editorial board had recruited Kepner in May to take over the job of providing news summaries for the magazine, a task he would fulfill until his resignation in the fall of 1960 (Kepner 1998, 3). Kepner immediately became bedrock for the corporation and a rising star in the magazine. As such, his talents and contributions deserve a more detailed introduction.

Introducing Jim Kepner

With Jennings gone, *ONE* needed an editor and Jim Kepner was recruited for the job. Kepner was ideal for the position in many ways. He was a talented writer who was trained as a journalist. He was adaptable and willing to write in a few distinctive "voices," thereby employing several different pen names representing various perspectives. Perhaps most important, he was relatively moderate regarding office politics, equally dedicated to ONE's growing educational mission as he was to the magazine. Some observers such as Vern Bullough have suggested that it was largely through Kepner's impartiality and cooperative efforts that ONE, Incorporated, survived the years after Jennings's removal.[2] Although he performed this moderating role admirably, it drained him personally, and Kepner would suffer for years, eventually sacrificing his income, education, career, and even his home for the sake of ONE's ideals and his work on behalf of homosexuals.

Because Kepner was to play a key role in the success of ONE for the next several years, he certainly deserves a proper introduction. His biological mother abandoned Kepner when he was an infant, although he did not learn of this until he was nearly twenty years old (Kepner 1998, 1). Mary Kepner discovered him swaddled in newspapers and left beneath an oleander bush in an empty lot in Galveston, Texas, on September 19, 1923.[3] He had probably been deserted because of his malformed legs and a clubfoot (Potvin 1998).

Mary was a nurse, and she and her husband, James Lynn Kepner, promptly adopted the child and arranged for corrective surgery. They continued to help their foundling son through the following difficult years of physical therapy (Gannett and Percy 2002, 125–26; Potvin 1998).

Although Mary had been raised in a strict Catholic tradition, young Kepner was raised a Protestant. According to his friend and fellow activist Ernie Potvin, he attended church school regularly and was thoroughly religious throughout his youth. During an interview occasioned by his having won a prize in Bible studies, twelve-year-old Kepner confessed to young *Houston Press* reporter Walter Cronkite that he aspired to become a missionary in Africa (Potvin 1998, 6). However, his education and the experiences of his early teen years, including an undeniable attraction "to other boys or to older men," caused him to question his long-held faith and religious beliefs (Kepner 1998, 1). Later in life, he acknowledged that he had felt a strong attraction to other males since age four, and he experienced his first crush on another schoolboy as early as first grade (Kepner 1998). Because of this, his religious faith became increasingly challenged, so the adolescent Kepner began exploring literature and found solace in books, especially science fiction.

An obituary by Kepner's friend Ernie Potvin, published in the winter 1997–98 edition of the *ONE•IGLA Bulletin*,[4] reported that Kepner had graduated cum laude from Galveston's Ball High School (Potvin 1997). Potvin repeated this in a later article, adding that Kepner had especially "excelled in English, Latin, history, and science" (1998, 6). But historian Paul Cain found that some of Kepner's other colleagues claimed he dropped out before graduating (2002, 20). Kepner had contrived the same tactic as Harry Hay to avoid gym (and having to shower with other boys) in high school: he joined ROTC, which, to his surprise, he enjoyed (although he later declined a lieutenant's commission). While in school, he worked as a soda jerk, a Western Union messenger, and an office clerk. He aspired toward college, but that would not become financially feasible until twenty years later, while settled in Los Angeles in the 1960s.

The national draft began as war became inevitable in the early 1940s. Just prior to his eighteenth birthday, Kepner tried to register as a conscientious objector (CO). But the Presbyterian Church was not pacifistic, and he could only register as a CO with denominational support. When called before the draft board the first time, he registered as a CO but was not asked to provide additional information, probably because of his persistent limp.[5] In 1942, he moved with his father to San Francisco, where he soon found and experienced the homosexual underground and had his first sexual experience—with a

Merchant Marine named Nial, who shipped out within hours after their encounter.[6] Ultimately, Kepner's crippled leg and his proclaimed homosexuality prevented him from military service.

While working full time for a milk carton factory, Kepner began to seek information on homosexuality in his off hours. Disappointed with his findings in the public library, he began sorting through used bookstores in search of a history to accompany all the people he'd been meeting. According to Potvin, one of the first books Kepner acquired was Radcliffe Hall's *Well of Loneliness*, first published in 1928. A sympathetic coworker told nineteen-year-old Kepner that if he was seen walking the streets with Hall's book tucked under his arm, his elusive gay brethren would soon recognize and embrace him, but this tactic failed (Kepner 1966, 4). Kepner also ordered two homosexual-themed "Little Blue Books" for a nickel each from Haldeman-Julius publishers of Girard, Kansas.[7] He ordered a slew of other titles from the Girard publisher as well, so as not to draw attention to himself (Potvin 1998).

Kepner found other homosexuals through San Francisco's science fiction clubs, which served as "surrogate organizations for closeted homosexuals during the forties" (Licata 1978, 56). The extent of the hiding frustrated Kepner, though, as did the flagrant persecution against those who refused to hide. Soon after arriving in the city, he witnessed a police raid at the Black Cat bar on Montgomery Street. Just as he had gathered enough nerve to approach the doorway, police rushed the place. Kepner hid in "a nearby doorway as they hauled out a dozen handsome huskies who went along as if they deserved arrest." He was especially impressed by the bravery exhibited by the dozen or so "queens" as the police ushered them out. "I can still hear one queen cry, 'Don't shove me, you bastard, or I'll bite your fucking balls off!'" he later wrote in his history of gay journalism, *Rough News, Daring Views*. "That queen paid dearly, and it took me a long while to understand why hearing that made me feel proud" (Kepner 1998, 399; also 1994, 8).

Kepner continued his participation in the science fiction clubs into 1943, although rumors of his homosexuality had affected his popularity and standing within the groups. He told some of his San Francisco friends that he intended to start a magazine for homosexuals called *The Gay Fan*; this idea offended (or scared) many of these contacts who promptly discontinued their association with him (Kepner 1989; Potvin 1998, 8). So he moved to Los Angeles, where he again sought out others interested in science fiction. He joined the Los Angeles Science Fantasy Society, becoming its secretary and then president. But once again, when rumors of his sexual proclivities began to proliferate, he was forced to leave the club. Undaunted, he decided to publish a fanzine of his own, titled *Toward Tomorrow*. For employment, he worked once again as a soda jerk; then he became a warehouseman for Pacific Electric Railway and next a machine operator, manufacturing airplane parts for an ironworks plant (Potvin 1998).

At some point in 1943, Kepner made contact with a pen pal from Rhinelander, Wisconsin. Wally Jordan had supposedly revived a nationwide organization of homosexuals called the Sons of Hamidy. The notion of such a network thrilled Kepner, but he soon discovered it was a hoax. Jordan had been writing to others listing Kepner as the organization's secretary before he had even formally consented to join (Cain 2002, 21; Marcus 1992, 46). Although there was no Hamidy, the idea of such an organization continued to inspire him: "I held on to the dream" (Kepner 1994, 7).

In 1945, Kepner helped to organize the Futurian Society of Los Angeles, inspired by a group of Marxist science fiction fans in Manhattan. He published the fifth and final issue of *Toward Tomorrow* in 1945, which had a strong Marxist leaning. Kepner made plans to move to New York to further his career as a writer, but his plan was spoiled when he discovered one of the other six Futurian Society founders was an FBI plant. Kepner eventually made it to Manhattan anyway, twice hitchhiking the entire way there. He became active in Communist Party activities and enjoyed listening to soapbox lecturers in Union Square and Columbus Circle. He got a staff job at New York's *Daily Worker* and began writing news bits and occasional film reviews. He participated in writers' workshops and even met one of his favorite columnists, Dorothy Parker. But in associating with professional New York writers, Kepner realized that, although he had a great passion for journalism, he was probably not skilled enough to make a solid living at it (Kepner 1994).

Kepner became an official member of the Communist Party in New York as the war came to an end (Potvin 1998). He marched in three Communist-led May Day parades in Manhattan, 1946 through 1948, and was inspired by the collective energy of the events. Twice, he turned to a friend he was marching with and asked, "Do you think we [homosexuals] could ever do this sort of thing?" and, both times, he knew the answer before hearing the reply: not in ten thousand years.[8] When party members discovered his homosexuality, they cast him out as "an enemy of the people." His landlady, who had helped recruit him to the party, told him that even though she liked gays, to admit them "would destroy the movement." However, she reassured him, "Come the revolution, you will be treated right."[9] Until then, however, Kepner was out on his ear.

Devastated, Kepner moved to Miami. Unable to find work there, he moved back to San Francisco, where he volunteered at the Communist Party's California Labor School library. In 1950, he and fellow traveler Mel Brown opened a store on Grant Avenue called Books on Telegraph Hill, which carried several "radical, Gay, and avant-garde books" such as *The Divided Path*, which Kepner recommended, and *Dianetics*, which he didn't (although it became the store's best seller).[10] During that time he married the bookstore's auditor. That relationship lasted a month, until he came home and found her having sex with one of his friends.[11] The store went out of business after eighteen months, and Kepner moved to back Los Angeles with Brown.

In 1951, Kepner and Brown moved into a rustic Craftsman-styled house at 2141 Baxter Street, one of the steepest streets in Los Angeles. Kepner was to live there until 1972—the longest time by far he ever resided at one location. He began hosting "twice-weekly gatherings of a mixed group of sci-fi fans, ex-radicals, and characters he met in Pershing Square." At some point in 1951, he ran his idea past some of his homosexual friends, including "Lisa Ben" (whom he had met through a Los Angeles science fiction club), his neighbor Betty Purdue, Mel Brown, and a man who happened to be the roommate of Bill Lambert. (Kepner would not actually meet Lambert until a later Mattachine discussion session.) Although Kepner's idea of a publication for "gays" appalled most of his friends, a few supported it. Purdue responded by taking Kepner to his first Mattachine discussion meeting, held in a Los Feliz residence. The topic of this meeting was "What can we do about those swishes and dykes who give us a bad name?" Although usually "timid in new groups," Kepner, remembering the brave behavior of the "nelly queens" arrested at the Black Cat in San Francisco, stood up for "the swishes." After all, "it was those obvious ones who established squatter's rights to the Gay bars the rest of us could sneak in and out of" (Kepner 1998, 3). After attending several more Mattachine meetings, Kepner was formally invited to join one of the five Mattachine groups, then called "guilds," with Bob Hull as his guild leader.[12] Soon after, he was recruited to work for *ONE Magazine*.

Kepner as Editor

Kepner's first article in *ONE* appeared in the March 1954 issue, published under the pseudonym "Lyn Pedersen." It was entitled "The Importance of Being Different," and as a debut article it was a zinger. "Are homosexuals in any important way different from other people?" he asked rhetorically, before clarifying his position on the matter: "*Vive la différence!*" But he cautioned his readers that divergent opinions on the matter had fractured the Mattachine Society, which had become "almost schizoid" over the question: "What can a Society accomplish if half of it feels its object is to convince the world we're just like everyone else and the other half feels homosexuals are variants in the full sense of the term and have every right to be?" Kepner had attended the Mattachine conferences in April, May, and October of 1953 and had seen firsthand what utter disasters they were. As Potvin put it, "People came with sky-rocketing hopes to these conferences and tore one another apart. Jim thought he was the only person in those gatherings who saw that they did not all want the same thing nor could they easily agree on how to get it" (1998, 9). Kepner acknowledged the dangers of that duality and its potential to polarize the movement, dividing its energy and resources by fueling conflicts from within. "Only by allowing the free action of individual groups within the structure of an elastic society can such diverse philosophies work together. But such schizophrenia is hard to handle." He believed all homosexuals should remember their unity in purpose and that they must sacrifice their differences to it. He concluded the article with a prescient observation: "With other minorities, racial and religious, similar dichotomies have forced into existence a variety of opposing organizations, each with its own clear-cut program. For homosexuals, as well, this must probably come, in time." For now, he concluded that although he would continue to advocate for "the right to be different," he acknowledged that, somewhere along the line, he had "picked up the notion that I can't protect my own rights in that quarter without fighting for everyone else's" (Kepner 1998, 9).

Kepner brought renewed ambition and optimism to the corporation. But having a vision and making it real are quite different, no matter how much enthusiasm one brings to a project. During Kepner's first year at ONE, he, Rowland, and Bob Hull attempted to coordinate a group of homosexuals in Mexico, but their efforts fell flat. (Rowland and Hull returned to ONE in early April 1954, soon after the expulsion of Jennings.) Kepner also attempted to start an organization in Tucson with Dave Schaffer, but that organization never materialized either. Still, the feedback he received from his readers encouraged Kepner. Some wrote to him that *ONE Magazine* had "saved their lives," and this knowledge moved and motivated him as it did the others (Potvin 1998, 9).

By the fall of 1954, *ONE Magazine* was being shipped monthly to 1,650 subscribers, most of whom paid an extra dollar per year to receive it in a plain wrapper. Through newsstand and other sales, circulation increased to five thousand. This rise in readership and distribution, however, did not immediately translate into increased revenue for the corporation. Because of a lack of funds, ONE's board cancelled the August and September issues, and all subscriptions were extended by two months as compensation.

Compounding their difficulties, the postmaster detained *ONE's* October issue on grounds of obscenity, despite the vigilance of attorney Eric Julber in his perusal of that issue, the cover of which prophetically said, "You Can't Print That." Government censors nevertheless "banned it under a law that forbade the mailing of any 'obscene, lewd, lascivious or filthy' publication" (Potvin 1998, 29) because of a short story attributed to Jane Dahr, "Sappho Remembered," which favorably portrayed a lesbian romance.

Deb Price and Joyce Murdoch point out that *ONE's* staff was not too alarmed when they first heard about the seizure because it had happened before with the "Homosexual Marriage?" issue of September 1953, delayed by the postmaster for several weeks. But this time, Washington, D.C., postal inspectors agreed with Los Angeles postmaster Otto K. Olesen's assessment that the issue was unsuitable for mailing. The officers of ONE eagerly desired to challenge Olesen in court, but the organization's financial situation prevented quick action. Although Julber decided to take the job pro bono and not charge ONE, Incorporated, for his service, it was nearly a year (September 16, 1955) before he filed his lawsuit.

Kepner Resigns (the First Time)

In February 1955, an exasperated Jim Kepner resigned from the corporation, taking his office furniture and several hundred of his books with him.[13] The trouble was that Chuck Rowland had proposed that ONE raise money to purchase a house to convert into a mission or home for wayward homosexuals, called the Walt Whitman Guidance Center (Legg 1994, 156). Kepner's frustration rose as the others discussed the idea. He feared that the resources needed would starve out the publications division. In a letter to the directors dated February 27, Kepner complained that he and others felt as though they had been "manipulated like puppets" and expressed their fear that "some aims of the corporation are likely to defeat . . . the magazine." He admitted that his frustrations had been building for the prior few months, but he decided to remain silent, fearing that what happened to Jennings could likewise happen to him: "[I feared that] any opposition on my part to Chuck's project would lead to my expulsion." He felt that the mission to provide a home for "the lost ones from Main Street" was an awful idea, yet when he spoke his mind, he was told to "mind his own business," even though the project would harm *ONE Magazine*.

Kepner further argued that, as editor-in-chief, he should have a vote in corporate policy. He complained that the "corporation's predilection for inter-departmental secrecy and intrigue made for impossible working conditions." As for Rowland or the others telling him what to do, he stated that it was only when his manager at Canco gave him orders that he felt compelled "to carry them out with minimum regard for my own opinions"—but, of course, Canco *paid* him for his work there. Kepner believed *ONE Magazine*'s editor-in-chief should likewise be paid, even if on a part-time basis: "A magazine that . . . can pay the editors enough to expect them to express the publishers' viewpoint down to the last letter is a bit different from a magazine that is asking the editor to contribute his services gratis and in his spare time, while earning his living elsewhere." Until ONE could afford to pay even a modest salary to its core faculty, the organization could only be "a cooperative venture" of "volunteers in a common cause." As a corporation, the stagnant ONE might be doomed to failure. He concluded his resignation letter with the cordial hope that he could work for *ONE* again at some point in the future, recognizing the possible prematurity of his departure given that some of his complaints had already been dealt with adequately. (Rowland's home for wayward homosexuals never materialized.) Kepner further assured his colleagues at ONE that both the corporation and the magazine had his "continued and hearty support." Although Kepner exited the organization for the time being, in the month prior to his departure an idea had been planted that would draw him back to *ONE*—and even provide him the requested income.

Chuck Rowland, however, did not fare as well, and he became disappointed when support for his project fell flat. Rowland resigned from ONE soon after Kepner, although I have yet to find his resignation letter. In a March 1, 1956, letter, Corky Wolf,[14] acting as ONE's chairman, accepted his resignation with regrets: "We believe that this unique and hazardous venture has endured during the past four years because ONE's members have given their unwavering loyalty to the principle of majority rule." Wolf admonished Rowland for having held meetings in his home that "encouraged the development of something entirely foreign to the assignment given you at the Corporation meeting February 1 [1956]." Because it was "not possible to be a member of the corporation without the willingness to subscribe to this fundamental democratic procedure . . . no other conclusion remains for us [but] that you have repudiated a movement and a leadership you only recently appeared to hold in such high esteem."

ONE Institute for Homophile Studies

On January 29, 1955, ONE, Incorporated, sponsored its first public function, a Midwinter Institute held at the Biltmore Hotel in downtown Los Angeles. The event was a resounding success. The morning session, open to voting and nonvoting members, convened at 11:00 a.m. and consisted of the annual meeting of the corporation followed by an informal luncheon. At 2:00 that afternoon, the Midwinter Institute convened, which featured three presentations. Featured attendees included UCLA psychologist Evelyn Hooker, ONE's attorney Eric Julber, and author Gerald Heard, who would soon begin writing articles for ONE under the name "D. B. Vest" (Legg 1994, 18).

In Legg's estimation (Legg 1994), the highlight of the event was a paper presented by San Francisco psychotherapist Blanche M. Baker entitled "A Psychiatric Evaluation of Homosexuality: Causative Factors and Therapeutic Suggestions" (Legg 1994, 34). Baker's talk and the ensuing discussions inspired ONE's directors to develop an educational division. The next spring, in May 1955, Harry Hay would propose that ONE implement an educational structure[15] that was considered but not adopted. In June 1955, though, ONE's officers compiled an outline for ONE Institute that was more in alignment with the ideals Dr. Baker inspired (Legg 1994, 19).

If the success of a ritual can be measured by the longevity of its continuance, then the 1955 Midwinter Institute stands among ONE's greatest achievements. Annually thereafter for the next twenty-five years, ONE's Midwinter Institutes would present speakers and hold seminars for audiences gathered from all over the world on topics such as psychology, law, religion, literature, history, and cultural diversity. Live entertainment such as dances, plays, and puppet shows would entertain the conveners year after year. Dozens and sometimes hundreds of Friends of ONE traveled from across the Southwest and other distant urban centers to participate in the annual event, always held during the final weekend in January—an ideal time for a pilgrimage to sunny Los Angeles.

In March 1956, Corky Wolf was promoted from managing editor to editor of ONE Magazine, a position vacant since Jennings's resignation two years prior. Wolf immediately tried to recruit more women writers and a larger female audience. She had worked for ONE since first volunteering for the organization in the spring of 1953 and had become chairman at the 1955 annual meeting. Wolf was one of ONE's most reliable and perhaps underappreciated volunteers at this time.

Although ONE's articles of incorporation had not specifically created an education division, the formation of ONE Institute helped to fulfill the second and third general purposes of the corporation, which called for research and education on homosexual issues. In the summer of 1956, the education division committee of ONE—including Kepner, Julian "Woody" Underwood, Lambert (as W. Dorr Legg), and retired USC professor Merritt M. Thompson—reported that a study they had conducted regarding the quality of existing education pertaining to homophiles and homosexuality "exhibited numerous shortcomings." These were later enumerated in the September 1962 issue of ONE Magazine: "(1) scholarly timidity in dealing with a topic considered socially distasteful; (2) almost complete absence in institutional budgets of funds for furthering study of the topic; (3) medical, psychoanalytic or other bias limiting the viewpoints of most research; (4) culturally conditioned bias concerning homosexuality on the part of most researchers; (5) low level of research work in the field in consequence of the above factors." To remedy these problems and misconceptions, the committee recommended that ONE Institute offer courses in homophile studies that would recognize such diverse fields as anthropology, sociology, biology, history, law, literature, and religion (Potvin 1998, 9).

Merritt Thompson, as "Thomas R. Merritt," was one of the most important figures in the development of ONE Institute. Thompson had been a professor at USC since 1921 and was best known for his often-republished work, *The History of Education* (1933). Through Thompson's guidance, the goals of the institute were elucidated and the committee remained on task. ONE's directors voted to accept the committee's recommendations on October 15, 1956, and one week later, ONE Institute of Homophile Studies began offering its first courses of study (Legg 1994, 22).

According to Slater's records, thirteen students enrolled in this first term, all members of ONE's staff. These included Slater himself, Legg, Kepner, Rudi Steinert, and Dr. Thompson. The first seminar, HS-100, met for nine weeks. In the spring of 1957, the course met for eighteen weeks with fifteen students matriculated, including a future director of ONE, Fred Frisbie (as George Mortenson). During this spring term, a vocabulary committee was created, headed by Dean Thompson, and a dictionary of homosexuality was planned as a future project. Twenty-five other students met for an eight-session extension symposium in San Francisco. That fall, the institute offered HS-210, the first of a two-semester course titled Introduction to Homophile Studies, which met for eighteen weeks. Slater's notes show that twelve students enrolled, including Wayne Placek, Stella Rush, and Barbara Sutton.

According to the 1958 annual report, two primary problems plagued ONE Institute in its first eighteen months of operation. The first was the considerable strain on the faculty of a very heavy workload for no pay. Another problem was the absence of a textbook, which called for "forced-draft measures on the part of the faculty" and "considerable misapprehension on the part of many students as to the scope and true nature of the studies undertaken." This in turn led to "careless study, or none at all, [due to] a dearth of original thought and a standard of scholarship not very high in most cases." But the leaders at ONE Institute would not be daunted by such trivialities as scarcity of resources and general lack of interest. "Perhaps this is to be expected," they reasoned, "dealing with a file so generally plagued by low standards of scholarship, beset by taboos and social disapproval." Under Thompson's leadership, the four members of the education division set out to break new ground by accomplishing what he called "structuralizing the field": "Not only must ONE Institute pioneer in devising methods of studying the homophile, but must also somehow awaken others to see the need for such studies and then hold the students to satisfactory standards of accomplishment."[16]

As noted, Thompson himself was relatively new to ONE. He had heard of the first Midwinter Institute in 1955 but had decided not to go lest he find "a small group of eccentrics, freaks, or what have you." He gathered the courage to attend in 1956, at the age of seventy-two, and was surprised to find the group comprised of "very normal, fine appearing young people, some of them college students." He was particularly impressed with Dorr Legg,[17] "a dynamic, highly intelligent, former college professor in the fields of art and aesthetics." Legg and Thompson immediately became friends. As educators, they agreed on "the fact that the biases, prejudices, and social maladjustments in general were so nearly always based upon ignorance," and therefore "the most helpful activity to the movement would be an Institute, a kind of specialized graduate school of classes covering the relation of sex, particularly homosexuality, to the larger field of culture" (Thompson 1969).

All four of ONE Institute's faculty "acknowledge[d] the great benefits to themselves from their study and researches in clearer understanding of the homophile and his place in society." With this came an increased confidence in their ability to combat "professional and popular errors concerning the subject." Thompson noted that the students had reported such benefits as well. He also noted that the mission of "structuralizing the field" had been facilitated through the "accumulation of much bibliographical material, quantities of little-known facts, new perspectives on anthropology, sociology, history, literature and a number of other subjects which deal directly with the homophile man or woman" (Thompson 1969). The organization owed much to archivists Kepner, Slater, and Gibson.

One of the first difficulties in establishing the institute was in coming up with a name. Although the editors of ONE Magazine, Slater in particular, were content if not entirely comfortable in using the word "homosexual" in the title, many remained uncomfortable with the word. Legg complained that the term was an awkward half-Greek, half-Latin amalgam rife with "medical connotations of mental illness, abnormality, and pathology" (Legg 1994, 25). He preferred the term "homophile," which was pure Greek (homos meaning "the same" and philos being "love for"). Legg pointed out that many of their European forebears had preferred the word, and Magnus Hirshfeld may have used the word as early as 1920. The word became popularized when Niek Engelschman used it in the August 1949 issue of VRIENDSHAP, published in Amsterdam (Legg 1994, 25–26). Legg declared that the European embrace of the word "was a Declaration of Independence empowering a hitherto stigmatized segment of society to define itself in its own terms." (This ignores the fact that the physician credited with inventing the term "homosexual" in the 1860s was himself a homosexual.) He wrote in retrospect: "The word 'Homophile' lifted discussion out of the age-old grip of medical, psychological and theological obloquy onto the levels of philosophical, moral, and ethical discussions, properly befitting full-fledged members of society" (Legg 1994, 26–27). Although Legg championed the term as a cathartic and welcomed moniker, the tacit conflict over these terms mark another early split in the corporation with those forming the core of the institute preferring "homophile" and the editors of ONE continuing to use the word "homosexual." Many in the early movement remained uncomfortable with either term, however, and both became increasingly problematic as the popular press began to use them later in the 1960s, as will be seen.

Legal Setbacks

Although ONE, Incorporated, progressed on many fronts, its legal battle against the postmaster continued, and in this arena things seemed far less sure. Julber presented his case against Postmaster Olesen on January 16, 1956, with District Judge Thurmond Clarke presiding. Julber's opening brief cited U.S. code, title 18, section 1461: "Every obscene, lewd, lascivious, or filthy book, pamphlet, picture, paper, letter, writing, print, or other publication of an indecent character; and . . . every written or printed card, letter, circular,

book, pamphlet, advertisement, or notice of any kind giving information
. . . of such mentioned matters, articles, or things . . . is declared to be non-
mailable matter and shall not be conveyed in the mail or delivered from any
post office or by any letter carrier." Julber countered that the magazine was
not "obscene, lewd, lascivious, or filthy" and that Olesen's actions had been
"arbitrary, capricious and an abuse of discretion, unsupported by evidence."
In refusing to distribute the magazine, the postmaster had caused "a depriva-
tion of Plaintiff's property and liberty without due process of law."

The following twenty-eight pages of Julber's brief laid out six key arguments. Apart from the complaints already mentioned, Julber noted that in
order to violate the statute in question, "a work must be lewdly simulative to
the average reader, and not to those of a particular class." He further stated
that "a comparison of other literature on the same subject being offered for
public sale at the same time as the instant work and freely transmitted in the
public mails shows that the instant work is not obscene, lewd or lascivious
under prevailing literary standards."

In defense of this statement, Julber included a sixteen-page appendix that
listed twenty magazines and journals that had published articles between 1951
and 1954. He also listed sixty-seven books or short stories that had clearly
pertained to homosexuality. Authors cited included Henry James, D. H. Law-
rence, Sherwood Anderson, Paul Bowles, Gore Vidal, Christopher Isherwood,
Fritz Peters, Herman Melville, and Willa Cather. Although most of the titles
listed were fiction, Julber listed Cory's *The Homosexual in America* and cited
Ruth Benedict's *Patterns of Culture*: "Western civilization tends to regard
even a mild homosexual as abnormal. We have only to turn to other cultures,
however, to realize that homosexuals have by no means been uniformly inadequate to the social situation. In some societies they have been especially
acclaimed" [see Benedict 1934, 242]. Julber's bibliography concluded with
an ironic flourish by citing Jack Lait and Lee Mortimer's infamous exposé
Washington Confidential (1951) for its "many references to homosexuals in
government positions, to fairy hangouts, queers, [and] perverts."[18]

Despite the concluding flourish, the strategy of Julber's appendix was logical
and sound. He concluded, "[I know of] no official action being taken by the
postal authorities to declare any of the magazines or works quoted from to
be 'non-mailable,'" and therefore *ONE Magazine* should likewise be allowed
postal distribution. However, his argument worked on another level as well.
According to linguist Jerome Bruner, literature, especially fiction, posits alternative but "possible worlds" that have the power to significantly alter the
way readers perceive their realities. As Bruner eloquently puts it, "The art of

the possible is a perilous art. . . . It challenges as it comforts. In the end, it has the power to change our habits of conceiving what is real, what canonical. It can even undermine the law's dictates about what constitutes a canonical reality" (2002, 94). Slater and Julber knew that fiction had this power, and my hunch is that the postmaster and the judges in the case knew it too.

Despite its merits, Julber's brief did not at all impress Judge Clarke. On March 2, 1956, Clarke entered judgment in favor of Postmaster Olesen, stating that the magazine in question had contained "filthy and obscene material obviously calculated to stimulate the lust of the homosexual reader" (Hansen 1998, 36). While totally ignoring Julber's arguments, which were well-grounded on precedent, Judge Clark added a new twist to the case: "The suggestion that homosexuals should be recognized as a segment of our people and be accorded special privilege as a class is rejected." This is puzzling, as nowhere in his brief did Julber suggest that homosexuals were a distinct class of people deserving special protection. Nevertheless, Julber and ONE were defeated—for the time being, at least.

The Divisions of ONE

In 1956, Kepner recommended that ONE rent an additional room in which to house their books and begin a library. To kick-start the process, Kepner donated four hundred of his own books which, according to Ernie Potvin, included "the core of his non-fiction collection," more than doubling the size of the corporation's library (1998, 10). Although Legg had written glowingly of the quality of ONE's library, in reality it had before this time "only consisted of no more than a few boxes of books behind couches at Corky and Joan's, or hidden away in Don Slater's closet" (Potvin 1998, 10). Slater and Jack Gibson were the corporation's first librarians, sharing credit in *ONE* as "Leslie Colfax." Potvin points out that "this was the first Gay library in the United States, but it would not be the last that Jim would be responsible for starting." Kepner did not donate to ONE all his treasured volumes, however, and his personal library continued to grow, becoming in 1975 the Western Gay Archives and later, in 1979, the Gay Archives: Natalie Barney/Edward Carpenter Library, with an office on Hudson Street in Hollywood. In 1984, the collection became the International Gay and Lesbian Archives (Potvin 1998).

In 1956, the corporation's divisions and subdivisions became firmly established. The four service departments of the corporation included the Book Service (through which patrons could purchase books related to homosexuality) and the Bureau of Public Information (a watchdog service that publicized news reports "of illegal acts directed against homosexuals by public and private figures and to correct published falsehoods about homosexuals"). The remaining two service departments were Education and Social Services.

The Publications Division assumed responsibility to print and distribute *ONE Magazine*. Through its Book Department, ONE had published two thousand numbered copies of James Barr's play, *Game of Fools*, in 1955. Barr had authored the homosexual-themed novel *Quatrefoil* in 1950, a story of love shared between two male navy officers, and *Derricks* in 1951, a volume of short stories. His works were important for portraying homosexuals "who were neither [sic] disgusting, fantastic, nor pitiable 'cases', but vigorous, healthy young American males, and extremely attractive to women" (Legg 1956, 2).

In 1956, the Publications Division published *Homosexuals Today: A Handbook of Organizations and Publications*, edited by Lambert/Legg as "Marvin Cutler." *Homosexuals Today* is a handsome publication, featuring a heavy black-cloth binding embossed with bold yellow type and a stylized face seemingly painted onto the cover. Others sketches by Corbin, drawn from the pages of the now-historic publications of *ONE* and *Mattachine Review*, decorate its 188 pages. Legg divided the content, a scrapbook-like history of the movement, into three sections: "The United States," "Europe," and "Homosexuals Today" (plus an index). The foreword, erroneously paginated as chapter 1, situated the reader in America 1950 where "attitudes toward homosexuals presented the faces of Janus—zealous repression, on the one hand, and awakening progress, on the other" (Legg 1956, 1). Next followed a speech Slater had delivered at the 1956 Mattachine Society convention in San Francisco concerning "The Homophile Press Today."

As for *ONE*, 1957 was a year of change, including a subscription increase. A "new look" for the magazine was unveiled for the June–July issue, reflecting a change in the way the magazine was printed. Formerly, publishers had used the offset method; the new production method would be the "speedier and more accurate" letterpress.[19] Also, *ONE*'s talented art director, Joan Corbin, who worked a full-time job elsewhere, was increasingly assisted by Dawn Frederick and Fred Frisbie, alleviating her workload and diversifying the style of the magazine.

ONE's third Midwinter Institute began on Saturday, January 26, 1957, with the theme "The Homosexual Answers His Critics." Wolf, Legg, and Kepner had been elected to the board of directors the prior evening. The institute included a dramatic presentation featuring scenes from an as yet unpublished play by James Barr. Harry Hay gave a two-hour lecture on "The Homophile in Search of a Historical Context and Cultural Contiguity" that was printed in *ONE Confidential*[20] the following fall and praised in the February issue of *The Ladder*, the publication of a lesbian organization called the Daughters of Bilitis (DOB) that had been founded in San Francisco in October 1955. Hay's speech is notable for its homage to anthropology, which he stated had "gone to some pains to demonstrate some physiological validity for this small minority." He mentioned both Ford and Beach's *Patterns of Sexual Behavior* (1951) and Ruth Benedict's *Patterns of Culture* (1934) as invaluable contributions to the betterment of homophile acceptance by society.

Hay spoke of the "berdache," a term he said had been "employed to represent the diversity of social employment of the Homophilic phenomena by varying social levels of Amerindian cultures." Hay said that the berdache played an important role as representing a folk pattern—"the vast substratal acculturation of the mass"—that had provided "the imperturbable foundation of all social and political complexes until astonishingly recent days." In other words, despite years of suppression by dominant European culture, the phenomenon continued to persist, and this fact, he claimed, was supported in the archaeological evidence from the Mesolithic and Paleolithic eras. Although V. Gordon Childe was disinclined to "adduce a patriarchic or gynarchic [*sic*] culture as a formative stage in the evolution of European Society, we will rely on much of his . . . solidly-rooted summarizations to reconstruct the emergence of the Berdache phenomenon as a constructive social institution" (Hay, as quoted in Legg 1994, 240). Although his message was impressive and inspirational, Hay's erudite and pedantic verbiage probably left many in his audience baffled.

This 1957 Midwinter Institute was a great success. With fifty participants, it was probably the largest gathering of homosexual rights activists yet, and the February issue of *The Ladder* devoted six pages of notes and reviews to the event (Gallo 2006, 33). New York psychotherapist Dr. Albert Ellis gave a talk "on how best to combat the antihomosexual culture of the United States" (Gallo 2006, 33). *The Ladder* announced ONE's intent to develop a program of undergraduate and graduate studies through a new division called ONE Institute. The DOB was also impressed with a presentation given by Blanche Baker, titled "The Circle of Sex," in which she said, "There is a growing awareness of the mixture of the male and female components in each of us. . . . Nature does not work in straight rigid lines, but rather in cycles of circles" (as quoted in Gallo 2006, 33).

Also at the convention, *ONE* contributor Stella Rush, then thirty-two, met thirty-six-year-old Helen "Sandy" Sandoz, who was visiting from San Francisco, and the two fell in love almost immediately. Sandoz and Rush were both friends of DOB founders Del Martin and Phyllis Lyon, and Sandoz became active in the group in 1956 after breaking up with her partner. As "Helen Sanders," Sandoz became assistant to the editor for *The Ladder* in December of that year and, in 1957, she signed the state charter for the DOB using her real name (Gallo 2006; Rush 2002). Rush became the Los Angeles reporter for *The Ladder* in April 1957 (still under her pen name of Sten Russell), but as their relationship continued to develop, Sandoz moved to Los Angeles by the end of 1957 and moved into Rush's Silver Lake home on Waterloo Street. In 1958, Rush and Sandoz organized the Los Angeles chapter of DOB. Both remained active in ONE as well, and Rush and Sandoz facilitated cooperation and communication between the organizations until Rush resigned from ONE in 1961. Their relationship would ultimately outlast both organizations, however; the two remained partners for thirty years, until Sandoz's death on June 7, 1987 (Gallo 2006; Saunders 2002).

Income and Remuneration

Around the summer of 1957, when *ONE Magazine* became subtitled "The Homosexual Viewpoint," ONE, Incorporated, began to pay two salaries, one to editor Don Slater and one to the business manager Bill Lambert. At a dollar per hour, the rate was hardly exorbitant, but it did strain the budget and angered Jim Kepner, who had been working full time at ONE for free while also working a full-time factory job five to six nights each week. Thus, in August, Kepner quit his night job, "took a heavy cut in his standard of living," and joined the "hurly-burly of ONE's daily office duties."[21] With three salaries now to support, ONE's deficit began to increase. Accordingly, on October 15, 1957, celebrated as the corporation's fifth anniversary, the directors of ONE confessed in their annual fund-drive letter to having amassed a deficit of $5,184.19 and asked their readers for help. The fault, they claimed, was the "long-unrealistic 25¢ price and $2.50 & $3.50 subs for *ONE Magazine*, and in some degree our earliest venture in book publishing," meaning that although *Homosexuals Today* and *Game of Fools* had sold very well, they had only netted "a theoretical profit of $752.99."[22] *Game of Fools* earned $895; however, more than 723 copies remained unsold. The fund drive itself proved mildly successful; by the end of 1957, the organization reduced its deficit by $1,500.[23]

Kepner and Slater participated in a public panel that autumn sponsored by a Hollywood organization called the Searchers entitled "What Does the Rise in Homosexuality Mean?" Slater stated that homosexuality was increasing for the simple reason that the population itself was increasing. He added that many individuals repressed or miserable with their homosexuality might have been emboldened by the Kinsey report, which had helped them "accept their deviancy."[24] A subsequent speaker, Dr. Arthur E. Briggs, author of *Walt Whitman, Thinker and Artist* (1952) and a member of the Ethical Culture Society of Los Angeles, "agreed [with Slater's] idea that the recent wars may have fostered an increase in homosexuality."

The next speaker, former vice officer Fred Otash, claimed to have invented the "peep-hole technique" used by LAPD vice to monitor public toilets while strongly disagreeing that the war had anything to do with it. He stated that, while he served in the Marine Corps, "the only fags we ran into were some Navy men who were doing women's work." He added that at Venice Beach in particular, the public had frequently complained of "being accosted" by male homosexuals in public restrooms. Homosexual men, he claimed, continually searched for "a real man" and therefore continually lured heterosexuals, especially young boys, into engaging in homosexual acts. Kepner countered by noting that far more heterosexual graffiti solicited sex on the bathroom walls than did homosexual graffiti. And if a man were propositioned, couldn't he just say no?

When Otash responded that he could not find homosexuality advocated in the Bible and that "either we should enforce the law as it stands, or else we should change it," Kepner reminded him that the Bible described the passion between David and Jonathan as "surpassing the love of women." Kepner quipped that if Otash "would care to do a bit of peeping in Pershing Square, he might find more Marines than sailors there among the male prostitutes and others who were seeking a bit of homosexual activity." Otash replied with the bizarre but commonly heard non sequitur, "The real men who offered their services to homosexuals couldn't really be considered as homosexuals in any sense." Briggs concluded the discussion by citing Goethe's assertion that "homosexuality has been around as long as men have." Then, citing Ford and Beach, he added, "It just might be quite common among animals as well."

The fall 1958 issue of *ONE Confidential* announced that ONE was preparing to publish two new books. The first was to be "a general survey of the homosexual field, quite unlike any other works so far in print, viewing the subject from different angles—the biological, anthropological, sociological, religious, legal, psychological, literary and philosophical viewpoints." The second would be more historical, with biographical profiles of notable homosexuals from the past.[25] This ambitious goal anticipated the comprehensive two-volume *Annotated Bibliography of Homosexuality* finally published in 1976 by Bullough, Legg, Elcano, and Kepner.

More Legal Setbacks

On February 27, 1957, a three-judge Ninth Circuit Court of Appeals panel in San Francisco confirmed District Judge Clarke's ruling that the October 1954 issue of *ONE* had indeed been obscene and therefore was not suitable for mailing. The judges were most disturbed by the short story "Sappho Remembered," which they deemed "nothing more than cheap pornography calculated to promote lesbianism" (Murdoch and Price 2001, 34). In addition to Clarke's commentary, the judges added that the magazine in question "has a primary purpose of exciting lust, lewd and lascivious thoughts and sensual desire in the minds of persons reading it." They added: "Social standards are fixed by and for the great majority and not by or for a hardened or weakened minority" (Murdoch and Price 2001, 33).

This setback certainly impacted the morale of those at ONE, Incorporated. As Joseph Hansen recalled, "Lambert began to have misgivings. ONE's directors grew restive. Some were ready to give up," but Slater and Julber continued to press on (1998, 36). Julber filed a petition for a rehearing on March 14, 1957, that was denied a month later, on April 12. Next, he wrote a Petition for Writ of Certiorari to the U.S. Court of Appeals for the Ninth Circuit, and filed it with the Supreme Court on June 13, 1957.[26] In the short, nine-page writ, Julber asked the Supreme Court to rule that the Court of Appeals had erred in finding the magazine obscene. It had misrepresented and incorrectly gauged "the moral tone of the community" and failed to take into consideration the bibliographic appendix.

Two days after ONE's fifth anniversary, on October 17, 1957, Corky Wolf presented her resignation to Lambert, Kepner, and Slater during a board meeting. Wolf had undergone surgery in early September, and six weeks later she still lacked the energy to continue her work for the organization. ONE printed a resignation letter[27] in the December issue, which featured a sketch of her on the cover by Corbin. In the letter, Wolf said that she had "for some years given a 'minimum of effort' to my employer and the 'maximum of effort' to ONE. The situation would remain this way had I any say in the matter. I have not." Although Wolf had never received payment for her work, her loyalty toward the corporation remained strong. The minutes of the October 17 meeting report that both "Corky and Vicki"[28] resigned immediately, though

Vicki would continue to "clean up loose ends on circulation correspondence." Slater was appointed a temporary third member of the board, and "Nancy"[29] would serve as the acting women's director, with "Woody" to manage circulation records, assisted by "Ginger." Slater was appointed to serve as acting editor, with Lambert and Kepner voting members of the editorial board.

Although Wolf's health had indeed taken a turn for the worse, Kepner stated that she had also resigned "due to growing distress with Dorr Legg's male chauvinism" (1998, 395). He also noted that with Wolf gone, Slater, Legg, and Kepner formed a "precariously balanced board of directors" as no two of them ever seemed to agree on the issues. Votes were often split two to one, and consensus was unheard of (Kepner 1998).

Toward the close of the year, on December 6, 1957, Legg participated in a seminar hosted by the Publications Department of San Francisco's Mattachine Society titled "Progress Survey, Workshop and Seminar." Dr. Wallace de Ortega Maxey, editor of a new publication called *Sex and Censorship* (1958), was the principal speaker. The main event was the morning session, tape-recorded and later broadcast on KPFA in Berkeley, pertaining to homosexuality. Other speakers at this morning session included San Francisco psychologist Blanche M. Baker; Hal Call, editor of *Mattachine Review*; and famed anthropologist Margaret Mead.

Victory

January 13, 1958, the Supreme Court reversed the Ninth Circuit Court's rulings in *ONE v. Olesen*. Though hoped for, this was totally unexpected by most of ONE's staff. When historians Joyce Murdoch and Deb Price contacted an aged Dale Jennings to ask how he felt when he heard of the victory, he replied: "My God, this is too soon! I'm supposed to be an old man before this happens!" Don Slater, a primary architect of ONE's strategy in the case, said that it was not as much of a surprise to him. "Because we were so sure of ourselves, in a way the decision was sort of anticlimactic." He stated that they "may have boozed it up a little more than usual," but there was no grand celebration. Slater certainly understood the ramifications of the victory: "It wasn't long after that outright advocacy of homosexuality burst into being" (Murdoch and Price 2001, 47–48). Murdoch and Price, in their comprehensive study of the history of lesbians and gays in the Supreme Court, conclude that

> The significance of *ONE's* three-year, largely forgotten legal battle is almost impossible to overstate. The written word has been the first path that count-

less gay men and lesbians have found out of isolation. The 1958 *ONE* ruling flung open the door for gay publications, which began to proliferate. Gay magazines and newspapers became a cornerstone for building gay communities and by encouraging people to come out, to connect with one another and to share a sense of identity and injustice. Millions of American gay men and lesbians have learned to hold their heads up high in part because an obscure little magazine successfully stood up for itself long before many of them were born. (2001, 50)

Ironically, this victory did not do much to improve the working relations between Don Slater and Dorr Legg. In retrospect, Jim Schneider wonders if this victory may have caused the first significant rift in the corporation. As he recalls it, soon after the victory, Legg began to get jealous and to feel that he was not getting enough attention around ONE. Slater, on the other hand, wanted to go gung-ho in pursuing lawsuits and challenging laws. He saw the magazine as a way to promote awareness and provoke social activism across the nation. Legg, however, did not care much for the magazine. At one point, when they were discussing content for *ONE*, he suggested that they simply copy something out of the phonebook. Legg was more interested in his school for homophiles, and the two men became increasingly at odds with one another as a result of these differences in ONE's basic mission and purposes.

Publication and (or) Education

During the business meeting prior to the 1958 annual meeting, the directors of ONE elected to make their combined knowledge and historical materials accessible to the public through the publication of a scholarly journal, *ONE Institute Quarterly*. The journal, which would publish and reprint articles, reports, and studies dealing with homosexuality, could be available to the public through subscription and could also be used as a reference in ONE Institute's courses. At the 1958 annual meeting, it was announced that the first issue would appear the following spring, "the first textbook of homophile studies ever written anywhere."

By the end of 1957, the impetus of the corporation had shifted away from the publication of *ONE Magazine* and toward a different and, for some, loftier goal: education. "The sexual variant needs education about himself and his place in society, if he is to become a happy and productive citizen," the 1957 annual report declared. "Few, if any, existing public or private educational institutions have provided this type of education. The general public needs to be educated about sex variation, in order to counteract ignorant prejudice and harmful discriminatory practices." It was for this reason that ONE Institute had been created and ONE Institute Quarterly of Homophile Studies (OIQ) would be launched, "designed for the serious student," its appeal scholarly, not "popular."

To help fund OIQ and to help alleviate the increased cost of printing ONE Magazine, the organization created a new three-tiered structure for membership, effective February 1, 1958. Those who contributed at least $15 per year would be annual members and would receive a one-year subscription to ONE Magazine and the quarterly ONE Confidential. Those who contributed $30 were contributing members, and they received the same benefits as the annual members plus a copy of the corporation's annual report. For $50, associate members received the above bonus plus "an additional Supplement, containing interesting material not available elsewhere." All members were invited to attend the annual meeting and the Midwinter Institute that followed.

ONE, Incorporated, hosted its sixth annual Midwinter Institute from January 31 through February 2, 1958, with the theme "Homosexuality—A Way of Life." Was the notion of a homosexual lifestyle as absurd as the psychiatrists and psychologists would have it? Viewed from a historical perspective, it was certainly "a novel idea, perhaps an American one; certainly of comparatively recent origin."[30] Other people in other times, places, and cultures had certainly made a place for their homosexuals: "Various ancient cultures fitted the homosexual into their patterns of living as the medicine man, the shaman, the priest, generally as 'the man like a woman,' or, 'the woman like a man.'" Nevertheless, the directors of ONE refused to consider such individuals as leading a homosexual "way of life." They maintained that it was not until the late 1800s that such writers as Whitman and Carpenter dared to "hint at some more stable position for the erotic love of a man for a man, or a woman for a woman," although "their approaches were both faltering and extremely vague." In the current era, they wrote, European homophile organizations were "developing pleasant social lives for their members . . . while many American homophiles feel that an aim of their groups should be a reduction in the incidence of homosexuality." ONE hardly championed such "reductionism": "[S]uppose that Nature (dare we even say God?) has intended or 'chosen,' for some very important and special reasons, a certain percentage of all men and women to express to the fullest extent the innate homosexuality we are told [by Kinsey] is a part of us all. Suppose that it should be discovered that by suppressing and repressing such men and women that traces and cultures have brought about their own slow suicide.

Suppose, most startling of all, that high moral values should be discovered in such a way of life. Does it not seem well worth our time and attention to discuss these matters[?]"[31]

To facilitate such discussion, the first issue of ONE Institute Quarterly was published and delivered to the Hill Street office on June 6, 1958. According to Kepner's 1959 annual editor's report, the Quarterly differed from ONE Magazine in a few significant ways. More serious in tone and didactic in purpose, it intended to "disseminate the results of the Institute's studies in the homophile side of history, religion, law, literature, and the sciences, and also to print or evaluate studies or researches by other scholars in the field." Dawn Frederick of ONE Magazine's art department was appointed OIQ's art director. The printing was done by the same firm that produced ONE, at a bid of $346 for five hundred thirty-two-page copies.

The first issue cost $.93 to print and mail each of six hundred copies (although ONE charged its subscribers less than $.88). The second issue, with five hundred copies printed, cost $.96 each, and the third cost $.84 with six hundred printed. An extra hundred copies were printed for distribution to university libraries, thanks to outside funding through a contributor. By the start of 1959, OIQ had attracted three hundred subscribers, with fifty more copies distributed through six newsstands and bookstores. Kepner estimated that it would take about 760 total subscribers to break even on costs for publication and distributions; five hundred more would be needed to recoup other office and editorial expenses. Clearly, as Kepner put it, the cost to produce ONE's third publication fell "well short of the break-even point." But was it worth the costs? Kepner and Legg argued in the affirmative, that it was time to till and sow the field of homosexual scholarship. They felt this project was ONE's new and urgent mission, expenses be damned. "We frankly admit that at times our sympathies and desires for prompt progress tempt us to move faster than 'sound business judgment' would approve," the board wrote to the Friends of ONE in the fall 1958 issue of ONE Confidential. "But if 'sound business judgment' had been at the helm in 1952, ONE would never have started in the first place."

Earlier in 1958, Stella Rush became chair of the Promotion Committee, and her first goal was to recruit expired subscribers to return to ONE Magazine, which Don Slater now described as "a propaganda device used to put the homosexual point of view across."[32] The magazine's tone had shifted somewhat since the 1957 meeting, where homosexuality was declared a valid, legitimate, and even noble way of life. With this given, ONE's focus turned to advocacy: "Can we, should we advocate homosexuality?" Dr. Blanche Baker was to address this topic in *ONE*'s January 1959 issue. As for the Education Division, ONE Institute hardly had a banner year. The 1958 summer classes were canceled because of lack of enrollment, and Slater's proposed fall seminar on English literature was likewise canceled. Legg, as director of ONE Institute, attributed the problem to "the serious lack of awareness on the part both of professional people and the homophile public of the value of systematic study of the subject."[33] He voiced his frustration over the lack of interest and seems to have lamented the situation by browbeating his audience, the Friends of ONE: "It seems patent to us that if the homophile is ever to be regarded as a part of society to be taken seriously he must begin by taking himself seriously and approach his whole mode of living with at least the same degree of care that other segments of society exercise. First-class citizenship requires first-class efforts. There is no easier way, unfortunate as this may be, to have civil rights and civil respect."[34]

The situation hardly improved the following year. In the fall of 1959, a class in Homophile Sociology met regularly but only attracted an average of eight students. A course called Landmarks in Homophile Literature was dropped after a few sessions because of low enrollment, but a seminar for faculty members pertaining to German history managed to convene periodically through the term. The officers and faculty of ONE Institute included Thomas M. Merritt as dean emeritus; W. Dorr Legg, director; and Alison Hunter (a pseudonym used primarily by Legg) was secretary. Faculty included James Kepner, Jr., instructor in history and psychology; W. Dorr Legg, A.B., B.M., M.L.D., associate professor of sociology; "Thomas M. Merritt," Ph.D., professor emeritus of philosophy; and Donald Slater, A.B., instructor in literature.

Running Hard and Standing Still

In July 1958, *ONE Magazine* reached an all-time low for subscriptions, falling below nine hundred. By comparison, nearly eighteen hundred subscribers had received *ONE* in its best month in 1954. This drop probably reflected frustration on behalf of the magazine's subscribers, who in 1957 had gone three months (nonconsecutive) without a magazine and then in one month received two issues—meaning they received ten issues instead of the anticipated twelve. Readers also appeared weary of the same writers and the same topics, month after month. "We have discovered that we have to work hard to sell this magazine, and like the treadmill in *Alice Through the Looking-Glass*, you find you have to run awfully hard just to stand still," Kepner wrote in his annual report as circulation director.[35] Progress had been made, though; 1958 saw twelve issues printed, and each distributed in the middle of the month of issue.[36] Ten issues had been produced in 1954, 1955, and 1957 and only nine in 1956. At the end of 1958, more than 55,000 back issues remained in stock, and only a few issues from the first few years of publication had sold out.

During a Monday, October 27, 1958, board meeting involving Slater, Kepner, and Legg, discussion ensued regarding the matter of ONE's tax exemption. Kepner and Slater wanted to know what the holdup was, and Legg stalled by discussing some pending court case that could have bearing on ONE's status. They decided not to pursue legal recourse for the moment but would have their attorney, Eric Julber, discuss his recommendations at the corporate meeting scheduled for Wednesday, November 12.

The corporation had managed to follow through with its plan to pay three wages in 1958, but not without some problems. According to the annual report, Slater had allowed ONE to reduce his salary from $47.50 per week to $42.50 in December. Lambert continued to earn $47.50 weekly, and, beginning August 1, Kepner received $75 per week as manager of the Book Department. At the end of the year, the corporation declared a net worth of over $15,000, nearly a $5,000 increase from the year before. This, however, occurred because the projected value of the library had been added to the assets, estimated at $5,000. Without this, the corporation's worth had actually decreased from 1957 by about $300.

All departments reported growth and smooth sailing for 1959 with one notable exception. Slater noted in his annual editor's report that the women's editor had resigned in order to attend school, and no one had stepped forward to replace her. ONE had prided itself on having women on its staff and in its membership, but "feminine interest began wandering over to the Daughters of Bilitis and their *Ladder*." Although *ONE Magazine* may have suffered for the paucity of female writers, Corbin had designed and illustrated half of the 1959 issues with Dawn Frederick available to work on alternate issues. As for ONE's library, the addition of a second room in the Hill Street offices provided the space needed for the library to grow. Former staff member Ben Tabor donated a large desk, and Fred Frisbie installed new shelves for the expanded library. Librarian "Leslie Colfax"[37] reported that two hundred and fifty new titles had been added to ONE's archive, including a donation by Reuben Bush of bound volumes of a complete run of *Der Kreis*, which had begun publication in 1937.

The 1959 report for *One Institute Quarterly* was less promising. In its third year, *OIQ* had "still not reached a level of circulation which eases its financial burden on the corporation." Readers had complained that the material in the first volume was too difficult for the readers of *ONE*. "A number of readers went into a state of emotional shock over their inability to read or comprehend some of the material in the first volume," lamented editor Kepner. "We have discovered to our sorrow that the mere fact that a manuscript is too long or too dense for *ONE Magazine* does not make it suitable for use in the *Quarterly*." Kepner announced that the forthcoming issue would be a double issue in order to "help us somewhat in catching up to schedule." The *OIQ* was never delivered on time. The fall 1959 issue was not distributed until January 1, 1960, and several subscribers complained of not receiving certain issues when, in fact, the late distribution and quirky numbering system confused many into thinking they had missed an issue.

Compounding matters, the printers, who had done a great job for ONE since 1957, were far less enthusiastic about *ONE*'s more intelligent progeny. Kepner wrote in his report, "They seem to have been distinctly dragging their feet with the last few issues, so with fear and trembling about going so far afield, we have arranged to have the *Quarterly* printed in England from now on, by the printer who did *The Keval*." Kepner further reported that the new printer estimated a cost of $200 per issue less than the previous printers, reducing the cost per issue to fifty-seven cents (as opposed to the ninety-seven-cent cost before). If accurate, the savings would be substantial, but Kepner failed to mention shipping and other fees that could significantly raise the price of production.

At the close of 1959, ONE, Incorporated, counted 248 nonvoting members, the Friends of ONE. People from all over the world came to visit the Hill Street office, pilgrims from as far away as New Zealand, Indonesia, France, Portugal, Brazil, Holland, Alaska, and most of the United States. ONE had clearly made an impression among the world's homophiles. In order to accommodate this newfound fame and recruit others into the organization, an awkward and ill-conceived effort to expand the board of directors was devised. ONE's attorney allowed for the interpretation of the bylaws such that each board member could be allocated half a vote, thus clearing the way to double the size of the board to eighteen. Two new voting members were expected to be nominated during the next annual meeting, in January 1960.

1960: Impending Change

On Friday evening, January 29, 1960, the board elected Ron Longworth and Clarence Harrison to be voting members of the corporation. As for the triennial election of officers, Kepner was elected chairman, Slater vice-chairman, and Legg became secretary-treasurer.[38] About twenty-five members and supporters attended the ceremony, including Blanche M. Baker and her husband from San Francisco. Kepner chaired the meeting, which convened at 8:15 p.m. and adjourned at 10:10 p.m.

The theme of the 1960 Midwinter Institute was "The Homosexual in the Community." Featured session conveners included the Reverend Stephen Fritchman of the First Unitarian Church in Los Angeles; Beverly Hills psychologist Zolton Gross; director of Southern California's ACLU, Eason Monroe; and UCLA psychologist Dr. Evelyn Hooker. For entertainment, actors performed James Barr's *Game of Fools* for the first time in the United States. The cumulative attendance of the eight sessions totaled 405 people—a most auspicious beginning for the new decade.

Kepner, however, would not last the year as a member of the corporation. He proffered many reasons for resigning, having been frustrated by the organization for a very long time. In his resignation letter, dated November 15, 1960, he blamed "a wide divergence of policy and purpose" that had emerged between himself and the other members of the board, especially regarding the "overblown claims made for the Institute, a general chip-on-the-shoulder attitude, . . . haggling about the *Quarterly*, the handling of the forthcoming Midwinter Institute plans, mismanagement of the book service and other serious financial questions, and some general personnel problems." Kepner concluded his letter: "Since the working conditions at the office have grown increasingly intolerable for me during the past five months, I now feel I have no alternative but to resign from membership in the Corporation." Billy Glover recalls that many of Kepner's issues in the office involved politics: he was a liberal Democrat, and Slater and Legg were both avid Republicans (as Jennings had been). But the one overarching reason that caused Kepner to resign from the corporation and begin a five-year vacation from homosexual rights activism was a letter he received from the IRS.

It seems that at some point in 1959, an agent of the State of California Franchise Tax Board came to ONE to peruse the corporate records. This man assured ONE that in his opinion, it should qualify as a tax-exempt organization. He pledged to help the organization secure federal exemption status (which had formerly been denied). Despite repeated halfhearted attempts, ONE, Incorporated, never would secure tax-exempt status, although ONE's attorney exhibited such confidence it would happen that he prematurely encouraged the Friends of ONE to deduct their contributions anyway. It later turned out that the reason that ONE failed to achieve federal tax-exempt status was not because the state had denied ONE's application but rather because ONE's business manager, Dorr Legg, had never submitted the required form designating "who would receive the corporate property if ever ONE dissolved" (Kepner 1998, 395).[39] When Kepner received a letter from the IRS that threatened to prosecute the organization—and him personally—"with criminal action if we kept claiming to be tax deductible," that was the last straw (Kepner 1998, 395). Kepner was out the door, for good this time.

It is not clear to me why Legg would fail to file the necessary paperwork to secure nonprofit status for ONE. Surely it would have been possible by this time—the Daughters of Bilitis had secured nonprofit status in California at the same time it filed its articles of incorporation, in January 1957, and later became federally tax exempt (Martin and Lyon 1991, 227). Legg's failure to file the requisite forms could only serve to put ONE in danger and to dissuade potential benefactors. Perhaps his distrust or disdain for government institutions might explain his lack of action? Perhaps Legg's failure to secure ONE's nonprofit status was somewhat akin to Slater's refusal to pay parking tickets in his days at USC? Surely Legg had invested too much in ONE to willfully or wantonly put the organization in danger. Yet, in effect, that is exactly what he did.

With Kepner gone, Slater—ONE's senior editor who preferred to operate from the sidelines—now found himself the undisputed senior editor of the magazine, even without the title editor-in-chief. Slater's allegiances, in accord with ONE's bylaws, resided first with the magazine and then with the institute. Increasingly, the magazine became Slater's domain and the institute Legg's realm. It seemed a healthy partnership: both Slater and Legg had proven themselves equally dedicated to the movement. Politically like-minded, they complemented each other organizationally as Legg managed the finances and Slater concentrated on the magazine. While these were their tendencies, their roles at this point were far from solid: Legg often contributed to ONE Magazine and Slater managed ONE's growing library. Both held seminars and courses under the auspices of ONE Institute (although the frequent cancellation of his classes because of lack of enrollment frustrated Slater). Moreover, in contrast to the stodgy and imperious Legg, Slater was more personable and charming—as Wayne Dynes put it, Legg represented structure and Slater nonstructure.[40] Although he may not have captained the ship, Slater made a great first mate, conveying to others a respect toward Legg that bordered on reverence. They were fighting the same battle, after all, and Legg had proven to be one of the corporation's most dedicated workers and intelligent tacticians.

5

Separation
(1960–62)

Life is defined through its extremes, where passions reign:
there is no middle ground of reason.
—F. G. Bailey, *Tactical Uses of Passion*

I HAVE COME to think of the late 1950s and early '60s as the golden years for ONE, Incorporated. Though plagued with personality conflicts and paucity of resources throughout its history, the organization had pulled though very difficult times and operations had become routine. After the dust settled, *ONE Magazine* emerged as the voice of America's homosexuals, and men and women from all over the country regularly turned to its pages for support, encouragement, and a sense of unity and fellowship. It was during this time that my primary consultants joined the corporation, Jim Schneider in the winter of 1959 and Billy Glover the following year.

New Blood and Fresh Perspectives

Jim Schneider was born on the family farm on April 4, 1932, the second of seven children. When he was thirteen years old, his father was incapacitated in a tragic accident involving a hay stacker. Through determination and hard work, Schneider and his older brother managed to keep the family together until their father's death in 1954.

Throughout his youth, Schneider always put the needs of his family before his own desires. Although his family was tight-knit and loving, he often felt isolated and alone. After his father's death, he left the farm and moved to Oakland, California, to live with one of his other brothers. After only three months' residence in the Bay Area, he realized that he could not tolerate the perpetual fog. He next spent a year in Fresno before settling in Huntington Park, a suburb southeast of Los Angeles. Jim Kepner described Schneider at this time as "a shy but determined young bachelor with a burning desire to 'get ahead in life'" (1971, 1). Disliking his newfound solitude, he tried meeting women through a dating agency, but nothing clicked with any of them. He became increasingly aware of his attraction toward men, and this awareness did not sit well with him.

Troubled by his lack of interest in women, Schneider visited a young psychologist named Dr. Timmer. The two met twice weekly for a period of months and gradually developed a rapport. A breakthrough came when Timmer introduced Schneider to *The Price of Salt*, a novel by Patricia Highsmith, writing under the nom de plume Claire Morgan. Schneider read this book about two women who fall in love with each other and, tearful at the happy ending, reconciled himself to his sexuality and set about learning what it means to be a homosexual. Dr. Timmer also told Schneider about *ONE Magazine* and suggested he obtain a copy. Schneider set out to do just that. Around Christmas of 1959, he got up the courage to call ONE's office. Editor Don Slater answered the phone. When Schneider inquired as to where he might find the magazine for sale, Slater directed him to the Florence and Pacific Newsstand close to Schneider's Huntington Park home. There, virtually in his own neighborhood, Schneider at last found a key to his own identity.

Schneider was intrigued by the cover of this December 1959 issue depicting two young men facing each other beside a campfire. One is crouched and leaning toward the other, his face and torso aglow as a burro looks on in the background. The cover art is attributed to the Swiss publication *Der Kreis* and the illustration to one Rico from Zurich. Schneider first read an editorial by Don Slater recapitulating a discussion among ONE's staff regarding what a homosexual might ultimately desire were he or she granted a Christmas wish. Slater's articulate and thoughtful response appeals to both the common or "same" aspects of homosexuals in society while simultaneously noting clear differences: "The homosexual like everyone else is concerned with the tax rate, the policies of armies, the practices of churches. . . . Like everyone else, the homosexual works and fights, plows the fields and harvests the grain—but as a homosexual. He plays and swims and skis and climbs mountains, dances and sings and drives cars as a homosexual. His homosexuality can be seen to affect his whole life. And this he must understand if he is to be gay, sure-footed—a happy lover who is able to succeed in his individual aspirations and his sex experiences" (4). Slater continued, "In matters of sex we may be said to be reaching a new kind of adjustment socially, better fitted to the homosexual and to our age generally." But with increased acceptance comes increased responsibility: "As individuals or in pairs we must be well informed about the whole range of possibilities if we are to make intelligent choices. We cannot continue to rely upon parents, the church, psychologists, or the police to determine what we want or should expect from life."

Perhaps, he notes, the right to marry might be one such consideration for some homosexuals. However, "faced with the many opportunities for experimenting as we are, we should be working out a code of ethics which insists upon our rights to express our sexual development and generally share in the common enjoyment of life." Basic rights should be asserted or fought for such as "the right to expect protection of our property and protection for the individual and homosexual family unit where it exists. We should probably expect military service, freedom of dress, and freedom from any sort of controls that link us with criminals and the maladjusted." Slater asserts that the homosexual should "use his intelligence and insist upon recognition of his overt behavior as one of the expected forms of deviation from heterosexual monogamy. He should also insist upon personal happiness, sharing things of the world, a defined position, and respectability."

Following this editorial is Jim Eagan's discussion of the possibility of homosexual marriage. Next, a romantic short story, "The Exiles," tells of two American Indians who fall in love and are caught in the act by Father Gomez of the Mission of San Luis Rey. When the padre banishes one of the boys from the mission, the other decides voluntarily to leave with him. The story ends with the two lovers, Esteban and Arturo, heading bravely together into the wilderness hand in hand, perhaps toward a distant campfire like the one blazing on the cover.

The concluding article is by Dr. Blanche M. Baker, a San Francisco psychotherapist with more than twenty-five years of experience in marriage counseling and a longtime supporter of ONE. In her response to an inquiry as to the merits of "gay marriage" and an accusation that ONE's editors had slighted the topic, Baker reminds the writer of an August 1953 issue on that very subject. She concludes that the ultimate reason that many homosexual relations are ephemeral is because of the "lack of self-confidence and appreciation of one's self as an individual." Should families and communities accept those with same-sex tendencies, homosexuals will then become "adjusted individuals who live quiet, creative lives in their own unique way and never find the path to the psychiatrist's office."

This was exactly the kind of information for which Schneider had been seeking. The articles were thoughtful and appealing; Joan Corbin, Dawn Frederick, and the editorial team produced an exceptionally tight issue that December 1959. Schneider again contacted Slater, and a few weeks later he attended a discussion group at ONE's Hill Street office where he met Slater face to face along with business manager William Lambert. Although the magazine moved him emotionally, Schneider's first encounter with ONE did not particularly inspire him. The building was old and shabby, the meeting room cramped and unkempt, and only a dozen or so in attendance including Slater and Lambert. Still, Schneider returned and became active in the discussion sessions for the next few years, eventually taking on the role of leader of the Friday Night Work Committee; after meeting his lover, schoolteacher Henry Lieffers, the two worked shoulder to shoulder for ONE until the organization split in 1965.

About the time he discovered ONE, Schneider began working for Bethlehem Steel where he taught safety and designed an effective training program. After leaving Bethlehem in 1980, Schneider started up Office Palace, a service that delivers office supplies to local businesses. Through his business experiences he has learned a great deal about management and administration—and he continued to learn and still operates Office Palace to this day. His application of that experiential knowledge greatly benefited ONE and HIC. Schneider has a rare and boundless compassion for people, demonstrated by his concern for the health and welfare of his coworkers. In accord with his concern for worker safety, his current expertise is in office ergonomics. One of his favorite assignments was to help offices retrofit to better accommodate workers while reducing repetitive stress injuries and increasing productivity.

ONE's other great workhorse, William Edward "Billy" Glover, also began working for Don Slater and Dorr Legg in 1960. Glover was born on September 16, 1932, in Shreveport, Louisiana. He grew up in Bossier City, Louisiana, and attended Bossier City schools. The high school is just four blocks away from his home on Monroe Street. He played flute in the band, which traveled during summers to Lions Club meetings. Glover received his diploma in 1950 and attended Louisiana State University in Baton Rouge where he "had more fun than learning." He graduated in 1955, and the army immediately drafted him into training at Camp Chafee, Arkansas. He transferred to Fort Riley, where he was one of the first soldiers to join the first division attending to troops as they returned from Germany. He later went to Fort Benjamin Harrison for further training in finance with the understanding that he would be stationed in Europe for his remaining time. When that failed to happen, he got upset, began acting up, and was subsequently caught in a suspicious encounter with another man. Though no sex was involved in this particular instance, the army discharged Glover over the incident in 1956.

Glover recalls having homosexual feelings and tendencies all his life. He was once caught fooling around with other boys under a wooden bridge near his house when he was four years old. He had sexual relations with several other boys in high school, later at Louisiana State University, and then within the army. But his sexual life peaked after his discharge when he moved to Los Angeles and drove his old Pontiac to Long Beach, Oceanside, or San Clemente in search of wandering sailors.

Glover had seen *ONE Magazine* on various newsstands in the late 1950s, so upon his arrival in Los Angeles he decided to contact its publishers. He first met Jim Kepner at the original downtown office on Hill Street and subsequently decided to attend Mattachine's 1959 convention in Denver. Inspired by the event, he sojourned to San Francisco where he stayed for a week with Hal Call, editor of *Mattachine Review*. He worked for a while at Call's Pan Graphic Press, and his review of the book *Advise and Consent* was published in the February 1961 issue of *Mattachine Review*.

Glover soon returned to Los Angeles and began volunteering at ONE. He became one of its first paid office employees shortly after Kepner's resignation late in 1960. His first assignment—self-appointed—was the inglorious task of painting the library floor with the only color at hand: bright red (Glover 1997, 27). Glover worked in all areas, very much the office gofer. He especially enjoyed delivering *ONE Magazine* to local newsstands, a task that often fell to him because Slater and Legg frequently had no functioning automobile. Glover also served on the committee that slipped the magazines into brown paper wrappers, and he often transported the bundled magazines to the post office.

When the differences between Don Slater and Dorr Legg culminated in the spring of 1965, Glover's loyalties remained with the magazine, so he joined with Slater, Sanchez, Joseph and Jane Hansen, and Schneider to incorporate the Homosexual Information Center in 1968. The IRS recognized HIC as a federally tax-exempt, 501(c)(3) organization in 1971. Prior to Slater's death in 1997, Glover decided to return to his home in Louisiana, and he continued to serve HIC from there. Until recently, he lived in his boyhood home, near his old school, surrounded by longtime friends and neighbors.

Calm before the Storm

As seen in the previous chapter, 1960 was a year of struggle and tenuous cooperation among ONE's directors, and at the end of the year, the organization was at a point of crisis. The December 1960 issue of *ONE Magazine* was the last to list Kepner, as "Lyn Pedersen," as associate editor. With Kepner's exodus, the tenor of the magazine was destined to change and the schism between *ONE*'s editors and ONE Institute's instructors would likely be exacerbated. All Schneider and the other associates could do was watch as power and resources became increasingly divided by these two separate divisions of the organization.

Following Kepner's resignation, Don Slater invited Ross Ingersoll to join the editorial board. Ingersoll accepted and soon began writing for *ONE* under the name "Marcel Martin." Slater and Ingersoll met when both attended a banquet at the 1958 annual meeting. The friendship kindled there remained warm ever since.

Ingersoll taught foreign language courses for a local college, and his first contribution to *ONE* was a translated article from the French magazine *Arcadie.* Although his pedantic prose was dry compared to Kepner's droll commentary, Ingersoll would prove a worthy replacement for Kepner as far as the magazine was concerned. He soon became a regular contributor, and he continued to work with Slater even after the split and subsequent transition from *ONE* to *Tangents.* According to Joseph Hansen, the highlight of Ingersoll's career with ONE was a six-page editorial published in the January 1962 issue that summarized the history of the magazine. Hansen lauded it as "one of the best articles *ONE* had ever printed" (1998, 27).

The corporation needed a new director to fill the remaining two years of Kepner's term on the board and so, during the annual meeting on Friday, January 27, 1961, the directors formally elected Fred Frisbie to the position that he had tentatively held since Kepner's departure. Clarence W. Harrison resigned during a corporate meeting on Monday, January 23, but no reasons were cited in his resignation letter, dated January 22. Joe Weaver, known consistently in corporate documents as "Joe Aaron," was elected to voting membership to fill the vacancy. Weaver had served as chair of the promotion committee since early February 1960.

During this annual meeting, Frisbie announced that some board members had attended the first annual convention of the Daughters of Bilitis (DOB), where Frisbie had been so impressed he reported that it had been "a fine Convention in all ways and put the men's organization to shame."[1] The promotion committee updated a brochure promoting *ONE*, distributing twenty thousand copies, and broadcast an advertisement for *ONE* on a Los Angeles radio station, which, to Frisbie's knowledge, was the first time that a "homophile organization had done such a thing."[2] Frisbie noted that a recent issue of *ONE Confidential* announced plans for corporate expansion and the costs involved. After many of the Friends of ONE responded by expressing concern that the corporation ran the risk of overextending itself, Frisbie acknowledged that perhaps it had been a "rash" thing to do.[3] The meeting adjourned at 10 p.m., at which time around sixty Friends of ONE and their guests were invited to the home of Rudy Steinert, a few doors west of Slater and Sanchez's home on Calumet.

In 1960, *ONE Magazine* posted its best subscription year since 1954 with an average of 3,805 copies distributed each month—nearly 1,000 more than the 1958 average. At the start of 1961, Ingersoll became the new international editor. "Alison Hunter" was listed as women's editor.[4] Slater noted in his annual report that bold stories such as "The Junk Dealer" and "A Beer, a Bath, and a Summer Night" had drawn both criticism and praise: "Our attorney has long been counseling us to keep moving farther in the direction of frank statement as well as literary merit. We don't want to go too far, but we don't want the magazine to be dull." Looking ahead, the editors set the magazine's primary goal for 1961 to attract more women readers, thus they planned to produce another "All-Feminine Issue."

As for the magazine's artwork, Dawn Frederick designed five issues and contributed thirteen illustrations. Joan Corbin designed six issues and contributed thirty illustrations. In her art director's report for 1960, Corbin expressed gratitude to Slater for his assistance: "The truth is that Don Slater, in addition to all his other duties, is often forced to act as art director and, due to the inaction of Eve Elloree, does all the soliciting for new material. Don handled the entire January 1961 issue, a very fine accomplishment, especially for one not familiar with the pitfalls of paste-up, further proof of his versatility."

The directors agreed in early 1960 that the layout artist would be paid $35 per issue. Both Corbin and Frederick received this payment a few times, but the goal of a permanent salary proved unrealistic. Corbin complained, "It remains to be seen which burden is more tolerable: that of the hourly insistence of a moral responsibility to pay for value received, or that of having made a commitment and NOT BEING ABLE to meet it."

Why did Corbin remain so involved with *ONE* if she felt inappropriately rewarded? She worked a full-time job as a drawing-board artist elsewhere, she explained at the annual meeting, but "when weekends come I am ravenous for a different kind of activity." She said it took "a minimum of two days to do a satisfactory issue" and that she had taken on the task as often as possible. "All of us at ONE work under extreme difficulties," she added. "Compared to the stress and strain of the rest, mine have been nothing." She announced, however, that she and her partner had purchased a house and property in the foothills north of Glendale and were in the process of upgrading the property. As a result, she could only commit to four issues for the coming year. Regrettably, Dawn Frederick would be unable to assist at all. Corbin ended her report by again thanking Slater "for his infinite patience and understanding."

ONE Institute's 1960 spring lecture series enrolled sixty-six students, and the fall series had eighty-seven. Slater lectured on "Petronius Arbiter and the First Gay Novel," with actor Morgan Farley reading from *The Satyricon*. Ann Holmquist, as "Ann Bannon," led a talk entitled "Some Secrets of the Gay Novel," and Harry Hay gave a heady lecture, "The End of a Dream: The Semantic Impasse." By invitation of the San Francisco Mattachine Society, Kepner, Slater, Lambert, and Clarence Harrison "conducted seven two-hour Extension classes [on successive weekends], brief capsule-summaries selected from the Institute's class-work." A total of ninety people attended these four seminars. As for regular classes, ONE Institute offered and conducted three courses in the spring: Freud's Theory of Homosexuality, The Gay Novel, and The Sociology of Homosexuality. Two hundred and thirteen people enrolled, and fifty-one two-hour sessions comprised a course. The fall term included classes titled The Theory and Practice of Homophile Education, The Gay Novel, and Homosexuality in History. Each course consisted of fifty-eight sessions, and one hundred eighty-two people enrolled. This was clearly the most successful year yet for ONE Institute of Homophile Studies.

The *ONE Institute Quarterly*, however, faced tougher times. Printing in England proved more problematic than expected, so a new local printer was selected. Lambert admitted that, even still, "its circulation has by no means yet attained a figure which makes its production relatively economical." The *Quarterly* still required significant subvention, and with Kepner out of the picture, Lambert had to stand in the gap alone to justify the journal's existence:

Attendance at classes and the circulation of the *Quarterly* show clearly how difficult it is to arouse serious interest in the study of homophile questions. To put it bluntly, homosexuals would appear to care very little about their own welfare, to judge by this evidence, but this does not imply, as we see it, that the attempt to awaken them should be abandoned.[5]

Frustrated but determined, Lambert would continue to educate the homophile, whether or not others appreciated his efforts and no matter the cost.

ONE vs. DOB: The Homosexual Bill of Rights Disaster

The primary purpose of the convention during the Midwinter Institute of 1961 was to produce a Homosexual Bill of Rights, which was intended to unify and rally all present. Thus, ONE's leaders were surprised when Del Martin wrote the following in the January issue of *The Ladder*: "Such a "Bill of Rights" is unnecessary, irrelevant, and likely to set the homophile movement back into oblivion. . . . [It] implies that this document would be a statement representative of this entire minority group. Nothing could be further from the truth. . . . It implies that we want exclusive rights—yet we want no rights for ourselves which we would not extend to others" (in Masters 1962, 119–20).

In preparation for the Midwinter discussion, ONE and Mattachine issued thousands of four-page questionnaires. The first two pages asked questions pertaining to the respondent's opinion regarding the Homosexual Bill of Rights and the social standing of homosexuals in general. The second two pages asked more intimate, optional questions. R. E. L. Masters correctly assessed that "[i]t is not unlikely that this portion of the questionnaire, along with a lack of enthusiasm for the proposed Bill of Rights and perhaps fear concerning its consequences, was in part responsible for the small number of questionnaires returned" (1962, 122), and his description of the fallout from this meeting is, unfortunately, the best I have found in print. Those contacted returned only 325 questionnaires but, suspiciously, the officers of ONE had not tabulated the results before the meeting.

Lambert had anticipated that DOB would provide the loyal opposition to the plan, but Del Martin later reported that most present at the convention agreed with DOB's perspective. They had hardly been in the minority at all, yet the assembly leaders refused to let Martin and others change the preordained format of the meeting, nor would they consider modifying or eliminating the title of the proposal. DOB president Jaye Bell withdrew that organization from the proceedings "unless the Bill of Rights form were to be abandoned. W. Dorr Legg of ONE, imminent [sic] authority on Paleolithic sodomy rites and other matters, made it clear that this would not occur" (Masters 1962, 125). Lambert later wrote the dissenting lesbians off as "assimilationists" and accused them of furthering fracturing the movement. He pointed out that Jim Kepner had resigned "a couple of days before the Midwinter Institute started," suggesting that he had left for ideological reasons (Legg 1994, 39). He made no mention, of course, of the IRS fiasco.

With Kepner's departure, the stability of the board of directors became increasingly precarious. Along with Kepner, two other voting members, John H. Lawson and Don L. Plagmann, also resigned. With many good people leaving the corporation and a dearth of viable talent available for replacement, 1961 became a year of exodus. Over the next four years, ONE would continue to fracture from within as diverse politics, policies, and philosophies intensified like tectonic pressures beneath a fault. "Was this some kind of watershed in a movement trying to discover and define itself?" Legg would later wonder rhetorically (1994, 39).

Kepner's resignation was made final during the corporate meeting on January 22, 1961, and on the following day Lambert sent a letter to Lois Mercer asking her to work full time for the corporate office as bookkeeper. Mercer accepted, with the understanding that she would perform most of the work from her home near Eleventh and Normandy. During a meeting on February 1, 1961, the board decided to hire Ron Longworth to work full time because the corporation was "short handed and in need of staff replacement." Longworth refused the position, suggesting that ONE couldn't afford him. He recommended that the corporation "devote all its energies to its most profitable operations" and that it outsource or abandon many of its secondary activities and services "until better times."

Lambert replied on February 15 that these comments had been well taken, though Longworth had not made clear which "secondary activities" ONE should sacrifice. Longworth had noted the *Quarterly* in his letter, but Lambert felt that "the general feeling seems to be that it is too important to drop." Lambert replied that the corporation's most important "income producer" was *ONE Confidential*: "It strongly cements the Friends to the Corporation." He suggested that *ONE Confidential* be shipped together with *ONE Magazine* in order to save funds. Lambert invited Longworth to help carry this out, but Longworth was not impressed with the plan so, on April 14, 1961, he resigned from voting membership.

Though shaken by the Bill of Rights fiasco, Stella Rush decided to stay on the editorial board of *ONE Magazine*. She had been a director of ONE for the previous five years and was also active in DOB. A sketch of Rush by Dawn Frederick graced *ONE*'s cover in June 1960. Nevertheless, Rush resigned the following year after discovering that an article published in the February 1961 issue and attributed to "Alison Hunter" had *not* been written by Alice Horvath, as had been assumed—nor by any other woman. Rush's resignation came about during a phone conversation with Slater on Wednesday, July 12, 1961. She explained her reasons in a letter to ONE dated Sunday, July 23, where she complained that the February editorial had advocated homosexuality as a means of birth control: "It is time to call for at least half the women of the world to do their duty and NOT have babies, at least not more than the world can support. We can think of no better way to ensure this than by encouraging more women to join in permanent and highly moral partnerships with one another."

Rush called the opinion presented "drastic" with overtones both "suicidal" and "fascist . . . a school of thought and action inimical to the liberty of all citizens." She was infuriated that "some of the male members of the corporation feel justified in writing the most drastic opinions under this feminine pseudonym [Alison Hunter] if a feminine editor happens to be lacking at the moment." She noted that the article contained "undertones . . . of the same school as the Lambert editorial which was relegated to *ONE Confidential* as a matter of personal opinion" and concluded, "I find this particular development distressing on more levels than I care to enumerate or you would care to hear, I'm sure." Thus ended Rush's five-year membership on ONE's board of directors. She had served on the magazine's editorial board for sixteen months.

Whereas the acknowledgment-of-resignation letters sent to Kepner and others who had resigned earlier in the year had been brief and cordial, the letter to Rush, addressed August 9, 1961, was more commanding than polite. Although signed by Frisbie as ONE's chairman, the prose certainly recalls Lambert's stern authoritarianism more than Frisbie's flowery and polite style: "Now there are two points we feel must be clarified in no uncertain terms. First, no one can serve two masters and do equal justice to both. Since the Daughters pursue a line of reasoning widely divergent from that of ONE, it follows that anyone active in the two organizations must find his thinking subtly tinged and influenced by both. Without elaborating further let it simply be stipulated that in the future voting membership and participation in Corporation affairs of ONE shall be extended only to those not so connected with another homophile organization."

The letter also lambasted Rush for her "regrettable tendency to be precipitate in drawing conclusions without making a sufficient examination of the related circumstances and qualifying conditions." Rush was reminded that, in 1954, it was editor Corky Wolf who devised those particular pen names, which were considered corporate property: "Leslie Colfax" as librarian; "Marvin Cutler," director of the Bureau of Public Information; "Robert Gregory," editorial secretary; "Armand Quezon," international editor; and "Alison Hunter," women's editor. The letter continued, "We sincerely wish it had been possible for you to grasp clearly the differences of policy in the use of such names (or titles) and in such personal pen names as Sten Russell, Marcel Martin, James Barr, Gabrielle Ganelle, Lyn Pedersen, Alice Horvath, William Lambert, W. H. Hamilton, and many others." As it was, Rush should have known that the views of "Alison Hunter" did not represent "the ideas of some particular person." The letter concluded by noting that the board had not acted upon her resignation and that, if she wanted to reconsider, they could meet to discuss the situation. The condescending tone of the letter ensured that was not likely to happen.

Clipped beneath a copy of Rush's resignation letter, I discovered in the HIC archives a note from Rush addressed to Lambert that might explain this prickly response. The note was dated July 27, 1961, penned by Rush after having had a "distracted long-distance phone call from Amanda S." the night before. It seems that "Amanda's" real problem stemmed from a letter Lambert wrote to her. Rush complained, "Honest-to-Pete, Bill, couldn't you think of some better reasons to keep her away from L.A. than by telling her lies about the women here. . . . After all, I don't know another pair than Cork and Vick who get drunk and beat each other up. Undoubtedly I could find some if I combed the bars! But what the hell." She continued, "You wonder where the trust, faith, and loyalty to ONE is going? Your letter to Amanda is an example of how to queer said trust, faith, and loyalty." She added that the Alice Horvath situation mentioned in her resignation letter was but one of many examples of how Lambert had violated the trust of the organization and its workers. She understood how difficult Lambert's life had been since he had dedicated himself to ONE and said she made "large allowances for this fact." Others felt otherwise, noting that Lambert was suffering the consequences of his own decisions. She asked, "Why should they have to pay for your unhappiness?" Rush concluded on a critical note that, according to her, stemmed more from her respect and admiration for Lambert than from ill will or bitterness: "It is hard to believe a man of your brilliance cannot look as scathingly at himself as he does the rest of the world."

Rush sent her original letter of resignation to ONE's chairman, Fred Frisbie (as "George Mortenson"), and mailed copies to all other board members,

"tired of people giving phony reasons 'til you chase them down in person.
. . . Corporation members have a right to know why they are being deserted
and not be given some Pollyanna story." She concluded with her best wishes
and hopes that she could soon afford to send a monetary donation and contribute to *ONE Magazine* again in the future.

I will leave it for others to assess the overarching significance for the pre-
gay movement that ONE and the other homophile organizations (except, of
course, the DOB) were so flagrantly male dominated. I hope that the facts
and details here presented will inspire thoughtful discussion as to the ultimate
causes and ramifications of this tragic fissure between men and women that
seems pervasive and even haunts the contemporary movement. For my part, I
find it sad that the women were not given the respect and remuneration they
so clearly deserved, and I admire them for their perseverance, fortitude, and
dedication to the cause. While I hesitate to draw overreaching conclusions
or to paint too broad a stroke with too coarse a brush, it seems to me that
the women were in the organization primarily for the cause and then for the
camaraderie, whereas some of the men shared these sentiments yet often let
their egos get the best of them.

With that said, perhaps it was the headstrong arrogance of the men that
kept ONE alive and at the forefront of the movement for well over a decade.
Could ONE have survived, let alone succeeded, without men such as Jennings, Rowland, Legg, Kepner, and Slater vying for control and pressing the
organization to further its goals and to grow? Or might ONE have persevered
longer, and achieved even greater accomplishments, had its directors been
more inclusive and welcoming of women and shared their meager resources
more equitably among them? In the pages that follow, we will see exactly
where the organization was headed as a result of Slater's and Legg's headstrong leadership. Had they taken action to keep such dedicated workers as
Kepner, Corbin, Wolf, and Rush in the organization, ONE, Incorporated,
might have weathered the '60s, redefined itself in the '70s, and provided a
beacon of hope through the tremulous '80s. As we will see, this was certainly
not what happened, and because of endemic rivalries and fractioning, the
organization became a laughingstock to many, and a disgrace.

There is plenty to chew on here, much food for speculation. I think it is
tragic that so many people came to ONE with such high hopes only to have
them ground to the dirt or dashed against a wall. Some people—both men
and women—never recovered from the emotional blows they endured in
caring for this cause and this organization, as will be seen. At this point, eight
years into the corporation's history, it was very clear that the men at ONE's

core, Legg and Slater, maintained their control and their incomes by sacrificing the needs of the others. Although both of these men deserve recognition
as the pioneers and leaders that they were, they also deserve criticism for
having put their own needs before ONE's and for allowing their differences
to tear the organization apart.

With Kepner, Corbin, Wolf, and Rush gone, the magazine again required
a fresh infusion of talent to keep it afloat. Thus, Slater began looking in
earnest for talented writers while Legg struggled to grow ONE Institute. As
before, they were able to draw from the abundance of dedicated and talented
homosexual folk in the Los Angeles area, and before long, ONE was again
revitalized. Although this new success was to be short-lived, ONE's recovery
was largely a result of the efforts of two newcomers to the scene, a somewhat
eccentric but dedicated married couple named Joe and Jane Hansen.

Introducing the Hansens

At some point in 1961, Wayne F. Placek, a relative newcomer to Los Angeles
from Wahoo, Nebraska, and student at ONE Institute, brought his lover Joseph Hansen to ONE's Hill Street office to meet Don Slater and see if Slater
might publish a story Hansen had written. Slater liked the story and agreed to
print a shorter version at a later date. Until then, Hansen had only published
poetry. In fact, he made his debut in ONE Magazine with three poems in the
March 1962 issue. In the June issue, ONE featured Hansen's shortened story
"The Chosen," attributed to James Colton, a pseudonym used under Slater's
insistence. Hansen's stories soon became a magazine mainstay. Slater required
Hansen to continue using the Colton pseudonym for his own protection,
although Hansen would later wish that he could have used his real name.
In any case, he was forever grateful to Placek and Slater for starting him "on
a career that would result in thirty novels and who knows how many short
stories, almost all of them accounts of what it is like to be homosexual in our
world and time" (Hansen 1998, 42–45).

Joseph Hansen was born on July 19, 1923. He spent the first ten years of his
life in Aberdeen, in the remote northeast corner of South Dakota, where he
began writing at the age of nine. His family moved to Minneapolis in 1933.
Three years later they settled in Pasadena, California, where he later became
editor of the school newspaper for John Marshall Junior High. Hansen attended Pasadena Junior College beginning in 1939 where he reported for the
school newspaper and often performed in plays and radio shows. After school

he worked for the public library (Hansen 1992, 237). He began purchasing and reading books by classic authors such as Shakespeare, Poe, Whitman, Thoreau, and Emerson. Walt Whitman's *Leaves of Grass* quite shocked him as it celebrated feelings that Hansen, an active Christian throughout his youth, believed sinful. "Whitman's manly ease with his sexuality eased my worries, and Emerson's 'Self Reliance' urged me to be myself, no matter what the world might think" (Hansen 1992, 237–38).

At this time, Hansen befriended Robert Ben Ali, whose play *Manya*, written when Ben Ali was seventeen years old, had achieved national notoriety and launched the career of boy actor Bill Beedle (who soon became William Holden). Ben Ali introduced Hansen to even more great literature, such as the works of Homer, Joyce, Cocteau, Rimbaud, and Baudelaire. Hansen described Ali at this time as "more than lover," being also "mentor, counselor, comforter, [and] a spellbinding talker." Reflecting on Ben Ali, Hansen recalled that he had always been lucky with his friends: "They have been my university—the only one I was to have or to want" (Hansen 1992, 238).

Hansen began working for the Pickwick Bookshop on Hollywood Boulevard in February 1943. Because the bus ride from Pasadena to Pickwick took over an hour, he moved out of his parents' house and found a room on Yucca Street near the bookstore. He continued to see Ben Ali, as he had for the past three years, but this changed when Jane Bancroft entered the shop one Saturday morning. Bancroft was from Texas, although her family line could be traced to John Winthrop, first governor of the Massachusetts Bay Colony. She had grown up around horses, and "her arrested vocabulary suggested the stables of Fort Bliss, the Army cavalry post at El Paso . . . and the stockyards, where she'd worked cattle from horseback." Her vulgar manner and style belied her lively, well-read, and sophisticated mind. An adroit reader with an amazing memory, she loved to discuss history, politics, religion, and philosophy. Hansen was surprised to find himself attracted to her body as much as her mind: "Slender, narrow-hipped, tall for a girl, she wore bell-bottom jeans and cut her hair short like a boy's. I found her a treat to look at" (Hansen 1992, 239–40). They married at the Los Angeles courthouse on August 4, 1943. Their daughter Barbara was born in July 1944. Although Joe and Jane had married, each identified primarily as homosexual and both pursued relationships with others of the same sex.

In the late 1940s, inspired by folk singers such as Burl Ives, Richard Dyer-Bennett, and Susan Reed, Hansen bought an Autoharp and began singing songs of his own. From late 1951 through 1953, he was featured on a weekly radio show called *The Stranger from the Sea*. The show did fairly well, and a record company named Tempo produced a couple of albums that sold well in the Los Angeles area but garnered little attention elsewhere. During this time, the Hansens lived in a house in the Hollywood Hills that Jane's mother had given them. Although living in the heart of the city, they again had the feel of the country because plenty of wilderness surrounded them in the canyons, and a neighbor with a horse let Jane ride when she wanted (Hansen 1992).

Hansen only wrote song lyrics and broadcast copy during the early 1950s, but he never lost interest in the craft and considered writing his preferred vocation. In 1955, he and Jane helped a friend write two episodes of *Lassie*, "The Greyhound" and "The Hungry Deer." The next year, John Ciardi published Hansen's poem about youth in South Dakota in *Saturday Review*. Two more poems with similar themes soon appeared in the *New Yorker*. These proved false starts, however, and no career seemed about to emerge. So Hansen turned to selling encyclopedias door to door until he secured a job clerking in Technicolor's shipping department.

Slater invited Hansen to join *ONE*'s editorial board in 1962. Hansen agreed to the job but insisted the magazine should cease speaking to the choir, as it were, and begin addressing the community at large: "Only through enlisting the understanding of people of good will in the heterosexual segment of society [do we have] a chance to gain equal rights in that society."[6] He felt this would provide a fresh, new approach that the magazine—and the organization—so desperately needed. Slater agreed, and Hansen helped to bring new life to *ONE*, a much-needed new voice at a time when many of the old guard were leaving.

Prelude to Disaster

ONE's tenth annual business meeting convened on Friday evening, January 26, 1962. Chairman Frisbie called the session to order at 8 p.m., introducing Slater as vice-chairman and Lambert as secretary. Fellow board member Joe Weaver was introduced as head of promotions and circulation; Billy Glover was secretary of social services; Joan Corbin, now seventy-three years old, was art director. Lois Mitchell, the organization's bookkeeper, was the final staff member introduced. The members of the various work committees were acknowledged for "their staunch support [for] without them the ship would be scuttled."

Next, Morgan Farley was nominated and voted in as a member of the board. All agreed that Farley, described by Joseph Hansen as "a fragile, white-haired man with a voice beautiful as the rustling of autumn leaves," had certainly earned the position (Hansen 1998, 46). Farley was a successful film actor with his first roles as early as 1929. In 1952, Farley appeared as the minister in the western classic *High Noon*. During the 1960s he would appear in television series such as *The Big Valley, Star Trek,* and *The Wild, Wild West.* Farley was a key player during his stint on the board, and he would help to usher the organization through the difficult days to come.

After Farley's election, Chairman Frisbie delivered a rousing speech to those convened in which he reviewed the organization's decade-long history. He spoke of how he once gave one of the editors some money for new shoes after seeing holes in the man's shoe leather. This man accepted the cash but said that he would "have half soles put on and apply the rest toward the printing bill." Frisbie continued: "With this kind of abstemious, devoted, dedicated will to serve—and go on serving come what may—so is it any wonder that ONE rocked along for ten years? The wonder of it all is that, in a measure, we did prosper. We made tremendous gains in serving a segment of humanity—and by this token, all humanity. We are a child of our times— we are a voice no longer in the wilderness but are heard in the cities—ever militant are we, and this is our strength. The milestones of achievement are passed by and remain as markers."

Lambert next presented a ten-year summary of business operations. He divided his history of the organization into four distinct epochs. The first was the period of "the launching of the Corporation." This ended after about eight brief months when ONE moved into its corporate office downtown. Then came the "period of professionalization" where the organization became departmentalized and workers were trained accordingly. Third was a period of expansion when ONE began "carrying out the stated purposes of the Corporation's charter." Finding it imprudent to rely only on income generated from only one source—magazine sales—so it was that in 1955 "another base of financial support was provided when the Corporation decided to begin the book-publishing operations provided for in its charter." Accordingly, in 1955, ONE held its first educational endeavor, the Midwinter Institute, which thence became an annual tradition. ONE launched *ONE Confidential* in 1956, and business records were "improved, unified, [and] made more accurate." ONE opened a book service for the Friends of ONE as well.

Lambert stated that the corporation had just begun its fourth period, that of "Corporate adulthood and consolidation," claiming as its defining characteristic "the close of the period of volunteer help (except for committee work) and of operations conducted from people's homes." ONE had recently created an entirely new bookkeeping system and "has now moved into the big-time by acquiring that modern hallmark of distinction, a tax attorney." Most important, Lambert concluded, "The Corporation's dependency upon the fluctuations and unexpected reactions of the sales of ONE Magazine have gradually decreased from a ratio of more than 90% of the Corporation's income in 1953 to just over 50% of its income in 1961. In view of the extremely hazardous record of many large publishing firms over the past 10 years and of the demise of some of the nation's very largest magazines this would appear to be a development much to the advantage of the Corporation's prosperity."

Although Lambert never went so far as to call ONE Magazine a liability for the organization (as the Quarterly had certainly become), it seems to have inconvenienced ONE's business manager. Lambert clearly believed that ONE could secure a more solid "financial structure" through reconsidering its apparently long-neglected mission statement.

The Venice Group
and the Rise of Professor W. Dorr Legg

In April 1962, the name W. Dorr Legg, as professor of ONE Institute, appeared in ONE Magazine, contributing a critical review of Irving Bieber's Homosexuality. Legg's name had appeared once before, in the April 1959 issue, where Slater had listed him as a speaker during the prior Midwinter Institute Saturday afternoon session on "Mental Health and the Homosexual." ONE's September 1961 issue introduced him as "William Dorr Legg, A.B., B.M., M.L.D. (University of Michigan), Associate Professor of Social Studies, trained in music and landscape architecture." The profile credited him with having pursued a career in "city planning and landscape architecture in Florida, New York City and on the West Coast." Furthermore, "he has been Assistant Professor of Landscape Architecture at Oregon State College [and] later owner of Dorr School of Design, Hollywood, with a faculty of eight architects, interior decorators, professional artists and landscape architects." Legg had allegedly contributed "to professional journals in the United States and abroad." It seems that while acting as business manager, Bill Lambert was the name he used. But when he was acting as professor of ONE Institute, he preferred to be addressed as W. Dorr Legg. This created some confusion because many, Don Slater in particular, had long thought that Lambert was his real name and Legg the pseudonym.

In the spring of 1962, ONE's landlord evicted the organization from its third-floor office on Hill Street, which was to be razed because of earthquake risks. Morgan Farley located and helped to secure a new office at 2256 West Venice Boulevard near downtown Los Angeles. The new location was much more spacious and serene than the two rooms they had downtown, with tall east-facing windows providing light and a view of tropical ficus trees. Farley may have paid the first month's rent out of his own pocket (Hansen 2002, 109). Fred Frisbie signed the five-year lease on April 12, 1962, allowing ONE, Incorporated, the use of the second floor of the facility for the purposes of setting up "publishers' offices." The rent was $160.00 per month—a rate ONE could easily afford. ONE INC. was soon stenciled onto the left entrance door with its four divisions—EDUCATION/PUBLISHING/SOCIAL SERVICE/RESEARCH—listed on the right. The organization settled into its bright new location on May 1, 1962, and the entire crew thrilled at their luck.

Although ONE's charter specified that its primary purpose was to publish *ONE Magazine*, the organization's emphasis continued to shift toward its ancillary purposes, research and education. According to Hansen, this occurred largely because Dorr Legg began to manipulate the purposes and resources of the organization toward his own ends. Because ONE Institute could not afford to hire faculty, it would make do with what it had. Slater, with his degree in English, would continue to teach literature; Morgan Farley, acting; Legg would teach the social-scientific aspects of homosexuality; and others could be used as needed as supporting faculty.

Professor Legg was especially pleased with the new office: "When a list of ONE's functions was painted on the door of the new place, education came first," Hansen noted (2002, 110). Legg began to imagine this improved but still sparse headquarters as converted into a school, a university for homophile studies that he would organize and direct. "He could hold seminars in it, conducted by himself" (Hansen 2002, 110). Perhaps Hansen's assessment is overly harsh—Legg easily found others to go along with the plan. Even Slater was excited about the new arrangements and looked forward to teaching classes on homosexual history and homophile literature. During a board meeting on July 25, 1962, Slater was officially appointed to ONE Institute's faculty and given the title "assistant professor." The title came, however, without pay, so Slater would have to continue to rely on Sanchez for financial assistance and to support himself through outside work.

On August 16, 1962, Legg, Slater, and Frisbie hosted a meeting at the new office to discuss several proposals to establish a foundation in honor of Blanche M. Baker, who had died on December 11, 1961. Dr. Harry Benjamin of New York was present, as well as Merritt Thompson and William F. Baker, spouse of the deceased, who had traveled from San Jose. These men (with the exception of Baker) resolved at an earlier meeting, held January 27,

1961, to "found and establish the Blanche M. Baker Foundation to conduct and to sponsor educational efforts, research, publication and counseling services in the interests of homophile men and women."[7] When it came time to nominate directors or trustees for the new organization, Legg, Slater, and Frisbie declined because of other commitments. Baker, pleased that a foundation might be created in his wife's honor, expressed his willingness to participate. Benjamin and Thompson agreed to accept a director's position, provided that the workload was minimal and other people, such as an executive secretary, would do most of the work involved. The State of California required at least three residents of the state to act as founding officers, but those who had offered to serve as incorporators lived so far apart from one another that someone suggested five incorporators, at least one of whom should be a woman.

Those assembled further decided that this organization should "maintain a publication for general circulation containing a Questions and Answers Department somewhat along the lines of Dr. Baker's own magazine column, 'Toward Understanding,' preferably to be conducted by a woman doctor or psychologist." The Baker Foundation would also feature a "program of public education by means of lectures and other activities somewhat along such lines as those developed by [Magnus] Hirschfeld at his famed Institute in Berlin."[8] It was also suggested that the foundation maintain a clinic that could provide psychological as well as medical treatments. Although they considered a training program for specialists who could run such a clinic, this "was felt to be not inappropriate, but too utopian for immediate consideration."

The group decided that the Blanche M. Baker Foundation would be as autonomous as possible (though it could collaborate with other organizations) and should consult with a professional publicist. It was proposed that the foundation be temporarily housed in the Baker's San Jose home, but the majority believed San Francisco would be a preferable location, since Dr. Baker had worked there. All agreed on the organization's title and that it should secure nonprofit status. They compiled a list of twelve people who would be contacted to help organize the Blanche M. Baker Foundation, including authors Aldous Huxley and Gerald Heard, Beverly Hills businessman Otto Oppenheimer, ONE's attorney Eric Julber, and psychologist Evelyn Hooker. The group agreed to expand the list of potential people and "active steps toward incorporating . . . should proceed forthwith."

Although this was a successful meeting and those involved had noble intentions, it seems no further action was taken, and the idea for a nonprofit organization devoted to homophiles and dedicated to Baker soon foundered.

ONE did, however, later change the name of its library to the Blanche M. Baker Memorial Library. And later, with the help of benefactor Reed Erickson, Slater and Legg formed an organization very similar to that envisioned herein, known as the Institute for the Study of Human Resources [ISHR], which still exists today.

School Days

The fall semester of ONE Institute for Homophile Studies commenced on Monday, September 17, 1962. Thomas M. Merritt headed the institute as dean emeritus, William Dorr Legg served as director, and Robert Gregory served as secretary. Morgan Farley, instructor in drama and literature, taught HS-134, a drama workshop conducting readings and dramatic representations of homophile poetry and plays, on Thursday evenings from 8 p.m. to 10 p.m., the hours of all evening courses. Don Slater, A.B., was billed as assistant professor in literature, teaching Writing for Publication (HS-136 and HS-137), which dealt with the "special problems of writing for the American and European homophile press." On Tuesday evenings, Slater also taught HS-140 and 141 (141S in the summer of 1963), a library workshop focused on "classification and use of scientific works and fiction in the homophile field" and discussing processes of cataloging bibliographic research. Legg taught HS-212 and 213. HS-212, a two-semester course on homosexual history, met on Monday evenings and dealt with "speculative, scientific, and philosophic trends" and the "emergence of a world-wide social movement." The second semester's course, HS-213, analyzed programs and ideologies of homophile organizations in the United States and abroad. The back cover of *ONE*'s September issue listed complete description of courses. Each course cost $15.00, and visitors could sit in on any particular session for $1.00.

What did this shift in emphasis bode for *ONE Magazine*'s future? "Education is one of the purposes for which ONE (a non-profit California corporation) was organized in 1952," *ONE* reminded its readers. "Its charter calls for 'dealing primarily with homosexuality' through research, 'educational programs,' publications and other such means as are enumerated in its charter." ONE, then, would not divert energy and resources away from the magazine unnecessarily. Rather, it would follow through on an earlier promise, making salient a hitherto latent purpose. One might easily come away with the impression that ONE intended to move toward a higher purpose. Another, though, might find ONE spreading itself too thin:

For the fact that the magazine had been the sole excuse for ONE's existence, had brought friends and supporters from all across America, had alerted the establishment that homosexuals were part of the warp and weft of society and had rights the same as everyone else . . . Bill Lambert suddenly cared nothing. He would build his hallowed Institute of Homophile Studies above that dusty saloon on Venice Boulevard, and teach the truth to a happy few (and few they always would be), expenses be damned. (Hansen 2002, 110)

ONE's December 1962 issue had a casual and homelike feel to it—a rare mood for the magazine. The cover featured a festive sketch by Corbin depicting two pixies festooning baubles and beads in an evergreen bough. An inside cover blurb introduced the organization by summarizing its mission and purpose as articulated in the articles of incorporation as it had for years: "A non-profit corporation formed to publish a magazine dealing primarily with homosexuality from the scientific, historical and critical point of view . . . to sponsor educational programs, lectures and concerts for the aid and benefit of social variants, and to promote among the general public an interest, knowledge and understanding of the problems of variation . . . to sponsor research and promote the integration into society of such persons whose behavior and inclinations vary from current moral and social standards."

The masthead listed Don Slater as editor and Robert Gregory as managing editor. Associate editors were William Lambert and "Marcel Martin." "Alison Hunter" was women's editor, and art director "Eve Elloree" was credited with the intriguing cover of a stylized Christmas tree (an image recycled from a prior issue). Staff artists Fred Frisbie and Antonio Sanchez complemented Corbin's art throughout the issue, as they had done for years. According to tradition, the December issue featured a short story, a fifteen-page tale by "James Colton" called "Kindness." This at last was the revised version of the short story that had inspired Wayne Placek to introduce Hansen to Don Slater in the first place (Hansen 1998, 56).

The December editorial, written by Legg, presented pretty much the same line it had for the past ten years. Forceful as Legg's statement may sound, after ten years of the same tune it may have begun to sound somber and humdrum to *ONE's* subscribers: "That mission is to help homosexual men and women to live a better life. They must be encouraged to think clearly for themselves and about the mainly hostile society in which they find themselves. If this means the administering of large doses of courage, even of belligerence, then this must be done, for at all costs they must be roused and awakened and to see themselves as citizens and as people. Secondarily, perhaps, the magazine must also concern itself with making the outsider understand the homosexual in his almost infinite variations and aspects."

A surprising obituary tucked toward the back of the issue, on page twenty-three, quelled the cheerful holiday mood: "To the Memory of Robert Hull . . . Dead by His Own Hand." Mattachine founder Henry Hay, who had presented Hull with his original "Mattachine idea prospectus" in the fall of 1950, contributed a rueful eulogy: "Bob, it was your stubborn search for logical function a decade ago, coupled with the passion and intensity of your belief in the first Mattachine idea, that helped create within the living and working relationship of the pioneer Seven a bond even closer and more precious than brotherhood. Somewhere, in the years that followed, we—who now scribble these pedestrian sentiments—failed you. Forgive us!"

6

Division
(1963–65)

We began to see, though it took a long time for most of us to realize it, that even if Lesbians and Gays were "in the same boat," we weren't always paddling in the same direction.
— Jim Kepner, "Goals, Progress and Shortcomings of America's Gay Movement"

Social Dramas

In prior chapters, we have seen that ONE, Incorporated, was a house divided almost from inception, two primary camps emerging as the corporation sought to define itself. At first blush, the shared sense of purpose and the excitement for the success of *ONE Magazine* blurred the underlying ideological differences. But in time core differences in ideology, identity, purpose, and audience made for a deep rift between the two factions who came to call themselves "homosexuals" on the one hand and "homophiles" on the other.

The homosexuals were determined to secure sexual liberty and equal rights for all individuals. This mind-set is best illustrated through the ideas and writings of Dale Jennings and Don Slater, both tireless in their dedication to *ONE Magazine* during their tenures on *ONE*'s editorial board. The other contingency, embodied by Dorr Legg and, to a lesser extent, Jim Kepner, was the homophiles, which Jennings called culturalists. These philosophical differences yielded different goals and purposes within ONE that increasingly emerged as rival factions after Kepner's departure. The homophiles increasingly desired to make ONE an educational institution—ONE Institute of Homophile Studies—that would serve the needs of the local community, those who would come to the facility and participate in its seminars and discussions. To the contrary, those who increasingly were content to call themselves homosexuals (and would ultimately found the Homosexual Information Center, or HIC) wanted to contest sodomy laws, fight for equal rights for homosexual individuals to serve in institutions such as the military, and have their relationships and families recognized as legitimate by the government and, ultimately, by the population at large. They felt that the right to sexual privacy should rank nearly as high as the right to sexual freedom, and they wanted to stimulate debate on these issues on both local and national levels through their magazine, which ideally should appeal to all people, homosexual and otherwise.

Although both homosexuals and homophiles managed to coexist within ONE for fifteen years, my research suggests that, more than any emotional duress or personality conflicts, it was these fundamental differences that caused the underlying convective currents that would increasingly separate the two factions and drive them to the point of division. As will be seen, I also found that the paucity of ONE's resources—a situation to which the corporation had long been accustomed—may have helped to hold the organization together, for it was soon after a legitimate benefactor came on the scene that Legg and Slater became emboldened enough to take action, one against the other.

Although some have rated the split of ONE as one of the great tragedies of the pre-gay movement, others have shrugged it aside as irrelevant and inconsequential. Harry Hay remarked that the whole matter revolved around "two dinosaurs spitting at each other and not realizing that dinosaurs had become obsolete" (Cain 2002, 8). Washington, D.C., activist Frank Kameny told Paul D. Cain that insofar as he was concerned, had both Legg and Slater "suddenly vanish[ed] from the scene now, or any time in the last decade or decade and a half, there wouldn't be so much as a ripple" (2002, 9). Judging by the minor commemorations that marked the deaths of these two men as opposed to the more significant occasion such as the extravagant memorial service for Jim Kepner (and more recently those of Harry Hay and Morris Kight), perhaps Kameny spoke accurately.

Tactical Passions

At the annual meeting of ONE, Incorporated, on January 25, 1963, Joseph Weaver, as "Joe Aaron," was elected chair and Dorr Legg vice-chair. Slater's friend and neighbor Rudi Steinert was elected to voting membership. Glover presented the annual report for both Social Services and the Promotions Committee, and Fred Frisbie gave his final report as chairman. Newcomer Monwell Boyfrank was elected first to voting membership and then as secretary-treasurer.

Not much was known about Boyfrank other than he had a long-term friendship with homosexual rights pioneer Henry Gerber that began in 1940. In later correspondence with Jim Kepner and Roger Austen in the 1970s, Boyfrank said that he was born in the Oklahoma Territory around 1900. Boyfrank was part Cherokee and described himself in youth as a "rolling stone" cowboy (Sears 2006, 57–61). Supposedly, Boyfrank pressed Gerber to restart the activities of the Society for Human Rights, which Gerber established in Illinois in 1924 and, after a hellacious ordeal involving his arrest and prolonged trial, never revived (Licata 1978, 53; see also Kepner and Murray 2002, 30–31).

As secretary, Boyfrank was more thorough and detailed than Legg had been, although he had a habit of listing names and dates incorrectly. Whereas Legg's minutes were hen scratches on colored half-sheets of paper, usually handwritten with a flat pencil and often very difficult to read, Boyfrank's minutes were much more legible, detailed, and ultimately typed. Boyfrank had a peculiar habit of playing with his moniker: sometimes he would spell his last name "Boyfrank," and other times "boyFrank." He signed the name with one long swoop and only capitalized the M: Monwellboyfrank. His writing style was elevated and hypercorrect, as when he wrote in the minutes from Sunday, April 7, 1963: "Father Bernard [of the American Eastern Orthodox Church in Las Vegas, Nevada] made a tentative proposal that his church assume the obligation, one evening of each month, of any of those who feel the need, from a moral standpoint, with idea of later, provided One sanctioned such idea, of an occasional discussion group." Boyfrank had immense respect for, and exhibited strong loyalty to, ONE's business manager and vice-chair. Following Legg's own practice, he referred to him as "Professor Legg" when speaking of his affiliations with ONE Institute and "Bill Lambert" when the topic turned to business affairs.

For the most part, 1963 was a relatively blasé year for ONE, Incorporated. Morgan Farley's drama classes were officially canceled during a board meeting on Friday, March 1, 1963.[1] Discussion followed as to whether or not to keep the office open on Thursday evenings when the class had been scheduled, but nothing was resolved. It was noted that the American Eastern Orthodox Church had expressed apprehension about its relationship with ONE. It was made clear that the organizations would remain totally distinct, and the church should not presume it would print *ONE Magazine.* Appreciation and allegiance to ONE's long-standing publisher, the Wolfer Company, was ensured.

On Sunday evening, March 3, 1963, the board announced that Father Bernard Newman would present the April lecture of ONE Institute, "The Way of Truth." A month later, on Sunday, May 5,[2] the Board decided to integrate the American Eastern Orthodox Church into ONE's social services division, asserting that "religious counseling as a part of One's social service work [should] be expanded." The directors also announced that the building ONE occupied on Venice was for sale for $67,500, and the board decided to investigate the feasibility of purchasing the property.

Weaver resigned as chairman of the promotions committee during a board meeting on March 31, and Jim Schneider was installed in his place. After missing several corporate meetings, the board notified Sanchez and Corbin that, if they did not attend the corporate meeting on July 28, they would be dropped from corporate membership. When that day arrived, Sanchez appeared but Corbin did not. After eleven years of dedication and service, Joan Corbin, *ONE*'s talented and much-loved art director, was removed from membership. Unlike Stella Rush, who left with a flourish, Corbin's exit prompted only silence, as if she had simply faded away. Another dedicated, long-term member—one of the core personalities behind the magazine—fell by the wayside.

Elections and Electioneering

In her famous study of the day-to-day operations at a Jewish center in Venice, California, ethnographer Barbara Myerhoff noted that elections were particularly emotional times for center personnel. Months before an actual election, electioneering became intense. "Coalitions were formed and re-formed. Marginal members were assiduously wooed. Block votes of interest groups were sought. Every assembly of more than two was turned into an opportunity for speechifying." She added that most "definitive decisions" were made at nomination meetings rather than at the elections themselves

(1979, 120–21). This pattern also proved true in the case of ONE, but it was intensified in the fall of 1963 as tensions ran exceptionally high.

On November 24, ONE's directors gathered for a nomination meeting to discuss possible candidates for any vacancies for voting members in anticipation of the annual meeting, scheduled two months hence. It soon became apparent that the six current voting members split evenly as to which candidates they would favor. Slater, Sanchez, and Steinert wanted Billy Glover elected. Glover had staunchly supported the magazine for years and assisted the corporation in many ways. The other three voting members, Boyfrank, Weaver, and Lambert—all the officers—opposed Glover but mildly favored Thelma Vargas, Lewis Bonham, Reuben Bush, and Bob Winn.[3] Slater's group did not feel that any of these others had contributed enough to the organization to justify voting status and opposed each of them for this or other reasons. Most if not all directors agreed that two candidates discussed should be elected: Harry Hay and John Burnside. Getting those two on board was assured, provided they accepted. Before adjourning that night, the board agreed to place Burnside, Glover, and Hay on the ballot as primary candidates. They further agreed to vote on each candidate separately, one at a time, according to custom. Bonham, Bush, Vargas, and Winn would be on the ballot as alternates in case any of the three primary candidates declined nomination. Slater hoped to persuade Hay and Burnside to vote for Glover. Unless that happened, Glover's chances appeared dubious because the bylaws required a two-thirds majority vote to elect a new member. If all else failed, the Slater-Sanchez-Steinert coalition believed it could form a voting block, ensuring that none of Legg's preferred alternate candidates could win election, either.

On January 12, 1964, Legg convened a directors' meeting at 5:10 p.m. Weaver, Steinert, Sanchez, and Boyfrank attended. Legg gave a financial report, and Weaver discussed taxation rules. They discussed a prior meeting (of January 5) as well as ONE's upcoming European tour, which Rudi Steinert would direct. Next, Boyfrank abruptly announced his impending resignation because of ailing health. Boyfrank appears to have intended his resignation to take effect immediately, following adjournment. The directors agreed to ask Lewis Bonham, a Glendale resident, if he would accept nomination to the corporation's voting membership. They would also ask Bonham to typeset the forthcoming article, "Crime against Nature." This agreed, the session adjourned at 8:25 p.m.

Given the polarized state of affairs within ONE, it seems appropriate that the January 1964 issue of ONE Magazine was printed in stark black and white.

The magazine launched with Slater, of course, as editor. "Robert Gregory" was managing editor, and Glover, Ingersoll, and "Mac" O'Neal ("K. O. Neal") were associate editors. Staff artists included Frisbie, Sanchez, and Roy Berquist, as "Rolf Berlinsen."

Apart from the logo, date, and price (still fifty cents), the white cover of this issue simply states in stark bold print, "THE HOMOSEXUAL WORLD'S BEST-SELLING MAGAZINE 12th YEAR." In his editorial, Slater boasts that *ONE* was "the oldest U.S. Publication of its kind in existence today; and it is the most widely read in all the world." This is followed by an article by Donald Webster Cory and John P. Leroy entitled "The Echo of a Growing Movement," which reports on the American Psychological Association (APA) conference that had taken place in Philadelphia the prior Labor Day weekend. There, a coalition of East Coast Homophile Organizations (ECHO) lobbied for "enlightened discussion" on the subject of homosexuality. The theme for the conference had been "Homosexuality—Time for Reappraisal." In honor of the conference, which attracted around ten thousand psychologists, the *New York Times* boldly printed the word "Homosexual" for the very first time in an advertisement for the event.

Cory and Leroy comment in their article on a paper by R. E. L. Masters that was read in the author's absence in which Masters criticized homophile organizations for giving "little aid and encouragement to the effeminate homosexual, the transvestite, and the transsexual." Masters complained that these organizations were ashamed of the effeminate males among them, so organizational leaders shunned them and refused to allow them to participate in the movement. "In rejecting them," he maintained, "the organizations display bad faith, for the movement is presumably for the benefit of all homosexuals."

According to the article, Cory himself next addressed the assembly. After a brief historic overview, he criticized the movement for its ineffective leadership, neurotic tendencies, unreasonable if not abstract goals, and its proliferation of mediocre writers and false experts on the subject. On the upside, the dialogue regarding homosexuality at the professional and even popular levels had reached more sophisticated levels, and social attitudes appeared more favorable. As homosexual individuals made gains in social standing, homophile scholarship gained in credibility, and government agencies and the ACLU began contacting homophile organizations for input and cooperation. The movement had certainly made some progress; homophile participation in the Labor Day APA convention certainly indicated that a long-latent social force was mobilizing.

The Beginning of the End:
The 1964 Annual Business Meeting

ONE's annual business meeting held on Saturday, January 25, 1964, was a bizarre event indeed, which Slater later compared to Bedlam.[4] According to the minutes, forty-six guests and members attended, but many of them grew disgusted as disputes and rancor carried the meeting through the night and into the next morning. The directors listed on the roster consisted of Weaver, Boyfrank, Legg, Slater, and Steinert. Visitors included Frisbie, Winn, Schneider, Bonham, Glover, and Glover's lover Melvin Cain. People came from all over southern California to participate in the annual event: North Hollywood, Glendale, Burbank, South Pasadena, Torrance, Van Nuys, San Diego, Santa Ana, Culver City, Pico Rivera, and Palm Springs. William F. Baker, husband of the late Blanche M. Baker, traveled from San Francisco, and Father Bernard Newman came from Las Vegas. As in years past, each of these pilgrims came to ONE's annual meeting eager to witness and participate in the historic event.

Joe Weaver chaired the meeting, and Monwell Boyfrank acted as secretary despite his prior resignation. Three of the six other voting members also attended: Legg, Slater, and Steinert. Sanchez was absent because of a work obligation, but Slater secured permission to vote on his behalf via proxy.[5] John Burnside and Harry Hay were present; each was rapidly nominated and elected onto the board, leaving one vacancy to fill. The now eight voting members decided to choose between Glover, Bonham, and Winn to fill the remaining vacant position.

According to Slater's copy of the minutes, the directors cast six more ballots, but none of the remaining nominees received enough votes to secure a place on the board. They recessed from 11:15 to 11:45 p.m., and then Slater, Steinert, Burnside, and Legg each made a speech. Morgan Farley later told Glover that Slater tried too hard to pressure Hay and Burnside into siding with him on Glover's behalf, so they and some others in the room had responded with doubt and suspicion.

At some point after Hay and Burnside's election, Chairman Weaver sided with Boyfrank and Legg and decided to deny Slater the use of his lover's proxy. Making matters worse for Slater, the balloting procedure that night had been altered from the customary procedure. The directors abandoned their usual practice of voting on one person at a time; the new procedure, according to Weaver's instructions, required each director to write three names on one ballot, one for each vacancy. That is how they had elected Burnside and Hay, with each being named on four or more ballots, and how Glover had *not* been elected (probably having been one vote short). Slater questioned why Weaver cast a ballot in the first place, as tradition held that the chair would only vote to break a tie. Slater protested, insisting that the directors honor ONE's corporate customs. He also suggested that they cease debating their balloting procedures before such a large audience and moved for recess until the next day when they could continue the debate in a more private forum.

The directors defeated this motion, and Weaver pressed the vote. More speeches were made and more votes cast. Eventually, both Hay and Burnside grew furious with the situation. Both resigned on the spot and refused further nominations. After all the fighting, the group was back to square one with three seats remaining vacant.

At 12:45 a.m. on January 26, 1964, the directors took another vote, again generating no conclusive results. Slater continued to protest the voting methods and insisted Glover was the only legitimate candidate. Legg then addressed the meeting and another vote ensued, but still no majority prevailed. At 12:55 a.m., the directors decided to break in order to allow Sanchez time to arrive after work and cast his vote in person. At 1:30 a.m., with Sanchez present, the meeting resumed. The chair again instructed directors to write in three names, as they had done previously. After two more ballots were taken, Weaver pronounced Bonham and Winn elected as voting members. According to the minutes, the directors took three more ballots after this but failed to elect a ninth board member. At 2:03 a.m., the meeting recessed until the following Sunday, February 2, 1964.

According to Legg, the directors cast seventeen ballots that night.[6] As a result, the board apparently increased its membership by electing two new members. But, in the process, it made a mockery of the corporation and alienated some of its most talented and dedicated supporters.

Election Woes

Proceeding home after this disastrous annual meeting, Sanchez, Slater, and Steinert compared notes and found that none of them had voted for Winn or Bonham. If true, neither had truly been elected to the board. Unfortunately, at that late hour and after all the confusion, it seems Slater had not thought to examine the ballots during the meeting—though later, in a court deposition, he recalled that he could not have done so anyway because all ballots were secret. According to their accepted rules, no motion would be in order "that violates the privacy of a balloting procedure other than the show of hands or ayes or nays."

As it was, one of two things probably happened: either one of them had indeed voted for both Winn and Bonham, or Boyfrank misrepresented the vote and in effect helped Legg maneuver a coup. Slater clearly believed the latter scenario; Legg later stated that he thought Steinert probably defected.[7] In either case, with Steinert, Slater, and Sanchez in steadfast denial of having voted for those two men, Slater and his faction insisted that Bonham and Winn had not been properly elected and thus were *not* duly authorized as voting members of ONE. Slater and Sanchez repeatedly made this assertion and challenged the election at corporate meetings throughout the rest of 1964, but the majority ignored them with the chairman's permission.

According to Slater's notes from the trial, Legg consequently threatened that if Slater discussed the issue with anyone "outside the corporation proper he would be dropped from membership." In later correspondence with his attorney Ed Raiden,[8] Slater acknowledged soliciting outside council for advice. Attorney P. Z. Deutsch told Slater, "Founders of such a movement as the homosexual is engaged in, because of the nature of their persons, usually kill each other off or are eliminated by their followers and officers when they get in the way of progress." Although one assumes Deutsch was speaking metaphorically, suggesting a social rather than an actual death, the severity of her metaphor confirmed Slater's dire situation. Legg's pattern appeared all too clear. First, Jennings had resigned when confronted by Legg's stern authority as ONE's business manager and first chairman. Then Kepner and Wolf exited, both complaining of Legg's haughty attitude and imperious behavior. More recently, Rush, Farley, and Corbin also left, all having complained about the situation at ONE, and now Hay and Burnside became alienated. As Slater saw it, more than a few good workers had left the organization because of Legg's misconduct. Now, it seemed, his own job lay on the line, so indomitable Don Slater braced himself for a fight.[9]

On Sunday, February 2, 1964, between 1:30 and 2:20 p.m., the voting members of ONE (except for Winn) gathered to discuss the situation. Much debate ensued, but nothing was resolved. During the next board meeting on February 16, with seven voting members present, Slater proclaimed that an error had been made in the annual elections, but he was again outvoted and the board approved the minutes as presented.

Harry Hay attended this meeting to act as witness and parliamentarian. According to Legg, Hay also was there to witness that the proceedings were conducted in accordance with *Robert's Rules of Order*.[10] Although this may seem inconsequential, this was actually a deft move on Legg's part. The corporation had established many traditions apart from *Robert's Rules*, such as the policy that the chair never vote unless to break a tie and the method of balloting, which Slater complained Legg had altered to his advantage. Although Legg appeared to enforce the standard, many of the "rules" and "traditions" Hay moderated that day were actually new to the corporation, while the board cast long-standing traditions aside as they inconvenienced the new majority. After all of Slater's planning, Legg still seemed a step ahead. Slater was stymied, and the corporation was at an impasse.

On August 12, 1964, Slater mailed a letter of complaint to Boyfrank: "It is becoming increasingly difficult to reach the Board of Directors. On more than one matter in which I asked the board's consideration I have had no reply. I would like to suggest a corporation meeting to facilitate communication and action." Boyfrank answered with a very peculiar two-page letter: "Dear Don, I think I see what you're driving at in your valued note of the 12th, and you have good company in your dissatisfaction. We are paralyzed." He continued with a comment evocative of Slater's impish stature: "Our most loved and respected corporation members have an elfin disdain of mere money. That is part of their charm, and without it I imagine *One* would never have got started. Time was when that what-the-hell, let's-go-for-broke attitude was appropriate and availful [*sic*]. You didn't know what the future held, you did not have so much as a shirt to lose, you could improvise then and modify later according to developments and you were young and full of mustard. You felt a powerful urge to start something and you started something." But, Boyfrank admonished, through all of these brash actions, there had been no real attempt to make money. "Our magazines don't make money for us: they're a drain on us. And you're an older man by twelve critical years in a world where youth is at a premium and age is an embarrassment and a calamity."

Boyfrank next declared that Slater only wanted people working for ONE who were likewise "courageous, extroverted and a little scrappy": "You want all men to be Don Slaters. That would be a delectable world, but it is not the world we happen to live in. You're not going to change, and any hint that you adopt less of a damn-your-eyes policy in the magazine's format will only make you more determined to express the pure, absolute or 200–proof Don Slater with no concessions to conventions and cowards."

As for calling a meeting, Boyfrank flatly rejected the request:

> Let me ask, Whom do you know among the members of the corporation
> who will change any more readily than you will? What argument can you
> advance that hasn't been used already? For example, could you tell Mr. Good
> anything that would make him confident that your magazine will become a
> money-maker for him and for us? Could you bring yourself to make changes
> that would enable more firms to advertise in *One*?
>
> To ask these questions is to answer them. Each man's behavior is a func-
> tion of his principle, his character, his self-respect. That being true, there is
> no use in calling meetings. We are at a deadlock. It may be deplorable, but
> any man who might consent to the sacrifice of his principle would expect a
> disaster to result—and he might be right.

A letter from Steinert[11] to Weaver dated nearly a month later, on September
9, 1964, complained that ONE had not held a corporate meeting since June
or July. Steinert requested Weaver to call a meeting before he left for Europe
later that year. A corporate meeting was finally called for September 25, during which Steinert warned the board that he might not return in time for
the annual meeting, scheduled for Friday, January 29, 1965. He requested an
absentee vote should he not make it back on time, and the directors granted
his request.

On October 4, 1964, the Friends of ONE convened at the Waldorf Astoria
Hotel in New York to see Steinert and fourteen others off on a three-week
European tour. According to an article on "Social Services" by "B. W." that
appeared in the November 1964 issue of *Confi*,[12] around fifty people attended.
Steinert, a European expatriate, spoke first after an hour of food and social-
izing. He gave a rousing speech on how homosexuals in America should
"come courageously into closer fellowship with and support of each other"
and "shed all pussyfooting and mask-wearing, to stand up and be counted as
self-respecting homosexual citizens."[13] Chuck Thompson, as tour manager,
spoke briefly, to be followed by Dorr Legg, who encouraged the audience
to "enlist support for ONE" by sending news clippings to the Venice Street
office and by reporting on local court cases and legal issues. After a ques-
tion-and-answer session, Legg introduced Reed Erickson, a female-to-male
transsexual who had been a patient of Harry Benjamin's and was president
of the Erickson Educational Foundation (EEF), a philanthropic organization
based in Baton Rouge, Louisiana. Legg then made a grand announcement:
a new corporation had been formed in Los Angeles called the Institute for
the Study of Human Resources, or ISHR. Erickson would preside over this
organization; Don Slater would serve as vice president, and Legg as secretary-

treasurer. Unlike ONE, ISHR was a tax-exempt corporation "legally prepared to receive contributions from those wishing to take substantial tax deductions for their gifts." Quite simply, individuals and corporations could receive tax advantages by donating to ISHR, which in turn would make contributions to ONE.

Reed Erickson is more properly introduced in chapter 9, in which the creation of ISHR is presented in more detail. Erickson had first contacted ONE in July 1964 and arranged for Legg to come and visit him in Baton Rouge, Louisiana. Legg cautiously complied and was surprised to find that Erickson, though clearly eccentric, was a legitimate millionaire and established homophile philanthropist. ISHR was established in August 1964 at Erickson's prompting and expense. By the time of the New York send-off, Erickson, through the EEF, had channeled $3,000 to ISHR. Beginning in January 1965, ISHR would receive $1,000 a month, and over the next twenty years, Erickson would continue to donate a great majority of ISHR's revenues, providing $200,000 in grants and more to Legg and other individual researchers (Devor and Matte 2004).

Legg stayed in New York from Saturday, October 3, through Wednesday, October 7, 1964. While there, he met with Donald Webster Cory and New York Mattachine president Julian Hodges. Legg noted that New York's Mattachine office resembled ONE's first two-room office in downtown Los Angeles. He dined with Dr. Harry Benjamin, a close friend of the late Dr. Blanche M. Baker. Barbara Gittings and Kay Tobin, editors of *The Ladder*, came up from Philadelphia to visit with the Los Angeles contingency. A visit with Clark Polak, editor of a new publication called *Drum* published by Philadelphia's Janus Society, did not go well; Polak accused ONE of "rank 'parochialism and provinciality.'"[14] Still, Legg must have been on cloud nine with all of the attention lavished upon him. And, with money rolling in, a new day seemed to be dawning for ONE, Incorporated.

While traveling through Europe and India later that fall, Steinert wrote to ONE's corporate office requesting an update on corporate business, but ONE's secretary did not respond until December 26, 1964. According to Slater's notes, Boyfrank's letter advised Steinert that he "would not be allowed an absentee ballot after all, and the corporation was considering by-law changes of a quite serious nature." Clearly, Legg, Boyfrank, and Weaver were staging a second attempt to take over the organization. Steinert did not receive Boyfrank's response until Thursday, January 14, 1965; by then it was too late for him to make it back in time for the annual meeting, scheduled for January 29, 1965.

ONE's directors held a corporate meeting on Friday evening, January 15, attended by Slater, Sanchez, Bonham, Legg, Boyfrank, and Weaver. Erickson was also present, visiting from Louisiana. A tape recording was played of Slater's recent lecture at California State College. Next, the directors decided to rename ONE's library as the Blanche M. Baker Memorial Library. They also decided, under protest from Slater and Sanchez, to convene the annual meeting at 8:00 p.m., as usual, but that they would adjourn promptly at 10:00 p.m. and resume at 2:00 p.m. the next day.

During a board meeting the following week, on January 22, Bonham, Legg, Boyfrank, and Weaver met and selected as the slate for nominees for the election at the upcoming annual meeting "Greg C., Keith D., Billie G., Bob N., Johnnie N., Chet S., Jim S. and Thelma V." All participants prepared for another showdown.

The 1965 Annual Business Meeting

ONE, Incorporated's, thirteenth annual business meeting, on January 29, 1965, adjourned early as planned—before completion of the scheduled business. This enraged Slater and Sanchez. In a note to the other board members, Slater reminded the directors that many Friends of ONE had traveled a great distance to attend and had "made it a point to be in attendance throughout the sessions." In addition to the voting members, twenty-five nonvoting Friends of ONE were present, including Hay, Burnside, Morris Kight, Betty Purdue, and Jim Schneider's partner Henry Lieffers. The minutes list Robert E. Newton and Greg N. Coron as a couple. Fifteen guests had also been present, but voting members Slater, Steinert, and Winn did not show. Some reports were given: Ingersoll reported on the status of the magazine, and Bonham reported on finances and circulation. After Roy Berquist addressed the status of ONE's art department, the meeting adjourned promptly at 10:00 p.m.

When the meeting reconvened at 2:00 p.m. the next afternoon, January 30, no business was conducted because of the lack of quorum. Voting members present included Bonham, Boyfrank, Legg, and Sanchez. Schneider presented two reports, one on the social services division's rehabilitation activities and the other as chair of the Friday night work committee. The nine nonvoting members present included Hay and Burnside, Coron and Newton, and Kepner. The minutes note John Nojima,[15] Legg's partner, as a visitor. Without a quorum to conduct further business, "the meeting adjourned to the earliest hour at which a quorum can be secured." The secretary would notify voting members as to where and when the next corporate meeting would convene. This second session of the annual meeting adjourned at 5:00 p.m. on January 30, 1965.

The third session of the annual business meeting convened Friday evening, February 5, with Weaver, Bonham, Boyfrank, Legg, Slater, and Winn present and Sanchez and Steinert absent. According to Boyfrank's minutes, Dorr Legg, acting as chair, began the meeting by reading excerpts from *Robert's Rules of Order*. Slater objected to this, and rising to a point of order, read aloud a letter he had addressed to certain members of the board, dated February 3, 1965. When Slater's objections were overruled, he withdrew from the meeting in protest. Boyfrank then proposed a motion to dismiss Slater from corporate membership, which Weaver seconded, but the motion was tabled. The board decided, however, that "any member who is outside the state for sixty days, so that he cannot attend meetings, shall have his vote and status as a voting member suspended during such absence." This motion carried unanimously, clearing the way for the bylaw changes proposed in Boyfrank's December 26 letter. The board raised the number of voting members to fifteen and elected to have five officers rather than ONE's traditional three. According to schedule, the board would elect the new voting members and officers at the next annual meeting, in January 1966, and again each third meeting thereafter.

The directors proceeded to elect new board members per the newly modified bylaws. They first elected Kieth [*sic*] Dyer, Chet Sampson, and Jim Schneider. Gregory Coron and Robert Newton were elected next, followed by Lew Bonham.[16] Last, the directors discussed the dismissal of Don Slater, but again tabled a decision, as they would again during a subsequent meeting on Sunday, February 14. On Friday, February 12, Newton, as chairman of the advertising committee, recruited Dick Spellman to assist as a member of that committee.

On Sunday, March 21, ONE convened its third corporate meeting at the Venice Street office. Bonham, Boyfrank, Coron, Weaver, Dyer, Legg, Newton, Sanchez, Sampson, Schneider, and Winn attended with Slater and Steinert absent. After the minutes of the prior meeting were read and approved, Sanchez addressed the assembly and proposed a motion, "the purpose of which was not clear." When the motion failed to receive a second, Sanchez left in frustration. Newton next discussed his recent lecture at Claremont College, and Legg reported on his recent meeting with the ACLU. Chet Sampson, who owned a travel agency, reported on a forthcoming trip to Europe and suggested that Slater be invited to go with him with Kepner as backup. This motion carried unanimously. Schneider reported on the progress of the Friday night work committee. Then Weaver moved that the board appoint Dyer to be the associate editor of ONE Magazine "to represent the corporation on the editorial board." The motion carried, and Dyer agreed to serve as a liaison between the editors and the directors—an act that would have dire consequences.

On March 23, a note was sent to Kepner advising him that Slater could not go to Europe with Sampson. Despite the airfare to and from New York being provided, Slater, it was said, could not afford the other expenses. When presented with the opportunity, Kepner eagerly accepted. The note to Kepner, probably sent by Legg, asked that Kepner address the European organizations on ONE's behalf and then write an article on the journey upon his return. The opportunity thrilled Kepner who, although he had been given short notice, welcomed the chance to tour Europe while perhaps rekindling his relationship with ONE in the process. He probably did not realize that tensions within the organization were approaching the boiling point.

On March 24, Dyer resigned as associate editor of ONE Magazine, stating that he felt unqualified for the job. In an attached report of the proceedings of the editorial staff meeting he attended on Monday, March 22, Dyer stated that the editors had at first welcomed him, but when he told them that the board had appointed him associate editor, a lively discussion ensued. The editors took offense that the board had appointed Dyer without their approval, and they decided "immediate action would be taken to make necessary adjustments in the Magazine Staff personnel." In the meantime things would stay as they were with Slater as editor-in-chief. Dyer was asked to remind the board that, if the directors felt out of touch with the editors, then article 3, section D of the bylaws empowered them to invite whomever they wished to attend their meetings. As it was, the corporation's move seemed to puzzle the editorial staff because they had always experienced "a satisfactory working relationship between the Magazine and the Corporation and Board of Directors."

Dyer concluded his report to the directors by agreeing with ONE's editors, stating that "the Magazine has and is functioning in a most satisfactory and responsible way, internally." Legg personally responded to Dyer on March 25, reminding Dyer that Slater had no power to appoint his own editors. Only the board could make appointments and fill positions within the corporation. This made Slater's position as editor-in-chief advisory, at best.

The next corporate meeting convened on April 11, 1965. Bonham, Boyfrank, Coron, Weaver, Dyer, Legg, Newton, Schneider, and Winn attended; Sanchez, Slater, and Steinert did not. It was announced that Kepner would be going to Europe in Slater's place. Dyer reported having met with ONE's editorial board, which had resisted his appointment. Accordingly, he formally resigned his position as associate editor. Bob Waltrip spoke about the magazine's "editorial problems." Bonham moved that the corporation "express dissatisfaction with the failure of the editorial board of *ONE* to adhere to corporate policy." Weaver seconded this motion, and it carried. Coron and Dyer proposed that a representative of the editorial board attend all corporate meetings, but this motion was tabled. Dyer then moved that "the editorial board, in the absence of Don Slater, rotate the position of editor-in-chief monthly among all of its members." Winn seconded this motion, which carried unanimously. The board decided that Legg would advise the editorial board of these decisions during their next board meeting, to be held in ONE's offices the following night. This meeting adjourned at 8:40 p.m.

"Night of the Long Knives"

Tensions had been running exceedingly high within the corporation, and Slater's position had become precarious, his influence greatly diminished. Legg, Boyfrank, and Weaver in particular were furious at the editors' refusal to admit Dyer to their ranks. In turn, the editors were annoyed that Legg would resign from the editorial board and then attempt to dictate policy as chairman. Legg attended the editors' meeting the following night and told them of the board's disappointment. Ingersoll described the occasion in detail:

> Slater, Hansen, Mac McNeal and I were holding a regular editorial session, probably arguing, with Mac's shrill, angry voice loudest of all. And suddenly Lambert stormed into the room, drew himself up in his imperial majesty, and began to lay down the law, letting us know that we were underlings, and were not empowered to discuss policy, let alone make it, and to tell us what we could and could not do, and what we would and would not be *allowed* to do.
>
> Mac, who was wearing a stunning camel's hair coat that night, jumped up, shrieked at Lambert that he wasn't going to take any more of "that shit" and slammed out of the room. Lambert went on, unfazed, and soon Hansen got to his feet, announced quietly that he too had heard more than enough, and walked out. I was just as indignant, but I simply sat there and said nothing. Don had sat through the whole thing without saying a word, and I didn't want to do or say anything until I had a chance to talk to him. (Ingersoll 1997, 12–13)[17]

Hansen likewise recalls not staying to hear the end of Legg's rant. "I left while he was still raving on, convinced he was out of his mind." Hansen had heard about the "shady revisions of the corporation bylaws," largely because of Slater's absences and the "almost endless 1965 annual membership meeting." As he saw it, within a few short months of becoming chair, Legg "had dumped most of the legally elected board of directors and replaced them with lackeys 'elected' by no one but himself" (1998, 53–54).

Hansen's assessment seems correct in many ways. As it stood, Legg clearly had Boyfrank and Weaver on his side—or perhaps even in his pocket. Although Legg did not pay them for their services—they were not his hirelings—they did stand to gain in their relationship with Legg. As sociologist F. G. Bailey has observed, relationships between a leader and a follower typically involve both a moral element and a transactional one (2001, 44). The moral element of their bond is clear: to further the needs of the organization with a particular emphasis on expanding the social services and education divisions. The transactional element is less obvious: although no money was exchanged, a considerable amount of power was involved. Boyfrank and Weaver were, after all, the corporation's senior officers. For Legg, fond of structure and nearly obsessed with hierarchy, this made them the undisputed corporate leaders. As Legg had reminded Dyer, only the board could make appointments, fill positions, or determine corporate policy. At this time, the three officers had gained total control over the board, a situation unlikely to change. Legg and Slater would remain at odds. But so long as Legg led a unified coalition of the corporation's officers, the cards were clearly stacked in his favor.

There could hardly be anyone more unlike Dorr Legg than Don Slater. Even physically they were distinct: Legg tall and lanky; Slater short and puckish. Whereas Legg loved formality and thrived on authority, the casual and easygoing Slater appealed to a different sort of person than those drawn more toward Legg. To borrow from Victor Turner, one might say that Legg represented "structure" and Slater "anti-structure" (though enshrouding Slater in the accompanying cloud of liminality and communitas would take the comparison a bit too far) (1969, 175–76). Although some were attracted to Legg's regimented business philosophies, others gravitated to Slater's good humor and more personable ways. Slater preferred to lead through example; he had not sought power but, in fact, had avoided it. While he was proud to have become the senior editor of *ONE*, it was never a position he coveted or actively sought—Slater was content to progress slowly up corporate ranks. He was always respectful to others, especially his elders, and he enjoyed sharing power and authority with the other editors. He loved to engage in intellectual discussions and preferred to make decisions based on debate, consensus, and common sense.

Both Slater and Legg, fiercely intelligent people equally dedicated to the cause, clearly held contrary visions of the corporation's primary missions and purposes. They were each experienced in social activism and had won a significant gain for the rights of homosexuals in Los Angeles and in the United States through the Supreme Court decision. Each had learned the inner mechanisms of the legal system, and neither feared to use the courts to achieve his goal. Together, they formed a formidable alliance. Apart, they could be redoubtable adversaries.

Once Mac McNeal left after that meeting, he never returned. This substantially set back *ONE Magazine*, which he had supported financially. McNeal had taken over the *Tangents* news column, *ONE*'s most-read column since its inauguration by Kepner. Now, that job, and "the rumpled brown manila envelope stuffed with clippings from readers all over the country, all over the world" became Joe Hansen's responsibility. Hansen would not let Legg bully him out of working for *ONE* and standing fast beside his friend and colleague, Slater. Ingersoll, however, wrote his letter of resignation to ONE's board the next day, the morning of April 13, 1965. "At the conclusion of the meeting last night—and I am sure that by now you will have learned of all that transpired at that meeting—I announced that I was not walking out on the meeting nor on the magazine. I hope that this resignation will not be considered a denial of those words." Ingersoll concluded that if he felt his presence would help the situation he would stay, but he could see no reason to stay.

When Slater heard of Ingersoll's resignation, he called Ingersoll to tell him that he had been "working on a plan he thought would straighten things out and make it possible for us to work together again." Slater asked Ingersoll to sit tight and suspend his resignation for the time being. He asked Joe and Jane Hansen to kindly sit tight as well.

It was Glover who, in retrospect, compared Legg's actions in "firing" the entire editorial board to the "Night of the Long Knives"; Glover's surviving HIC compatriots nod and smile at the comparison. Although Slater had not been murdered, as Ernst Röhm had been on the night of June 28, 1934, when Hitler began ferreting homosexuals out of his army (Dynes 1985, 103), the comparison signifies the severity of Legg's action and the dire repercussions for the organization. The Dyer affair had angered both the officers and the editors. Even though Dyer himself had the best intentions at heart, his action set off the social drama, causing anger and grievance to both sides. Now, clearly distinct factions gathered around two leaders, Legg and Slater. During the meeting of April 12, 1965, when Legg barged into the meeting of the editorial board, he had effectively thrown down the gauntlet: the desires of ONE's officers outweighed the needs of the magazine's editors. The editorial board had no right to discuss or try to influence corporate policy; if the editors did not agree, then they would all be fired.

From Slater's perspective, the prediction of the psychologist Deutsch was coming true. ONE Institute had clearly become a higher priority to the corporation than *ONE Magazine*. Slater also knew that with the financial support of Erickson and the EEF, ONE Institute could probably survive without the magazine. And if ONE no longer needed *ONE Magazine*, then it would also no longer need its editors, him in particular. Slater saw the writing on the wall. He knew how Legg liked to operate—Slater clearly saw his expulsion from ONE pending. Unless, of course, Slater could preempt it, which is exactly what he set out to do. A confrontation between them was imminent. Together with Sanchez and Glover, he laid out a plan to reverse the situation. Another coup loomed—only this time, Legg would be in the hot seat.

Mutiny[18]

On Wednesday, April 14, 1965, Slater and Glover, claiming to represent ONE, Incorporated, rented warehouse space from Atlas Screen and Manufacturing Company, 3473 Cahuenga Boulevard in Hollywood, across from Universal Studios. It was a simple facility and a simple lease: after a $75 deposit, Slater could occupy the space for $75 a month for the first six months and then pay $100 per month thereafter. The new address for Slater's ONE would be 3473½ Cahuenga Boulevard. In sealing the deal, Atlas agreed to install a swinging door and replace the existing sliding door entrance.

Slater had already cataloged and inventoried most of the library, which he and Kepner had worked hard to compile. Because the accounts were in order, Slater and his crew could easily pack up the materials on Saturday night and move them to Cahuenga before Legg arrived at the office to prepare for the board meeting scheduled for Sunday afternoon. Slater had earlier conferred with his attorney, who assured him that although his plan was certainly unconventional, the law was on his side (Hansen 1998, 55). Then Slater, Glover, Cain, Sanchez, and a friend of Slater's who owned a moving van, Jano Cybulski, met at ONE early on Sunday morning, April 18, and they cleared out the Venice Boulevard office, taking everything to the new office on Cahuenga (Hansen 1998, 55–59).

Hansen has provided a rich description of the ensuing confrontation. After the move, an exhausted Slater left Glover asleep on the sofa in the new office to take Sanchez home. Once there, "[Antonio] dropped exhausted into bed, while Don fed the cats, took a shower, and changed his clothes. [Slater then] drove the old Studebaker back to Venice Boulevard, climbed the stairs again, found an overlooked chair, placed it in the middle of the sunny morning vacancy, and sat down on it to await the arrival of Bill Lambert, knowing he would come early to make ready for the big meeting at which he would at last strip Don Slater of any part in ONE, Inc." (Hansen 1998, 57).

Legg must have been flabbergasted when he crested the stairs to find the office bare. He no doubt became furious when he realized the office was completely vacant except for a single office chair and a seated Don Slater, exhausted but smiling. Slater relished this moment, later telling Hansen he had "never lived a better moment in my life" (Hansen 1998, 57). After the delicious silence, Legg began ranting, "But you can't. . . . This is outrageous! This is *robbery*. Grand larceny! I'm calling the police!"

But he didn't call the police. Slater suggested that they calm down and work out a compromise, but Legg refused to engage in any negotiations, stating: "I don't compromise with thieves." Still, Slater proposed that if Legg would "restore the legally elected board, and agree to resume ONE's activities on the old footing," then they could meet with Slater's attorney the next day to sign papers that had been prepared, and he would return the office, library, and mailing list. Legg stood fast and refused Slater's terms. He opted to take the matter to court—and to ONE's membership. While Slater spoke of compromise, to Legg it sounded more like an all-or-none ultimatum—which is exactly how he presented it to his fellow directors later that day (Hansen 1998, 58).

Slater felt he had won, but at what price? He successfully turned the table on Legg, staging a closed-door coup of his own, which put an entirely new twist on the ritual. To again borrow from Turner (1969, 170–78), rather than a ritual of status elevation whereby the power and influence of one was furthered by the elimination of the other, Slater had converted it into a ritual of status *reversal* whereby the underdog—Slater—reversed the situation in order to leverage a compromise. Though daring, the outcome of Slater's move was far from certain. Legg was every bit as stubborn as he.

Later that afternoon, during the business meeting and after Slater went home to catch up on sleep, Legg began a smear campaign against Slater that would continue for the next twenty years. With Boyfrank's support and encouragement, an entirely new board, and funding from their newfound philanthropist Reed Erickson, Legg hired Beverly Hills lawyer Hillel Chodos. Together they would relentlessly pursue Slater and his Tangent Group, dragging them in and out of court for the next five years, as I detail in the chapters to come.

In the five years following Kepner's resignation, ONE had become increasing polarized between those who supported ONE Institute and those who favored *ONE Magazine*. In the end, Kepner's prediction that the movement would in time fracture into different organizations, each with its own clearcut mission and purpose, had come to pass. Rather than a metaphor of vessels and ships, Kepner believed a corporation was more like an organism capable of growth and even division. As F. G. Bailey correctly notes, "periods of faction-fighting, like adolescence, precede maturity." If a faction can survive long enough to develop a core of constituents, then "a new kind of group, which is no longer a faction, has come into existence" (2001, 53). As we will see in the next chapter, two new groups did come into existence, although the fighting would intensify and continue. To extend Bailey's metaphor, both of the new organizations would undergo a prolonged adolescence.

Two Years of War
(1965–67)

Jarndyce and Jarndyce drones on.
—Charles Dickens, *Bleak House*

THE IDEAL OUTCOME would have been for the 1965 division of ONE, Incorporated, to mark both the end of one era for the Los Angeles movement and the dawning of a new, more productive one. Theoretically, the infighting over, each group had the chance to start afresh and focus on what it did best, with the Tangent Group continuing to publish the successful *ONE Magazine* while the Venice Group developed its Institute for Homophile Studies. To Legg and Slater, sadly, such accommodation became impossible. The situation soon developed into a zero-sum game where only one group could continue as the bona fide ONE, Incorporated. Hostilities that had simmered for the past two years now boiled over and the Friends of ONE found themselves split clean down the middle with only two individuals, Jim Kepner and Vern Bullough, remaining independent enough to maintain working relationships with both organizations.

For the sake of clarity, I employ the terms "Venice Group" and "Tangent Group" throughout this chapter to distinguish the two factions. Although Legg's Venice Group won the legal right to keep and use the name "ONE" early on, the compromise agreement of settlement signed in the spring of

1967 concludes that both factions were legitimate halves of one whole. Therefore, to call the Legg's group "ONE" and Slater's faction "Tangents" as other writers (and the factions themselves) have done perpetuates the idea that Legg's faction was the more legitimate of the two. My research, however, suggests this to be more a matter of opinion than actual or legal fact. Herein, I call Legg's faction the Venice Group simply because the offices remained on Venice Boulevard. This is not a native referent for, indeed, Legg's faction never ceased to call itself ONE.

Of Pots and Kettles, Heroes and Knaves

The first action the Tangent Group took after moving to Cahuenga was to host an open house on May 2, 1965. Using the coveted mailing list, the Tangent Group next distributed a ONE Confidential to the Friends of ONE announcing the new Cahuenga address and attempting to clarify "the recent changes that have taken place and the reasons behind those changes" by publishing a litany of complaints. The newsletter claimed that ONE's board of directors "had become a rubber stamp for its chairman. And under his direction ONE was failing." Matriculation in the courses offered by the Education Division had been "falling off drastically." As for the Social Science Division, ONE Confidential described it as "no longer vital" and claimed that the Publications Division "had failed to keep a verbal contract with an author after announcing that his book would be issued" despite the fact that it had accepted advance payments. Subscriptions to ONE had "fallen off dangerously" after a policy change made membership in ONE mandatory after the first year of subscribing. To make matters worse, the corporation owed an immense debt to the printer and "constant appeals for financial aid could not keep ONE out of debt." The letter continued as follows: "To Don Slater . . . the situation appeared increasingly alarming. . . . Many other alert and intelligent and forward-looking Members shared his conviction that action would have to be taken to stop the downward spiral. The Chairman of the Board, however, arbitrarily blocked any and all attempts at free discussion and arbitration. His dictatorial frame of mind was nowhere more evident than in his unilateral attempt to gain complete control over ONE Magazine and its editorial functions. This resulted in the resignation of the editors of ONE, some of whom had been with the Magazine from its founding, others for periods of up to eight years."

The Tangent Group had moved the physical assets of the corporation "in order to save the organization and the principles for which it stands." The move intended to guarantee continuance of ONE Magazine, which was "the most important—because it was the widest reaching—arm of the organization." The Tangent Group further announced that the "Social Science Division, the Lecture Bureau, the Book Service, [and] the Library are again at the disposal of all Members, Friends and Subscribers. All policies of exclusion are ended."

Slater described the new office of ONE, Incorporated, as perched "on the inner edge of Hollywood proper." He wrote of the gully across the road and an old riverbank recently converted to a highway that ran from downtown Los Angeles all the way up the coast to Santa Barbara and beyond. To the northeast, looking across the freeway, one could view "green hillsides scattered with Eucalyptus and underbrush . . . the whole scene is a little bit of Old California, our visitors agree."

On May 2, Legg, Bonham, and Boyfrank, acting as the directors of ONE, Incorporated, distributed their own letter to the Friends of ONE wherein it was declared that "any statement that ONE has moved its offices is false." The letter made claim that ONE Magazine's "former editor" Don Slater "illegally entered" the corporate offices "using keys which long had been entrusted to him" and, with the help of unnamed others, removed property valued in excess of $10,000. This property, the letter continued, included volumes from ONE's library, the inventory for the book service, all correspondence, office furniture, equipment, and supplies. Denying any reasonable explanation for such behavior, Legg's letter attributed the rash action to Slater's "present disturbed state of mind," whereby he had convinced himself and a few others that he was acting appropriately. "Slater has not been on ONE's payroll since November, 1964," Legg declared, and "he has not held any office in the Corporation since 1963."[1]

Legg further asserted that Slater had previously all but resigned from his editorial work on the magazine although it retained his name on the masthead as a courtesy "in the hope that he might resolve his subjective problems—whatever they were—and again function as active editor." In the meantime, ONE intended to "regain possession of all of its property." Legg also hoped Slater's "many relatives living in this area can also be safeguarded against embarrassments arising from his conduct, if this can be managed." Legg's tone implied that the Friends of ONE who received this letter should take heart that the madman would be tempered, the property returned, and ONE, Incorporated, would continue on as before after weathering this annoying, unfortunate incident. "If the more irresponsible and impetuous elements are removing themselves from our midst we shall be all the stronger for the cleansing." The board of directors stood "solidly together in this resolve."

One reply to Legg's letter came to the Venice office from two Friends of ONE, Robert Mernagh and Richard Yamamoto, strongly defending Slater's group. The letter began by attacking Legg's leadership ethic: "A good executive knows how to delegate authority" and should act "more as a coordinator than a meddler. He realizes that the end product is the summation of the group working as a whole rather than of the individual's glory." As for the accusation that Slater had resigned because of "subjective issues," Mernagh and Yamamoto held that Legg's imperious attitude had led to the separation. "In our opinion he [Legg] has lost the drive and vision of the movement and subverted and exploited it to meet his own emotional needs." Mernagh and Yamamoto described the others on the "lax, shortsighted, do-nothing board" as Legg's lackeys with neither historic nor contributory relevance to the organization. "How many of you are hiding behind pseudonyms? How much of your position in the corporation is more than token? What actual voice have you, other than the right to parrot the responses of Mr. Lambert?"

Schneider's Attempt at Mediation

On Tuesday, April 20, 1965, Jim Schneider wrote a letter to Slater expressing his puzzlement: "You have made your move and have brought a man to his knees. While I may have disagreed with you over devices and methods used, I may also have been an incapable judge since I have such inadequate knowledge of the personalities and inner conflicts involved in ONE's past. May I suggest that you do not fail to be charitable to Dorr in your time of supremacy . . . ?" Schneider continued by asking if Slater would consider moving the corporation back to Venice Boulevard if Legg resigned from the board: "I am now interested in learning whether Don Slater's ship will be any different in ways of admonition, permissibility, charity, and general conduct over that of the other regime." He added that he had never "been interested in taking sides except as necessary, but rather, I am only concerned that ONE should move forward to help others. To this progress I am devoted and am willing to spend my efforts when called upon to do so."

The next day, Schneider wrote a letter to all board members[2] calling for both Legg and Slater to step down from the board so that ONE would not remain divided: "I have no concern over who may damn me if I do, and who may damn me if I don't. However, I'll be damned if anybody is going to tell me that I can't speak my mind. Unless drastic action is taken by all concerned parties to bring about a prompt solution to the dilemma at hand,

ONE's death will occur and ONE's funeral will commence within 10 days. . . .
ONE is about to be murdered by self-inflicted wounds (a bitch fight amongst
homosexuals) in a petty little power struggle over control and policies."

Schneider called upon both Slater and Legg to recall their commitment
to the homosexual rights movement and not to their own "distaste of each
other's prejudices, attitudes, acts or personal feelings." He urged both to resign
their positions immediately. He reminded his fellow directors that, without
incoming mail, ONE effectively could not conduct business; the post office
would withhold ONE's mail until the postmaster could adjudicate Slater
and Legg's conflicting claims of corporate legitimacy. He further urged all
members involved to devise "a compromise solution over such policies and
functions between the two opposing factions."

Schneider then proposed that each board member compose a list of griev-
ances and meet informally to discuss them at his home on Saturday afternoon,
April 24, 1965. He called for a brainstorming session where they (i.e., the
board members) could "enlist every possible new idea they can think of for
resolving this problem." Perhaps, he suggested, Slater could take complete
control of ONE Magazine and oversee Glover's employment while Legg could
manage ONE Confidential and the Quarterly. Schneider added that he had
prepared a written resignation, which he intended to submit at the corporate
meeting on Sunday, April 25. He urged others to do the same, but to first
discuss the matter in his home.

The Venice Group convened for an emergency meeting on Sunday, April
25, 1965. Schneider surprised everyone present by moving that W. Dorr Legg
resign as chairman of the board. The motion lost on a five to four vote. The
slim margin made Schneider believe that perhaps his idea had merit, but his
timing was off: others were not ready to break ranks. Besides, what would
they do in Legg's absence? Schneider believed his motion was defeated "only
because of the absence of time to develop any workable formula or solution
to replace the resignation of W. Dorr Legg."[3]

On May 8, 1965, Schneider wrote a nine-page letter to his fellow board
members. He had spoken to all involved, reached some solid conclusions,
and was now ready to propose sound resolutions. He began by illustrating
the rancor being fomented, citing "the reckless charges and counter charges
hurled" between Slater and his followers and Legg and his: "Dictators, thieves,
manipulator of minds, lust to play God, unlawful acts, criminal, the damned
great white father [Legg] is leading innocent children on a collision course
with disaster, the damned psychopath [Slater] is determined to have everything his way or ruin ONE for good, illegal acts, irregular maneuvering for

control, contriver of the personality cult, perpetrator of perpetual confusion and dissension, and etc."

Schneider noted his difficulty in piecing the story together because both Slater and Legg "are most sensitively aware of the entire history of each other and ONE, Incorporated, and its growth and development since its beginning. But both are distrustful of anyone making any inquiry of past happenings, lest that person be an agent of the other." Nevertheless, Schneider managed to piece together a thorough and accurate summation of the pertinent griev-ances on both sides. Slater contended that problems started with the Novem-ber 23, 1963, meeting where Legg had secured sufficient influence within the board to "secretly change the voting procedure on January 12, 1964, so that more than one candidate would be voted on at a time." Slater further stated that the chairman had violated long-standing "assumed tradition" by actively voting on the candidates himself. The permission—and then refusal—to al-low Slater to use Sanchez's proxy vote was "most irregular," and when Slater moved for a recess, "which is a privileged motion and must be ruled on by the Chairman in accordance with *Robert's Rules of Order*," Legg had not called the question to vote but rather simply continued the meeting.

Legg, in turn, described Slater as a sore loser who "simply refused to abide by the majority vote." Slater countered this by saying that Legg had "rigged things up so much against him, and has packed the corporate membership and board with so many 'stooges,' that any affirmative vote in favor of any proposals of Don Slater is impossible."

Slater lodged many complaints against Legg's management of the 1965 an-nual business meeting. First, Slater argued that the required thirty-day notice had not been properly given to each corporate member. (Steinert had not been so notified during his stay in Europe.) The third session, on February 5, 1965, was invalid because "no meeting can be recessed or adjourned unless it specifies a designated time and date for reconvening prior to the time of adjournment or recess." If this meeting was therefore illegal, then "the five newly elected voting Corporate Members who were elected at this continued meeting were also illegal, and so are the amended By-Law changes which were voted in." With this said, Slater contended that his "present action was the most honorable under the conditions imposed on him and was done for reasons of preventing embarrassment to innocent people in a public court action." He added that, if Legg decided to take legal action, he stood prepared to defend himself.

Schneider had intuited that things were amiss within ONE about the time of his own election to the board because Slater was never around. Schneider once approached Slater to voice his concerns, and Slater replied that he felt any attempt to apprise the newer board members of the situation would prove ineffectual because they simply did what Legg told them to do. Slater specifically referenced Legg's persuading the board to appoint a representative to the editorial board when none had been requested. Slater had taken great offense and felt it would be a "severe blow to the integrity of ONE Magazine and a further attempt by W. Dorr Legg to 'take over' all the affairs of ONE, Incorporated." It also riled Slater that Legg asserted that none of ONE's publications actually paid for themselves. "This is a damned lie," Slater insisted. "ONE Magazine has more than supported itself for years." Thus, Schneider added, the new corporate members found themselves totally in the dark, "having to deal with heavy charges and counter charges being flung between Don Slater and W. Dorr Legg in a most disturbing and disrupting manner."

Schneider next provided an astute assessment of the corporation's bylaws, which he found to contain some "startling undemocratic" elements. The three officers of the corporation truly held a great deal of power; all of their decisions bound the entire corporation with no opportunity for change or override on behalf of the voting members. He believed that article 4–C, allowing for any voting member to be stripped from membership by "the unanimous vote of the Directors present and voting at any regular Directors' meeting," might prove unconstitutional because it did not include any "process of appeal" for the member in question. "Thus, an alleged 'packed' or 'stooge' Board might remove a Member or employee it doesn't like, and that Member had no process for which to appeal to the Corporate Membership at large or to an impartial outside hearing officer for a reversal of the Board's decision." Conversely, had the board agreed with the director's decision, the board could not express its concurrence.

This system frustrated its corporate members who wanted to participate actively in the affairs and operations of ONE and bred "lack of interest, lack of stimulation, and lack of participation in the many affairs and activities of ONE." Most of all, this separation contributed to the current lack of rapport within the corporation. Schneider's letter further stated that neither side was truly talking—nor even listening—to the other and that if one faction succeeded in knocking the other faction off, then "the Thomas Carlyle phrase 'A mystic bond of brotherhood makes all men one,' shall have lived and died in vain."

To prevent ONE's demise, Schneider proposed a compromise solution with twenty-one stipulations. Basically, Schneider called for Legg and Slater to resign from their positions as board members and act more in the capacity of corporate employees or advisers. Future voting would be conducted "by secret ballot or in the absence of both" Slater and Legg to diffuse any rancorous feelings and diminish the level of politicking. Schneider proposed that the board amend the bylaws to allow the voting members to "nullify a decision of the Board of Directors by a 2/3 vote of all voting Corporate Members" (including absentee votes), and likewise establish a system of appeal for members dismissed by the board. The directors should report all decisions to the voting members each month and distribute minutes of all corporate meetings to each member in a timely manner. Schneider suggested that the corporation find "a better and easier understood parliamentary process for the conduct of meetings than *Robert's Rules of Order,*" adding that he hoped all involved would consider his compromise or propose similar solutions of their own. He concluded with ten arguments in favor of the proposed compromise, whose purpose would be to bring both of the current warring factions back together while strengthening the corporation and rendering it more democratic by adding a system of checks and balances. The governing control of ONE would leave the hands of both contending factions, and the board itself would become more fair and impartial. In his concluding paragraph, Schneider wrote that he and his partner, Henry J. Lieffers, prepared this agreement after consulting with the office of Charles E. Rickerhauser Jr., the state deputy commissioner of corporations. Schneider included with each letter a ballot whereby each member could vote for the agreement as offered or with suggested changes, or vote against the measure while offering suggestions.

When Schneider talked to Slater about this letter, Slater admitted that the idea had merit but would not likely come to pass. Legg responded by having Schneider removed from the board—and from the corporation. Schneider received this bombshell in a letter dated May 10, two days after he had dispatched his proposed compromise. Boyfrank summoned Schneider to dismissal proceedings scheduled for May 16, 1965. Schneider responded the following day, May 11, asking if Boyfrank could change the time to 3:00 p.m. from 4:00 p.m. and whether Schneider could bring a witness to "give evidence and testimony on my behalf." He also requested clarification of the specific charges against him. Schneider expressed his puzzlement regarding the action since Boyfrank had sent him a glowing letter of appreciation just six months prior on December 8, 1964. "It is neither healthy nor wise to purge a voice of dissent," Schneider added, "nor is it hardly fair or democratic." He never received an answer to his letter.

On Saturday, May 12, a beleaguered Schneider sent another note to Don Slater, "I have watched your mutineered ship (as you call it) sail, and I have been greatly concerned." He asked, "If there are those alleged Corporate Members to be left behind, who are relatively newcomers . . . then there is the question of whether anything is left for them to look forward to or pursue." Slater interpreted this as Schneider's awkward way of asking to be pulled from the corporate flotsam and permitted to board the new vessel. Sure enough, Slater graciously invited Schneider to join his group and to help continue production of the magazine. In his May 14 response, Slater complimented Schneider on his "calm perseverance," which "had a certain nobility about it." He said that no one, in his opinion, had really been "left behind." They had simply failed to keep up. He added that "newcomers" in particular were rarely "left behind"—old-timers more commonly lodged that complaint. Unfortunately, in the case of ONE, Slater felt that in some ways it was the newcomers that had let the organization down the most: "At an age when I was old enough to be their father, I had to negotiate a second revolution in my life, when I had wanted to rest, and when it should properly have been the responsibility of the younger ONES. After all, Bill, Tony, and I had done our work years ago when we founded ONE. Why should any one of us have to be called on a second time?"

Slater reminded Schneider that he had never "said that the persons voted into corporate membership this year would not make good members." But since the meeting on Sunday afternoon, April 18, 1965, shortly after his private encounter with Legg, Slater found himself appalled by the newcomers' lack of understanding of ONE's history and its mission, their failure to realize that "a blow had been struck." After this insight, Slater came to regard them all "as fools without a spark of life." He continued, "You think I was hard on them? You think I was enraged? I was too easy on the lily-livered bastards. I was not enraged, I was outraged—because I found it inconceivable that after what had happened they still would endure the fiction that their interests were in control."

As for the mention of blackmail, Slater denied ever having done such a thing. The subject had been raised at the meeting that afternoon, but not by him: "Look at the record. All public statements about the situation originating from 3473½ have carefully avoided personalities. Not so the statements of the 'board' of ONE of 2256. That statement read before the audience of May third and later published is loaded with intimidation by public accusation."

On Thursday, May 13, Schneider reported to the directors that he had received a letter from Chet Sampson postmarked from Copenhagen, Denmark, two days prior. Sampson reported that the gay European tour had proceeded "splendidly." He had received Schneider's nine-page letter and other correspondence and had felt bad to be abroad at such a critical period. He commended Schneider and Lieffers for their time and effort and declared it absurd that anyone should question their loyalty to ONE. He said that he had enjoyed his three-year association with "Dorr, Don and Billy" and appreciated each of them individually. But he felt they had all done a lousy job of public relations and that the five of them—Schneider, Winn, Coron, Dyer, and Sampson—through their financial contributions and their actions had unquestionably demonstrated their loyalty to ONE and their merit as voting members. "Who else could they name who has better rights to be on the Board?" Sampson further stated that he might manage to contribute $1,000 a year to ONE, once he returned and the situation stabilized.

As for Schneider's proposals, Sampson found "a great deal of merit in most of the items, and most of them involving By-Law changes sound excellent." He liked the idea of the voting members acting as an adjudicating body on the matter, hearing both Slater and Legg voice their grievances and deriving some sort of resolution through the process. Sampson, however, felt that neither would agree to "such a resignation—turning over to *OTHERS* control of what *THEY* built up." That was Sampson's only real reservation; other than that, he agreed with most of what Schneider proposed. He wished Schneider the best of luck in reunifying the corporation but expressed doubt that either Legg or Slater would relinquish control of the corporation they had created. He was right.

Legg's Venice Group voted to remove Slater from membership in ONE on April 23, 1965, and similarly expunged Sanchez and Steinert on May 16. During that April meeting, Dyer dissolved his Dramatic Arts Service and resigned from all duties and responsibilities within the corporation, "due to existing conditions of ONE, INCORPORATED failing to uphold its own standards." On June 14, the Venice Group sent a letter to the Friends of ONE stating that the organization had not "split." "Instead, there has been the cheap, criminal theft of property generously contributed to ONE." The letter continued, "This contemptible theft has been the work of cynical opportunists and their dupes." The directors asked that none of the Friends of ONE give his or her address or personal information to the "counterfeit" organization and to request that their names be promptly removed from the renegades' mailing list. As for the articles duplicated in the two versions of *ONE Magazine*, the Venice Group argued that the counterfeit editors had used the stories "as a measure of economy because they had long been typeset, not for their intrinsic merits." Readers were assured that the perpetrators of this brash crime were being properly hounded and "each will have to answer for his acts in due time."

Legg Files Suit (and Heists the Heist): Case Number 864824

On July 21, 1965, Beverly Hills attorney Hillel Chodos filed a lawsuit on behalf of the Venice Group, which called itself "ONE, Incorporated, a California Corporation." Chodos filed the suit, assigned case number 864824, against "Donald Rutherford Slater, Antonio Sanchez, William Edward Glover, Joseph Hansen, Rudolph N. Steinert, Bank of America, and Does[4] One through Twenty-Five" for possession of property, damages for conversion, and conjunctive relief.

Significantly, no individuals were named as plaintiffs, just the organization ONE, Incorporated. This tactic clearly gave the Venice Group the upper hand by preempting any legitimacy the Tangent Group may have had to claim itself to be a legitimate aspect of ONE.[5] The complaint cited three causes of action. In the first, Chodos asserted that "management of plaintiff's affairs shall be vested in a board of three directors," namely a chairman, a vice-chairman, and a secretary-treasurer. Further, "a voting member may be removed from membership, after notice and an opportunity to be heard, by the unanimous vote of the directors present and voting at any regular directors' meeting." Chodos declared that defendants Slater and Sanchez, who had in actuality been voting members of ONE continuously since 1953, had been "duly removed from membership by the unanimous vote of the directors at a regular meeting, after notice and an opportunity to be heard." The complaint added that neither Slater, Sanchez, nor any of the other defendants listed "has been an officer or director of plaintiff since January, 1963."

The lawsuit asserted that at some time between 2:00 p.m. on Saturday, April 17, 1965, and 3:00 p.m., Sunday, April 18, 1965, Slater and the other defendants used a key with which Slater had been entrusted to access the offices for the explicit purpose of removing all the corporation's property, valued at $10,000. Slater, the lawsuit infers, betrayed the corporation's trust. Further, the lawsuit falsely suggests that Slater entered into the offices under suspicious circumstances and without proper authority.

Chodos noted in his second cause of action that the defendants moved the property to 3473½ Cahuenga Boulevard in Hollywood, California, and diverted mail to that address in the name of ONE, Incorporated. Furthermore, posits Chodos, the defendants changed the telephone listing from ONE, Incorporated, to *ONE Magazine* and "caused the telephone company to direct telephone calls intended for plaintiff to them." Slater's faction had begun publishing a rival magazine with the same title as that published by the plaintiff and had profited by doing so, accepting payments and making deposits in the plaintiff's name. Chodos asserted that the defendants undertook these actions "fraudulently, willfully and maliciously, with a design to oppress, harass and injure the plaintiff; and the defendants have at all times well known that they were acting fraudulently and without any claim or color of right." Rather than the $10,000 property assessment, these damages amounted to the far greater sum of $50,000. The suit also called for "exemplary damages" of $200,000.

For his third cause of action, Chodos asked the court to take immediate action in order to prevent defendants from continuing to operate in ONE's name. He further requested that the court issue a permanent injunction restraining Slater and the other named defendants from "holding themselves out to the members, subscribers or contributors of [ONE, Incorporated] as the duly authorized officers, directors or representatives" of ONE. Nor could they publish a magazine with "*ONE*," "*ONE Magazine*," or any similar name as title. The defendants were to restrain from soliciting or accepting mail or donations on behalf of ONE, Incorporated, nor could they enter into any contracts or otherwise identify as ONE, Incorporated, or in any way claim to act on ONE's behalf.

As a separate action on the same day (January 21, 1966), Monwell Boyfrank, acting as ONE's secretary, filed a declaration for claim and delivery of personal property as part of the action for the case. The list of items is repeated here in detail:

(a) Office equipment, including a Rex rotary mimeograph; an IBM electric typewriter; an Adler typewriter; a Royal typewriter; an Underwood typewriter; a Burroughs adding machine; an Elliott addressing machine; an office desk; a shipping table and associated equipment; numerous office chairs; and approximately ten steel file cabinets.

(b) Files and records reflecting the operations and activities of [ONE, Incorporated] since 1952 including, among others, the following: master correspondence files comprising four four-drawer file cabinets; files relating to the ONE Institute, a research organization sponsored by plaintiff; master card index file of names and addresses of members, subscribers and others; members' financial card file; social service files; and editorial files, comprising approximately six file drawers containing manuscripts, photos and similar materials.

(c) A complete set of addressograph plates, or address stencils, containing the names and addresses of members of [ONE, Incorporated], subscribers to the magazine, former members and subscribers, and other persons receiving material from plaintiff on a regular basis.

(d) Business records, equipment, and documents including checkbooks, bank endorsement stamps, banking records, news dealer financial records . . . ; ledgers and journals from 1952 to the present; federal and California tax records; invoices showing accounts payable and records showing accounts receivable; financial statements and similar material.

(e) The business licenses of the corporation.

(d) [sic] The corporation seal; and the minutes of the meetings of the director, and of the voting members, of this corporation since 1952.

(f) Book service stock, consisting of a supply or inventory of books held by plaintiff for sale to its members and other interested persons.

(g) Research library, consisting of approximately 3,000 bound volumes; 1,000 paperback volumes; papers, documents and manuscripts; approximately 100 tape recordings; card index; and general library equipment including shelving, librarian's desk, and chairs.

Boyfrank's declaration further asserted that these items were in the possession of defendants Sanchez, Glover, Hanson [sic], and Steinert. It declared that "none of the said defendants has or asserts any legal ground, nor has any claim of color or right to either the title or possession with respect to the said personal property" and directed the sheriff to confiscate the listed items from 3473½ Cahuenga Boulevard in Hollywood.

On the next day, July 22, the court issued a temporary restraining order (TRO) against Slater, Sanchez, Glover, Hanson [sic], Steinert, and the Bank of America. This TRO summoned them to court on August 3, 1966, at 9:00 a.m. to show cause why the court should not issue an injunction against them prohibiting them "from holding themselves out to the members, subscribers or contributors . . . as the duly authorized officers, directors or representatives" of ONE, Incorporated. They were never to publish, print, or circulate any magazine called ONE or ONE Magazine nor could they "solicit or receive any mail, communications, manuscripts, checks or funds addressed to or intended for ONE, Incorporated." The TRO instructed the defendants to forward any such materials received to 2256 Venice at once. The court issued the TRO upon Chodos's filing a $1,000 bond.[6]

In a memorandum added to the TRO, Chodos, sounding a lot like Legg, wrote the following: "The wrongful quality of the Defendants' acts is compounded by virtue of the fact that, as alleged in the verified complaint, plaintiff has long reposed trust and confidence in the defendants Slater and [Sanchez], who have previously been officers and directors, and who have been privy to all of [ONE, Incorporated's] business operation and confidential files. . . . [This action could] constitute 'unfair competition' and therefore ONE could be entitled to 'injunctive relief.'"

Chodos's memorandum further stated that "Slater and [Sanchez], and their confederates, have actually physically appropriated [ONE's] personal property and removed it from its previous location to offices obtained by them." Chodos complained that Slater et al. had been "holding themselves out generally" as ONE, Incorporated, and had thus been "diverting contributions from plaintiff's long-standing members, subscribers and contributors, including both funds, correspondence and valuable research data, to their own use." He further alleged "that the acts and conduct" of the defendants had "been done . . . without any claim or color of right." The memorandum further stated: "None of the defendants has been an officer or director of [ONE, Incorporated] for more than two years prior to the inception of their plan of usurpation."

The court dissolved this initial TRO on July 30, 1965, because none of the defendants had been properly served by that date. That same day, however, Judge Harold F. Collins of the Superior Court ordered the defendants to appear in the courtroom of department 47, 111 North Hill Street, at 9:00 a.m. on August 13, 1965, to show why an injunction should not be issued barring them from acknowledging themselves as directors or representatives of ONE, Incorporated; from publishing *ONE Magazine*; from receiving payments or mail as ONE, Incorporated; or from entering into any contracts on ONE's behalf.

The court's summons was accompanied by an application for a new TRO, superseding the previous one. It also included a declaration by Chodos that stated Slater had threatened ONE's officers by saying he would destroy the property in question should they attempt to recover it. For that reason, Chodos urged the sheriff, as directed by the court, not to tell any defendant of the pending action until after he had recovered the possessions. The sheriff's department had originally suggested that they would complete this task by July 28, 1965, so Chodos refrained from serving Slater et al. until that time. As of July 30, the sheriff had not yet confiscated the materials, although his office planned to seize the goods at noon on August 2. Accordingly, the court would issue the new restraining order on or after that date.

On August 2, 1965, Slater apparently received his copy of this new summons, combined with the original complaints filed on July 22, a date written on the front page of Slater's copy of these documents. According to plan, the sheriff's department successfully confiscated the materials as or before the summons and restraining order were served. Slater would need to secure a $20,000 bond to retrieve the materials.

Slater had lost everything—or so it seemed. While the sheriff held the majority of the materials, Slater's friend Rodney Hee secretly held the mailing list and other crucial documents in his home. According to Glover,[7] Slater was furious that Legg had the sheriff confiscate the materials, not only for the value of the resources and their use to either faction but because the mailing list of subscribers was top secret information that should have been protected at all costs—especially from the police. Putting the mailing list in the hands of the sheriff would dangerously violate the movement's most sacred pact: the right to the privacy of its members. Because Slater had acted preemptively by storing the most sensitive and valuable materials at Hee's residence, the mailing list remained secret, and neither Legg nor the sheriff recovered the list of subscribers at this time.

According to Sanchez, however, Glover slipped and told some of Hee's neighbors about the nature of the materials they had stowed. One morning not long thereafter, someone pelted Hee's house with eggs. A professional musician who collected rare and valuable pianos, Hee feared that someone would set fire to his house. While Sanchez and Slater thought Hee's fear a bit extreme, events to come would remind them that although many of their Los Angeles neighbors were becoming more tolerant of homosexuals, others still hated them and would not hesitate to intimidate or harm them if given the chance. But after Slater allayed Hee's fears, the sensitive materials remained in Hee's Hollywood home near the Tangent Group office for about a year.

Nevertheless, on August 15, Slater wrote an impassioned letter to Raiden stating that, insofar as he was concerned, the sheriff currently possessed the true "heart" of ONE. Though others, most notably Joe and Jane Hansen, felt ONE Magazine was the only thing that truly mattered, Slater valued the historic assets he had accumulated over the years. He treasured his collection of legal rulings, case histories, diaries and memoirs, newsletters and publications of other homosexual organizations, the rare books, and other incunabula related to homosexuality and the history of the movement. Homosexuals throughout America could turn to no organization before ONE. No homophile press existed before ONE Magazine (although at this point, Slater reported, more than twenty homosexual publications circulated in the United States). Partially as a result of ONE's persistent activism, California was updating its own penal code (a process completed by 1969). Truly, ONE, Incorporated, had made history and this archive had recorded much of the process. "If ONE has any assets this is it. Damn the future of its publications, but the fate of this material is important." Slater wrote that he hoped that in the future, after he "gave up the battle lines," he could "retire to a place where I might organize and digest the material collected, and produce some sort of worthwhile result." Although his days as a leader and advocate for homosexual rights were far from over and many victories still lay ahead for Slater, he never did find the place or the time to sort and organize the materials as he had desired.

Luck was with him, however, insofar as rescuing ONE's archives was concerned. Thanks to a loan from a wealthy friend, he was soon able to secure the funds needed to post bond.[8] The materials were soon returned to the Tangent Group, which still maintains and guards them to this day.

August 1965: The Tangent Group Retaliates

The Tangent Group would not give up the fight easily. Early in August 1965, Raiden helped Slater, Sanchez, Glover, and Steinert file their answers regarding Legg's claims and his three calls for action. They disagreed with some of the claims made by Chodos, asserting for example that ONE Magazine's circulation was closer to four thousand than the five thousand figure claimed (eight hundred of which had been distributed through subscription and the remaining through newsstands). Also, the research library contained two thousand rather than three thousand volumes; five hundred paperback books instead of the thousand claimed; and a more reasonable estimated value of $2,500, which was much less than plaintiff's $10,000 evaluation. Concerning ONE's board, Slater and Sanchez claimed that they remained voting members because they had never been legally removed. As for Legg's assertion that neither of them had served as voting members since January 1963, they denied this claim, asserting that through 1963 and part of 1964, Slater, Sanchez, and Steinert had "constituted three of six remaining voting members and during part of 1964 and since April 23, 1965, have been three out of five remaining voting members of ONE, Incorporated." Slater and the other defendants had moved the named materials on April 17 with the intention of continuing to run the affairs of the corporation from the new location. The defendants further denied "that the transfer and change were made without the consent and against the will of plaintiff, ONE, Incorporated, but allege on the contrary that the three defendants, Slater, Sanchez, and Steinert, appearing hereby constituted a majority of the voting members of the said ONE, Incorporated, and were therefore entitled to act for the corporation." In conclusion, the defendants claimed to be "the legal and proper and controlling members of ONE, Incorporated." As such, many if not all of the claims and allegations made by the plaintiff were denied.

Slater's preparatory notes clarify his strategy in his battle with Legg. He planned to focus the court's attention on the fraud and intimidation that had taken place during the 1964 elections. Further, Slater planned to show that the directors had failed to protect Sanchez's proxy vote and that the chair had "failed to permit or entertain my motion for a recess to the following day." He also hoped to show that the "election" of Winn and Bonham had "not represented the will of 2/3 of those members present and voting."

On August 12, 1965, a counter summons was served involving the case, which named cross-complainants "Don Slater, Antonio Sanchez, and Rudolph H. Steinert, and ONE, Incorporated" against cross-defendants William Lambert, alias W. Dorr Legg; Monwell Boyfrank, alias Manuel Boy Frank; Lewis Bonham; Gregory Coron, alias Gregory Carr; Bob Newton, alias Robert Earl; and Chet Sampson, alias Chuck Thompson. According to this summons, the cross-defendants had ten days from the date of service of the complaint to appear in the California Superior Court and answer the cross-complaint. In this cross-complaint, Slater, Sanchez, and Steinert asserted themselves as the true majority of ONE, Incorporated, noting Sanchez was "one of the original organizers and has been a director, an officer or a voting member of said Corporation from the time of its inception to the present time; cross-complainant Don Slater has been [a director] since shortly after its inception, and is still a voting member and the editor of its magazine continuously for the past ten years." Steinert and Boyfrank had each been voting members since January 25, 1963. The cross-complaint listed Legg and Weaver as the remaining two board members as of January 1964, although it noted Weaver had officially resigned on or about April 23, 1965.

Up to this point, Raiden and Slater's strategy had been, predictably, to meet Legg's faction point by point and to make their arguments based on facts verifiable by personal records and letters, many of which the sheriff then possessed. In the fifth paragraph of their cross-complaint, Raiden concluded that based on the facts presented, ONE, Incorporated, had "so divided into factions that [it would have been impossible to] agree upon or elect a board of directors consisting of an uneven number." It followed that the factions had the corporation "so deadlocked that its business can no longer be conducted with advantage to its members." Slater and Raiden therefore proposed a new solution, one that would ultimately be their downfall. They suggested that the court liquidate the corporation and appoint a "receiver of the corporation as provided in Section 4656 of the Corporations Code." This receiver would "take over and manage the business and affairs of the corporation and preserve its property pending the hearing and determination of this cross-complaint for dissolution." Alternatively, they suggested, the court could reunify the organization by appointing "a provisional director as provided in Section 4655 of the Corporations Code." As will be seen, these ideas were not well received by one of the presiding judges during the upcoming trial.

The Trial (August 13, 1965): Will the Real ONE Please Stand Up?

The court convened as scheduled at 9:00 in the morning on Friday, August 13. As the trial began, and Hillel Chodos and Edward Raiden appeared before the bench. Also present was Lequita McKay who represented Hirsh-Graphics, the printer Slater had used to publish ONE Magazine. A detailed record of the hearing survives as a reporter's transcript on appeal. Edward M. Altman was the official court reporter, and the Honorable Ralph H. Nutter was the presiding judge.

Judge Nutter began by noting the filing of a cross-complaint the previous day, scheduled to be heard on August 23 by a judge in Department 16. Raiden asked to move the trial from 9 to 10 a.m. as Chodos had some other business to handle until that time. McKay then chimed in that her clients, Mr. Hirsh and Hirsh-Graphics, opposed any motion of continuance and should not have been included in the dispute in the first place. Here the judge made a startling turn. He called Chodos to task for having made a rude telephone call the previous night. "I would like to make a suggestion that, when you call in the next time, courtesy on the telephone is always helpful. I happen to be the one who received the phone call."

Chodos apologized, stammering that he had no recollection of what he had said. "It was very abrupt, almost rude orders," Judge Nutter replied. "Maybe under those circumstances you would rather have it go over to sixteen. Frankly I was a little bit shocked by the tone of the address." Raiden spoke up at this point, stating that Chodos simply wanted the restraining order continued until August 23. Raiden said that he had no objection to the continuance in part though he did object to the "phase of the restraining order which restrains the defendants and each of them from holding out to the members, subscribers or contributors that they are officers, directors, or representatives of ONE, Incorporated." Then Raiden added, "We should have the same rights that they have." Judge Nutter agreed that the dispute should be consolidated and, since Chodos had not had significant time to respond to the cross-complaint, the case certainly should not be heard that morning. In the meantime, Nutter vacated the part of the restraining order that pertained to Hirsh-Graphics, adding that the printers could conduct business with whomever they pleased. When Chodos protested, Nutter stated that the plaintiff might bring a separate suit against Hirsh-Graphics for damages but repeated that he could see no reason to hold them regarding the matter at hand.

Raiden again made clear his willingness to "keep everything else in status quo" except for the objection he had raised regarding his client's right to claim to be officers of and affiliated with ONE, Incorporated. He reminded the court that all of the corporation's equipment and records remained with the sheriff. "We are now litigating on the question of the surety. That is why the Receiver will be the ideal determinative." Raiden agreed with Judge Nutter in that "one judge should decide the whole thing" and agreed to the continuance with the reservation that "the restraint against [our] saying we are ONE, Inc. is far too expansive." As for paragraph two of the restraining order, pertaining to publishing *ONE Magazine,* and paragraphs three and four, which prohibited the Tangent Group from doing business as or receiving mail or donations on behalf of ONE, those terms he could accept and let stand.

When the judge suggested this compromise to him, Chodos politely refused to delete the first paragraph from the restraining order. "Then," answered Judge Nutter, "we have to have the hearing this morning." Chodos balked, "Does your Honor wish to proceed with it right now at this time?"

"I *don't* wish to proceed with it," Nutter responded. "But if you refuse to stipulate that the matter may go over, I guess we will have to hear it this morning." But first, the judge decided to attend to other matters, so he called a recess to the case.

When they were next summoned to the bench, Raiden informed Judge Nutter that he and Chodos had discussed the matter in the hallway during the break. Raiden had explained to Chodos, "We are concerned that we are not permitted to tell the members and the contributors our position, and we want to be able to do that." He claimed that under those circumstances, Chodos had agreed to strike elements of the first paragraph and to continue the matter to Department 16. With this said, the court deleted nearly three lines of the TRO's first paragraph, these lines being, "One, restraining the said defendants from holding themselves out to the members, subscribers or contributors of the plaintiff as the duly authorized officers, directors or representatives of the plaintiff." The rest of the order remained in effect, and the matter was to continue to Department 16 on August 23, 1965, at 9:00 a.m.

Clearly, this action nearly derailed Legg's faction. For Raiden to hit them so effectively this late in the game was setback enough, but to find that Chodos's rude actions the night prior to the trial had so biased the judge against them must surely have shocked Legg and Bonham, who could only stand by in frustrated silence as Judge Nutter summarily dismissed their claim against the publisher and struck a key component of their restraining order. For Slater's faction, this small victory provided crucial leverage. They could change the name of their magazine readily enough. But most important, they still *were* ONE, Incorporated. Slater's Tangent Group had prevailed in its insistence that they were a legitimate aspect of the corporation and could continue to claim to represent the majority of the legally elected board members of ONE, Incorporated, as of the January 1964 elections. They would print this claim in every issue of their newly titled magazine: "*Tangents* is published monthly by the majority of legally elected voting members of ONE."

From this point on, then, there were two ONEs: the Legg group and the Slater group. *Both* were legitimate aspects of ONE. The division had been just that: a split, not a robbery (as Legg would continue to claim). A legitimate corporate fission differs dramatically from a madman's coup. Judge Nutter had seen enough to recognize a true separation, a corporate divorce of sorts. He seems to have approached the case with a skepticism that, while fueled to some extent by Chodos's phone call, also came with the territory. As linguist Jerome Bruner reminds us, "law stories" are often and wisely "distrusted . . . by those who must judge between them." After all, no matter how principled the attorney, lawyers are paid to "tell stories committed to an adversarial rhetoric" (2002, 42). As such, Judge Nutter determined that this was a civil matter as no one had committed any crime. His decision gave Slater the green light to proceed with his own case, which Slater did with renewed determination.

Although the court battle would continue, as will be seen, I should note here that this "status quo" is to a great degree how things would remain. Ultimately, the Tangent Group kept the archives, or the great majority of it, which is currently being added to the Vern and Bonnie Bullough Collection of Sex and Gender, a special collections archive within Oviatt Library at the California State University, Northridge (CSUN). The Venice Group continued to operate under the name of ONE, Incorporated, focusing on educational seminars and courses until Legg died in 1994. Each group continued to take potshots at the other for the next twenty years, and the vitriol between them escalated so severely that few in the Los Angeles movement could truly remain neutral or bipartisan. The sharpness of the cleavage between the factions suggests that the corporation had indeed been fractured for some time, and the schism was most likely inevitable. Perhaps Judge Nutter perceived this as well.

Legg Responds, and the Battle Drones On . . .

On August 19, 1965, Legg, Boyfrank, Bonham, Coron, Newton, and Sampson filed their answer to the Tangent Group's cross-complaint. These cross-defendants asserted that Slater and Sanchez had indeed at times been officers and voting members, but they claimed that they had removed Slater as a voting member on April 25, 1965, "duly and properly, after notice and opportunity to be heard." They further claimed that Slater had not edited ONE Magazine for "ten years, but only from January 1959 until April 22, 1965," citing more technicality than actuality. As for Sanchez and Steinert, they had "duly and properly" removed them as voting members of ONE, Incorporated, on May 16, 1965. Legg asserted that he himself had been a voting member of ONE since its inception in 1953 and an officer/director during that entire time. Boyfrank had served on the board since January 25, 1963. Bonham had been a director since January 1964 (Slater would refute this) and became an officer that December.

Legg's faction, of course, denied that Slater's faction had ever comprised a majority of the voting members, especially at the time of the filing of the cross-complaint, by which time, Legg asserted, they had all been removed from membership. Legg also asserted there were *seven* voting members of the corporation as of January 1964, listing the obvious six plus Bonham. (Legg made no mention of Winn.) Legg further asserted that during that time the board of directors consisted of three officers—namely himself, Boyfrank, and Weaver. Bonham had been an officer since Aaron's resignation in December 1964.[9] The officers since then had included Legg, Boyfrank, and Bonham. The cross-defendants further asserted that Slater and his crew did not deserve any of the relief they had sought, having "come before this Court with unclean hands" because they had stolen the property in question.

On August 19, Legg filed a separate declaration in opposition to Slater's application for a receiver and in favor of the preliminary injunction as filed by Chodos. This declaration asserted that Legg had frequently contributed to the magazine and "occasionally used the pen name of William Lambert." This use of a pseudonym was not uncommon. "Each of the other individual parties to this action have occasionally used a pen name, with the exception of Manuel Boyfrank and Lewis Bonham," he continued. "Donald Rutherford Slater," as Legg knew him, also wrote as Leslie Colfax and Gregory James. Steinert went by R. H. Stuart, and Glover wrote as W. E. G. McIntire. Legg attached a copy of the articles of incorporation and a copy of the bylaws, which had never been amended "except to the extent shown in the minutes of the 1965 regular meeting," which were also attached.

Legg's declaration was a hodgepodge of fact and fiction. Legg deliberately misled the court by portraying Slater as second-rate office help who had—probably as a result of unrelated hardships—gone bonkers, taken advantage of the corporation's trust, and hijacked the entire enterprise in the name of some fool's crusade. This must have infuriated Slater, who stuck to the facts and trusted common sense and logic to prevail. Legg's declaration made many misstatements. For one, he refers to the annual meeting of January 29 and 30, 1965, as a "regular meeting," understating its significance as an *annual* meeting. Legg stated that he chaired the board for that meeting when in fact Joe Weaver had done so. As the alleged chair that night, Legg stated that he had in no way deviated from the traditional methods, nor had he in any way violated the standards as set forth in *Robert's Rules of Order*. Moreover, the chair had even adjourned the meeting to allow Sanchez to return and cast his ballot (though Legg failed to mention Slater's denied use of proxy). After this, the directors elected Bonham and Winn to voting membership—the implication in Legg's statement being that perhaps Sanchez had not voted as Slater had expected he would. Legg also denounced Slater's claim that the February 5, 1965, meeting had been illegal and presented Boyfrank's minutes to show that Slater had shown up, made an impetuous motion, and left upon that motion's defeat.

Legg, of course, did not mention the editors' meeting, which suggested to the court that Slater had performed his brash act only because he had felt slighted by the board. Also, Legg made no mention of the pending motion to remove Slater from corporate membership. Legg's version of ONE's history as reported by Chodos jumped right from that February meeting to the April mutiny: "Between the afternoon of April 17, 1965, and the afternoon of April 18, 1965," Slater and the other defendants came to ONE and removed the items, as stated. This marks the time between Legg's leaving the office on Saturday and returning the following Easter afternoon. Chodos implied that Slater and his crew had snuck in at night like criminals with a key entrusted to Slater by the directors.[10]

This declaration continues that on April 22, 1965, the directors officially informed Slater that a "regular April meeting" had been set for April 25 to discuss his dismissal from the organization. (Slater later insisted that this had *not* been a regular meeting of the directors but was instead a special meeting.) Chodos attached a copy of the notice as Exhibit G. The meeting had convened as scheduled, and Legg and Boyfrank voted to cast Slater from the organization. On April 23, Legg and Boyfrank sent another letter to Slater, this one dismissing him as editor of *ONE Magazine*.

During a board of directors meeting on April 30, 1965, Legg and Boyfrank wrote to Sanchez and Steinert telling them to appear before the directors on May 16 to give reason why they should not be removed from ONE's voting membership. The directors sent a similar letter to Jim Schneider on May 10. Legg's declaration concludes that the directors indeed met on May 16, and although he could not produce the minutes (the sheriff still held most if not all of the records), Legg assured the court that neither Sanchez, Steinert, nor Schneider had appeared, "and that they were duly removed as members of the corporation on May 16, 1965." According to Slater, this account of the meeting was not accurate. Schneider had shown up and addressed the board; however, the board would not allow him to present his witness. I will relate details of these events presently.

Back to Court

Both factions of ONE convened again in court on Monday, August 23, 1965, for a hearing regarding the Order to Show Cause for the Appointment of Receiver and the continuance of the previous Order to Show Cause. According to Raiden,[11] "the discussion on this day revolved almost entirely around the matter of election and the method of election of members, directors, and officers of the corporation." Judge Wells seemed incapable of deciding what to do, desiring to protect both parties. Raiden pointed out that giving Legg's faction the materials would have the same effect as deciding the case before it even went to trial. It was conceded that, in fairness, "each faction should have access to the equipment and material." But then Judge Wells became fixated on the fact that Slater's faction had filed a proceeding asking the court to dissolve the organization and appoint a receiver to act as arbitrator. Judge Wells concluded that since Raiden had asked for dissolution, restraint from operations must not have seriously damaged his client. Further, the judge stated that although he would make no ruling as to who should possess the materials in question, he did feel, due to the defendants' request for dissolution, that Legg's faction did indeed have grounds for a preliminary injunction, and he required a $10,000 bond. Raiden asked whether the individuals or the corporation had to post the bond, and Wells answered that he could make no other ruling "because of the request of the defendant faction for a receiver." He clarified, "I am granting their injunction as requested against your operating and against your hypothecation for the reason that what you are seeking here is dissolution. . . . You are claiming the right to continue operating pending dissolution. I am granting their request with the $10,000 bond with the additional provision that their injunction may include no hypothecation." Judge Wells added that he was "not making any disposition of the assets. I am not saying that they are entitled to them as opposed to you. . . . You can keep possession all you want. . . . I am not ordering you to turn anything over to them."[12] Nevertheless, this proved a decisive victory for Legg. Now Raiden took his turn losing face in the courtroom.

Raiden responded by filing a complaint stating that the court had not given him adequate opportunity to show evidence or to file a statement claiming that the declaration Legg had filed on August 20, 1965, was false. He claimed that Legg's faction had "secured a victory granting all the injunctive relief requested in their complaint, and one that accomplished the main purpose of the action in advance of a trial." He further added that Legg's faction had made no effort since the August 23 hearing to bring the matter to trial even though the action had been filed on July 22, 1965, and the issue was joined on September 21.[13]

The Interrogation of Lambert

Don Slater's deposition was taken at 1:30 p.m. on Thursday, September 16, 1965, in Chodos's law office in Beverly Hills. Very little of what he stated would have surprised anyone. He asserted that Bonham could not have been legitimately elected during the 1964 annual meeting for the reasons previously mentioned. Further, the directors had not legitimately continued the February 5, 1965, annual meeting; therefore, the changes made in the bylaws had been illegally ratified and the new members elected that night were not legitimate members at all. During the course of the deposition, Raiden often intervened to prevent Slater from incriminating himself, mindful of Legg's assertion that Slater had stolen the materials and Legg's resulting charge of conspiracy.

Dorr Legg responded to Slater's interrogatories in Chodos's office on Thursday, December, 23, 1965. Ed Raiden received his copy a month later, on January 26, 1966. The fact that Legg waited so long to answer Slater's interrogatories—over ten months—suggests that after his first unsuccessful day in court, Legg changed his strategy from one of aggressive offensive to one of prolonged delay. Under the circumstances, this could be expected. Because Legg's faction carried the name ONE, Incorporated, as far as Legg was concerned he could continue to propagate a version of history that validated his faction and vilified Slater's. The propaganda attack against the Tangent Group had gone exceedingly well. Legg knew Slater well enough to know that the man was stewing in his own emotional juices the entire time. It was unlikely that things would change for either of them in the next trial. Legg's faction would get to keep and use the name ONE, Incorporated, and the possibility remained that Slater would have to relinquish some if not all or of the coveted materials in the future. Meanwhile, Slater continued to do what he had always done: the logical thing based on the facts as he knew them. For Legg, this made Slater a difficult but predictable adversary.

As a part of the process of discovery in a case, interrogatories may be issued and verified under oath, but attorneys debate the utility of the practice: the other side can easily "hokey up the answers," as one attorney put it, which reaffirms Jerome Bruner's observation that "law stories simply are not, never have been, and probably never will be taken at face value" (2002, 42). It seems that further muddying the waters is exactly what Legg set out to do, though Slater did manage to nail him down on a few basic facts.[14]

As I read the transcripts of the interrogatories, I came to imagine a brightly painted chamber with scuffed walls and a long one-way mirror beside a single door. Because it took so long for Legg to respond to the initial request, these answers to the initial questions do not easily fit into the chronological narrative thus far related. In an effort to capture the spirit of the questions as they were written early in the trial cycle, I have chosen to present them in the manner in which I came to envision them—in the form of a noir detective mystery novel. I hope the reader will indulge my brief fictionalization of this part of the story.[15]

Lanky Dorr Legg sits uncomfortably in a wooden office chair in the center of the room, a wide-brimmed lamp dangling from a cord above him. Don Slater paces slowly around Legg wearing a leather pressman's cap, occasionally tapping his pencil on his yellow Spiro tablet. Slater exhibits a nervous urgency, determined to get to elicit some basic truths. Legg is sly, hard to pin down. Best to start with simple facts first, like names and dates. Turning towards the seated figure, he begins his interrogation.

"On what date was ONE founded?"

"October 15, 1952."

"And where does this take place?"

"At the home of W. Dorr Legg, at the corner of Dalton and 27th Streets in Los Angeles."

"Who were the founders of the organization? Who planned the Articles of Incorporation?"

"A large number of people contributed to the creation of the Articles and the Bylaws of ONE, Incorporated. Many made suggestions and contributed ideas."

"And what name did you go by at this time?"

"Dorr Legg."

Slater's pacing stops. "Dorr Legg"?

"Yes, W. Dorr Legg."

Slater leans closer to Legg's face, watching his eyes intently. Legg matches Slater's gaze, cocking his head sideways and back at an awkward angle. "Is that your *true* name?"

"Yes."

Slater stands up slowly, and turns away from Legg to face the long mirror, where he knows the attorneys are watching. "When and where were you born?"

"Michigan, 1904."

"How long have you been a member of ONE?"

"Since its creation on October 15, 1952."

"What do your consider your current status with that organization to be?"

"I am a Director of ONE, Incorporated. I am also a member of the Board of Trustees in charge of ONE Institute."

"I see. And what names have you recently used for your work with ONE Institute?"

"My own name, W. Dorr Legg. Not only recently but at all times."

Slater pauses. He certainly did not expect this answer. For years, he had known and worked with this man as Bill Lambert. Though many at ONE had used pseudonyms, often in an effort to expand the named list of contributors, Lambert, to Slater's knowledge, had always used his own name, just as Slater and a few others had. Slater always thought of himself and Lambert as special in that regard—they had voluntarily put their true names on the magazine from the start, without any pseudonym to protect them. It was one of the bravest things they had done.

"Then who is Richard Conger?" Slater asked.

"Richard Conger is a fictitious name devised by the management of ONE as a house name. It is used as a pen name for whoever is performing the functions of editor of *ONE Magazine* at any particular time."

"Who is the editor of *ONE Magazine*?"

"*ONE* does not have a single editor but is edited by a committee. I am a member of that committee."

"Have you ever been business manager of ONE, Incorporated?"

"Yes."

"Under what names have you acted in that capacity?"

"W. Dorr Legg and William Lambert."

"Do you teach at ONE Institute?"

"Yes."

"Do you have a college degree?"

"Yes. An A.B., B.M., and an M.L.D."

"Is ONE Institute an accredited school?"

A voice interrupts from over a speaker in the ceiling. It is Hillel Chodos, Legg's attorney. "Objection! That question is irrelevant and is not calculated to lead to any evidence relevant to this action. I advise you not to answer, Dorr."

Slater pauses and then scratches a dark line across his note pad. He proceeds with his questions. "What are the subdivisions of ONE, Incorporated, Mr. Legg?"

"The subdivisions are the Bureau of Public Information and Lectures, ONE Institute of Homophile Studies, ONE Institute Quarterly of Homophile Studies, Publication Division, Research Division, and the Social Services Division. The Research Division is currently lacking an acting director, so the board of directors of ONE, Incorporated is conducting its activities for the time being."

"Has the Research Division ever received any grants or gifts?"

"Yes."

"What is the relationship between ONE's Research Division and the Institute for the Study of Human Resources, known as ISHR, which you recently formed with Don Slater and Antonio Sanchez?"

"There is no relationship between ISHR and the Research Division of ONE, Incorporated, except that both organizations are concerned with the study of similar problems."

"Did ONE, Incorporated, pay for the incorporation of ISHR?"

"Objection!" the voice of Chodos boomed again. "That question is irrelevant and is not calculated to lead to any evidence relevant to this action. I advise my client not to answer."

"It's okay, Hillel," Legg responded with a flick of his hand. "I don't think any harm will be done."

"Okay Dorr, but without waiving my objection, I will permit you to answer a few of the coming questions."

"Thank you, Hillel. And the answer is no, ONE did *not* give money to help pay for the incorporation of ISHR."

"And who were the organizers of the Institute for the Study of Human Resources?"

"W. Dorr Legg, Donald Slater, and Antonio Sanchez."

"Is Don Slater still a director of ISHR?"

"No. He was removed on June 5, 1965. He was sent a notice of his removal from the board."

"Please name those individuals that you allege are present voting members of ONE, Incorporated."

"Myself, Bonham, Boyfrank, Robert Newton, Gregory Coron, and Chet Sampson."

"When was Chet Sampson elected to voting membership?"

"At our annual meeting in 1965."

"Was Jim Schneider elected at that same time?"

"Yes."

"Who removes voting members of ONE?"

"The Directors present and voting at any regular meeting if they vote unanimously."

"Are the voting Directors ever asked to vote on the removal of the voting members?"

"No."

"Were the alleged new corporation members elected at the February 5, 1965 meeting asked to vote on the removal of Don Slater from ONE at that same meeting?"

"No."

"Who voted on the alleged removal of Jim Schneider from membership in ONE?"

"The Directors, specifically Legg, Bonham, and Boyfrank, for reasons deemed sufficient by them including, among others, Schneider's continued assertions that his election to membership was invalid and his continued manifestation of a disposition contrary to that of the Directors. In my opinion, Schneider has obstructed the corporation's work and employed dilatory tactics for that purpose. This was explained to Schneider when he was removed on May 16, 1965."

"And was Mr. Schneider allowed witnesses at his trial that day?"

"The proceedings that resulted in Mr. Schneider's removal were not a trial.

No witnesses are ever allowed in the course of such proceedings. In any event, no request was made by Schneider to have witnesses speak in his behalf."

"Humph. The purpose of a witness is to do just that, is it not? It seems unlikely that you would not admit Mr. Kepner simply because he had not asked permission to speak on Schneider's behalf. So who was present when Mr. Slater was allegedly removed from membership in ONE?"

"As per the By-Laws, ONE's officers—myself, Bonham, and Boyfrank— were unanimous in the decision. Schneider, Coron, Newton, Dyer, and Winn, as voting members, were present as observers."

"Was Don Slater permitted to speak in his own defense?"

"Slater failed to appear at 4:45, the noticed time, and he was removed at 4:55 by unanimous vote. He appeared soon after, at 5:00, stated that the proceedings were a farce, and asked if anyone wished to hear his side of the matter. Nobody did."

"And were you also present when Rudi Steinert was allegedly dropped from voting membership?"

"Yes. As with Schneider, I voted against him for reasons deemed sufficient in accordance with the By-Laws, including primary disloyalty to ONE, Incorporated."

"And Antonio Sanchez? Were you present when he, too, was allegedly dropped form membership?"

"Yes."

"And what of Morgan Farley? Didn't he resign from ONE too? and Fred Frisbie? What of Stella Rush and Irma Wolf? Isn't it true that Jim Kepner resigned twice . . ."[16]

"Objection," echoed the stern voice of Chodos. "This line of questioning is off the point and is immaterial to any of the issues at hand."

"Indeed, Mr. Chodos," said Slater, "it is most certainly pertinent. But if you insist, I'll forgive Mr. Legg's declination to provide an answer. But it is true, Mr. Legg, that despite the ongoing exodus of so many others, you have remained a voting member of ONE from it inception to today?"

"Yes, I have already stated so."

"And have you ever opened a bank account under the name of William Lambert?"

"Yes, as ordered by ONE's Directors."

"Have you ever opened a bank account under the name of W. Dorr Legg?"

"Yes, as ordered by ONE's directors."

"Who presides at Corporation meetings of ONE?"

"The Chairman. He also presides at Board meetings."

"Did the Chairman preside at meetings during the first year?"

"Until the adoption of By-Laws, meetings were held informally; thereafter, the meetings were presided over by the Chairman."

"Is it true that a lot of the business of ONE is conducted by the general consent of those attending meetings?"

"As a rule, yes. But it should be pointed out that business is not conducted *by* the general consent of those attending meetings; it is normally conducted *with* the general consent of those in attendance."

"Are the voting members of ONE permitted to vote on all questions concerning ONE?"

"The votes of voting members, other than Directors, are advisory only, except with reference to the election of directors and the election of voting members. The advisory votes may be disregarded by the Board of Directors if they so choose."

"Do the Directors frequently change the vote of the corporation members after questions have been decided?"

"Objection!" Chodos again. "Your question is unintelligible and the word 'frequently' not defined. However, it should be noted that such votes are advisory and are, therefore, not 'changed' when advice is rejected."

"Did you, Mr. Legg, or any of the other directors of ONE, Incorporated, acting at the time of or prior to the 1964 Annual Meeting, change the nominees agreed upon by the voting members for the 1964 election?"

"Objection!" answered Chodos instead of his client. "Your question is unintelligible and does not indicate by whom the alleged 'agreement' was made. The order of voting was established in accordance with the By-Laws and *Robert's Rules*."

Slater kept his composure. The time to challenge this response would come later.

"Did the directors of ONE, Incorporated, acting at the time of or prior to the 1964 Annual Meeting, change the nominees agreed upon by the voting members for the 1964 elections?"

Legg answered for himself this time. "The procedure for electing voting members is set forth in the By-Laws and in *Robert's Rules of Order*. The directors make nominations, and the Chairman establishes procedure. Discussion and agreement among the members with respect to such procedure has been customary, for the purpose of advising the Board of Directors and the Chairman."

The questions that followed focused on the controversial 1964 annual meeting. When asked about Sanchez's vote by proxy, Legg stated that he did not remember whether or not Slater had used the proxy during the first part of the meeting, although he admitted that the chair might have permitted it. Slater asked why, then, there was no mention of the refusal to allow Sanchez his proxy in the minutes. Legg responded that during that meeting the directors elected Harry Hay and Burnside members but that they had resigned during that same meeting because of Slater's antics. Legg shrugged aside Slater's observation regarding the irregularity of the voting procedure. It was up to the directors to make nominations and the chairman to determine the order of procedures—as simple as that.

As guided by Chodos, Legg's strategy here was to deny that the directors of ONE had enacted any procedure contrary to *Robert's Rules* and corporate policy. Chodos helped to keep Legg on target here, ensuring that any question Legg answered regarding procedure more in accordance with what *should* have happened rather than what did happen, as when Legg answered that the chairman had always voted as a member of the assembly as authorized by *Robert's Rules*, whereas the custom since the early days of ONE was for the chair to vote only in order to break a tie. As for the February 5 meeting, Legg stated that the directors had indeed legitimately continued the annual business meeting and that "adjournments from each session to the next succeeding one were made in accordance with the By-Laws and *Robert's Rules of Order.*"

As for his accusation that Slater was a thief, Legg said, "Slater took and removed the personal property of ONE, Incorporated, with intent to deprive the rightful owner (i.e., ONE, Incorporated) of such property and its possession; and that, in my opinion, such conduct amounted to theft by Slater." Legg might as well have said, "I said that he stole something, but I did not call him a thief." Moreover, as Jim Schneider has frequently reminded me, any alleged theft of such magnitude should warrant the calling the police immediately in order to best prosecute the thieves. Schneider adds, "It is amazing that forty years after, dolts for Dorr are still parroting this thieving allegation." As Schneider and the others of the Tangent Group saw it, Legg had been elusive throughout the entire process, bending facts and language to suit his needs.

None of Legg's responses to his interrogators surprised Slater, but they certainly intrigued him. Slater, who continually strove toward a higher understanding of people, had no clue regarding Legg's true motivations. At one point—totally out of character for him—Slater even consulted an astrologer for advice on how to proceed. As it turns out, Legg's needs were fairly obvious: his newfound philanthropic friend proved less generous than anticipated and the Venice Group needed cash.

Although both factions of ONE filed many papers and volleyed charges at one another continually through the rest of 1966, neither side accomplished much. Raiden filed an appeal in July and Chodos responded with a brief on August 3, 1966. Legg's faction added to their complaint the fact that although their income prior to the split had been approximately $49,000 per year, it had since dropped to less than $24,000, a direct result of the "wrongful acts of defendants."[17] In November, the court held a hearing at Chodos's request in which he asserted that Slater was in contempt of court, but nothing was resolved on the matter.

Schneider wrote to Slater on December 10, 1966, urging Slater to follow Raiden's advice and file a libel suit posthaste. "It appears to me your flirting with compromise in public pronouncements and conversations only weakens your position and gives the other faction some propaganda advantages . . . i.e., why would you be offering to compromise and get out of a mess if you were so right?" Schneider told Slater that such negotiations ought to have been done privately and kept confidential, and that a defamation suit was certainly in order. Slater, weary of the process, decided to let the matter rest.

The Venice Group showed signs of fatigue as well. Legg wrote to Erickson on January 7, 1966,[18] of his restlessness to "get some action out of Hillel if at all possible." He stated that many of the Friends of ONE were "starting to get discouraged," and this meant they had stopped providing financial support. To make matters worse, the printer had "cracked down" yet again, as a result of their excessive debt. "Still," Legg continued, "we have to see to it that the Magazine is regular. For nothing is so panic-inducing in people as signs of weakness on our part."

At this point, both Venice and Tangent groups comprised surviving factions of ONE, Incorporated, although both had attempted to discredit the other as illegitimate. Every faction has a leader surrounded by either a core of morally committed individuals or a following of paid contract groups, or mercenaries (Bailey 2001, 28). In this case, Slater and Legg clearly headed two distinct groups. It is interesting to note in retrospect that Legg used promises of power and influence to lure people such as Weaver and Boyfrank to the board. When things did not go as planned, Legg's supporters jumped ship shortly after Slater's mutiny, only to be replaced by others who would continue to do (or vote) as he desired. Of course, Legg's greatest asset was his attorney Chodos, ONE's paid legal bulldog financed, ultimately, through Reed Erickson. In sum, Legg was surrounded by what F. G. Bailey would call a "following," a team recruited and maintained through contractual agreements (2001).

When we turn to the Tangent Group, however, we do indeed find the core of ONE, Incorporated—surprisingly intact, in fact, as exemplified by the dedication of these individuals to the magazine from the time of the mutiny on. The fact that all but one of *ONE*'s editors continued to support Slater illustrates the strength of their allegiance to him and their commitment to *ONE Magazine*. Moreover, the unwavering dedication of this core of activists—Bullough, Slater, Glover, Schneider, Steinert, Ingersoll, and the Hansens—would continue to contribute to the homosexual rights movement in Los Angeles, helping to keep it alive and thriving for the next fifteen years, as I illustrate in the following chapters. Legg's organization, on the other hand, though well funded through the generous contributions of the Erickson Educational Foundation, illustrates Bailey's point that factions, once established, are difficult to maintain. Legg had to spend much of his time and energy "keeping the fabric in repair." Bailey likens such an organization to a machine in which "seven-eighths of its output [is] spent on its own maintenance" with only a small fraction left over for politics and mission statements, as will be seen (2001, 45).

A Break in the Case

In the spring of 2004, ISHR secretary Reid Rasmussen invited me to peruse the archives at ISHR's offices on Arlington Boulevard in Los Angeles. Among these files were letters between Legg and Chodos dating from the spring of 1966 to the final court grievance pertaining to the split, filed December 26, 1969. These documents provide rare insight as to the strategy as planned by Legg and, to a lesser extent, by Boyfrank—and to their underlying grievances and motivations. This was an incredible windfall for my project because, although I had access to Slater's side of the story, before this I could only guess at Legg's strategies and motives. It also meant that through much of the time that Slater had been accused of hoarding ONE's historic documents and records, copies were indeed on hand at ONE Institute.

These documents revealed an underlying need for money on ONE's side— an irony because, soon after the split, Legg's faction established an enduring relationship with the wealthy and philanthropic Erickson and his Erickson

Educational Foundation (EEF), a nonprofit organization launched in 1964. According to a letter to Chodos from Bonham dated June 9, 1966, the Venice Group had received nearly $6,000 in loans and $2,500 in contributions since the day of the split, April 17, 1965. The European tours for 1964, 1965, and 1966 added $8,780.20, $7,058.32, and $5,740.42 to the annual gross incomes, respectively. Bonham included a month-by-month breakdown of the income for the twelve months preceding and subsequent to "the property removal." ONE's income dropped from $48,914.34 the year prior to the split to $23,642.50 the year following—a staggering loss of $25,271.84 and a reduction of more than half. With this said, I now return the reader to the main narrative of the legal battle between ONE and Tangents. From here on out I will integrate information gleaned from all possible sources.

On January 16, 1967, California Supreme Court clerk William J. Sullivan transferred the case (2 civil 30272) to the Court of Appeals, first district, in the State Building in San Francisco (renumbered 1 civil 24237). Slater sent a letter on January 23 to the new presiding judge, requesting that "the court decide this case as soon as possible" because "the preliminary injunction which has been in existence a year and a half now has had a decidedly hurtful effect on our work."

During the summer and fall of 1966, Legg sent all kinds of materials he had gathered pertaining to Slater's continued obstinacy to Chodos, which he called "ammunition" in a letter to his counsel dated August 5. In the same letter, Legg expressed frustration that Slater continued to use the corporate letterhead for his new business, only with the old address crossed out and the Cahuenga address typed above it. With a letter to Chodos dated January 31, 1967, Legg enclosed a copy of the recent *Tangents* magazine, the September issue distributed four months late. Someone in the magazine had written a book review using the pseudonym of Robert Gregory while "the originator of that pen name works here at the office daily, as is well known to everyone at Cahuenga." Legg also referred to Richard Conger and Sidney Rothman although neither of these men "had ever written anything for *Tangents*, or would." Worst of all, Legg pointed out, the masthead of *Tangents* continued to contain the statement "published by the majority of the voting members of ONE." He concluded, "All of this is very irksome, especially when it all is being published with ONE's money."

On Tuesday, February 28, 1967, Legg and Slater negotiated a compromise in Chodos's Beverly Hills office. They agreed that the library would be halved and portions of it returned to the Venice Group. Slater would return all book service stock as well as all business records and a file cabinet that Legg said properly belonged to ISHR. A "jointly framed letter of explanation of the terms of settlement, including their agreement to desist from any further use of or claim to the name ONE, is to be prepared and mailed out." All of these conditions were to be met before the Venice Group would withdraw its case, "otherwise we proceed on the 14th as scheduled."[19]

In a letter to Chodos dated the following day, March 1, Legg thanked his council for "a good, healthy seminar on realism last night." He urged Chodos to keep up the pressure and to make sure that "the determination that has kept us going operates here in the case-settlement." He suggested that they put the "squeeze" on Hirsh-Graphics, from which he would "be more than happy to accept typeset in any amount from $5 worth up." As for the Bank of America, "[W]hatever can be squeezed can go toward your bill. How to squeeze?" Legg suggested that they "forget the unbelieving judiciary" and deal on ONE's own ground, publication. He suggested that they "tell the story in full and sparing neither feeling, names or whatever unless B of A acknowledges their guilt and comes clean by way of some restitution." Legg concluded by stating that since it appeared no damages would issue from the case against Slater, "it is going to be a long, slow pull with your bill."

In a letter to Chodos from ONE's president dated March 6, 1967, Bonham lamented that not all voting members of the board had managed to participate in the compromise proceedings. Reed Erickson especially had questions regarding the arrangement, and members Les Collins, Bill Sutherland, Chet Sampson, and Monwell Boyfrank had not been asked for their input. After consulting with Erickson, Legg's faction decided that the Tangent Group should relinquish no less than $2,500 in damages: "We agree that when any member feels so strongly on a matter like this the other Members should stand together on the point. We have all (again except Chet and Manuel) agreed that if Cahuenga is genuinely seeking an out of court settlement it must be because it is to their advantage to do so. Therefore, it should be worth something to them to scratch around."

Bonham noted that three of the Tangent Group members owned property, and they could stand to lose a lot "by receiving judgments from the courts." Of this $2,500, $1,500 would immediately go to pay Chodos, and the rest would help with "urgent expenses here." If they went to court, they would pay Chodos's bill off at the rate of $300 per month "starting as soon as judgment has been rendered."

Bonham presented this letter to Chodos on March 6. The next day, Legg wrote to Chodos himself[20] to express his disappointment that Chodos had opted to forego the $1,500 they had promised him. In fact, he had decided not to push for a cash settlement at all, which annoyed Legg immensely. Legg went on to enumerate the known assets of the Tangent Group. They had heard Glover offer to advance the entire $20,000 needed for the repossession security after the sheriff had taken the materials. Schneider, they knew, owned a valuable home and maintained a substantial income. Slater could borrow something against his own home or sell one of his two cars if necessary, plus he had family "scattered all over the area here; none of them are without means." Legg concluded, "They have well-heeled supporters all over the area, apart from those with houses, any of whom could be counted on for a bit here and a bit there, if the need were shown. We just don't buy the argument that they cannot come up with the money, yours and ours both." Legg had spoken to Herb Selwyn, a mediator in the process, who said that it was "only a matter of [saving] face" at this point. But Legg disagreed: "I hope you do not underestimate the feelings all of us have had to live with for the past two years or the personal deprivations and strain we have experienced. Lew [Bonham] has had no salary for eight weeks! We already have given up far more than should be asked of us. We have nothing more to concede and, come what may, have to stand by our convictions."

On March 15, 1967, Bonham sent a letter to Chodos following up on a phone conversation the two had earlier that day where they had discussed the terms of the settlement with the Tangent Group. During a corporate meeting the prior evening, the board of the Venice Group passed a motion to approve the settlement provided the Tangent Group returned the complete mailing list "as evidence of good faith on the part of Cahuenga." Since the Venice Group had withdrawn their demand for a cash reimbursement, they insisted instead that the Tangent Group return "all property originally removed . . . that is, all Corporation records, minutes, education notes, etc., all Library books, manuscripts, Book Service stock . . . property belonging to ISHR, all equipment, and that a joint letter agreeable to both parties stating the terms of the agreement be sent to the complete mailing list of both parties." The letter notes that Raiden received a continuance nearly two weeks prior with the understanding that the Tangent Group would relinquish the list "within a few days." Bonham wondered, "Is the agreement a part of the court record, and can it be enforced?"

Agreement of Settlement

In April 1967, the directors of ONE and HIC decided to draft an agreement of settlement[21] in effort to resolve the matter out of court. On April 25, W. Dorr

Legg, Chet Sampson, Lewis Bonham, Monwell Boyfrank, Gregory Coron and Robert Newton (as first parties) and Don Slater, William Glover, Rudolf Steinert, Joseph Hansen, and Antonio Sanchez (as second parties) signed the agreement of settlement. The recital of the agreement stated prior to April 18, 1967,[22] that "all of the individual parties hereto were members of or associated with ONE, Incorporated." This statement should have ended the which-is-the-real-ONE wrangling because each faction, up to that date, had some legitimate claim to represent some aspect of the original organization. This document clarified this point, stating that since April 18, 1965, all of the above-listed parties had "engaged in activities directed to the advancement of the homophile movement but have done so separately."

Slater's Tangent Group agreed to return to the Venice Group a copy of the mailing list[23] and all of the business records of ONE including minutes, business correspondence, and financial records. The Tangent Group would also relinquish some office furniture, including bookshelves, file cabinets, and the Adler typewriter. The library books were to be divided equally between them. As for file materials and records, "either group may reproduce whatever they wish." Such copying would be completed by July 1967, but the sharing of materials in the future was encouraged. The Tangent Group would retain the wooden file that held the library card file "including the card index itself." It also retained the editorial files and the directory of homophile organizations. These actions were to be carried out "with all possible speed," and any further problems or complaints would go to a board of arbitrators. Outside of such arbitration, each side waived any future claim for damages "arising out of any matters occurring prior to the date hereof." The case, number 864824, would be dismissed without costs to either side.

The Venice Group would continue to have the exclusive right to use the name ONE, Incorporated. Members of the Tangent Group would "resign altogether from all offices and memberships in the said corporation." Nor would they use the pseudonyms of Richard Conger, Alison Hunter, Marvin Cutler, or William Lambert in any of their future publications. As a final provision, both parties together would draft, sign, and distribute a letter explaining the compromise "to all interested persons."

A final draft of this letter was dated May 8, 1967, and asserted that "the expense, delay and the bitterness always attendant upon litigation have been sufficiently disadvantageous to both sides and to the Homophile Movement as a whole, as to make a compromise desirable." The Venice Group announced that it would continue to operate as ONE, Incorporated, and to publish *ONE Magazine*. The Tangent Group, operating from Cahuenga Boulevard, would "henceforth conduct its affairs, including the publication of *Tangents Maga-*

zine, under the organization name, Tangents." Lewis Bonham, president of ONE, Incorporated,[24] and Don Slater, editor of *Tangents,* signed the letter.

More than just a compromise, the agreement and its accompanying letter suggest that the two organizations had struck a legitimate truce. Neither side declared a victory; neither had lost the right to *be* and to *have been* ONE, Incorporated, albeit from that point forward ONE would exist as two distinct organizations. In a letter dated April 27, 1967, Chodos wrote to the clerk of the Court of Appeals in San Francisco, telling him that Case No. 2 Civil 30272 "had been settled and dismissed" on that day in the Superior Court of Los Angeles County. The deal had been struck, and ONE was now two.

The Founding of ISHR, HIC, and Christopher Street West (1965–70)

Those were the golden days, although we didn't know it.
—Billy Glover (referring to HIC's days on Cahuenga Boulevard)

While the Battle Raged . . .

Since the 1965 division of ONE, Incorporated, many have debated whether the split ultimately benefited or injured the homosexual rights movement in Los Angeles and in the greater United States. Legg's loyalists first branded Slater's mutiny a tragic crime and then a substantial blow that had been heroically overcome. Others called it a calamity from which the Los Angeles movement never recovered. This chapter presents brief historical vignettes, a series of independent battles demonstrating the significant gains made by activists for homosexual rights both in Los Angeles in particular and the nation writ large after the infamous schism of ONE, Incorporated.

John O'Brien, who participated in the Stonewall uprising and helped found the Gay Liberation Front in New York soon thereafter, believes that post-split both ONE and HIC "hobbled along for the next thirty years living mainly on their past important accomplishments." In his executive director's report to ONE/IGLA (International Gay and Lesbian Archives), presented to the directors on April 3, 1997, O'Brien made the following statement: "This feud was based upon the stubborn individual control exerted by Dorr Legg, that cost our Movement many activists and their lost energies. Most people fled this bitter battle for control of ONE, which wound up in the U.S. courts. Only shells of previous activism, vibrancy and creativity were left with both camps being suspicious (and jealous for control) of new people and energy."[1]

Although one could conclude that the division of ONE, Incorporated, polarized (and paralyzed) the Los Angeles movement for years afterward, I have concluded otherwise. As this chapter shows, each surviving faction of ONE—the Venice Group and Tangent Group—continued to function after the split, and each played vital roles in the ultimate success and longevity of the local movement.

As I have noted, ONE, like its progenitor Mattachine, was volatile from the start and division may have been inevitable as the organization expanded and matured. Sociologist F. G. Bailey (2001) observed that factions might arise (or intensify) when a "new kind of political resource" emerges that intensifies competition. My research suggests that the political differences within ONE intensified when new resources became available through the financial contributions of Reed Erickson and the Erickson Educational Foundation (EEF). These new resources may have emboldened Legg to the extent that he attempted to fire the editors and destroy ONE Magazine to further the interest of ONE's educational division, ONE Institute for Homophile Studies. Slater, who had seen Legg similarly depose prior editors and contributors such as Dale Jennings, Jim Kepner, and Corky Wolf, anticipated his own expulsion and acted preemptively. Slater's mutiny of April 18, 1965, was therefore a desperate act, but it was not deemed criminal in nature. Slater probably intended to gain leverage and force Legg into a compromise. Instead, Legg used the money channeled through the EEF to wage an extended court battle against Slater and the Tangent Group.

Many of the events to be described in the first part of this chapter occurred before ONE's division, during the two-year court battle. However, I found it too confusing to attempt to dovetail the histories described herein—especially that of the creation of the Institute for the Study of Human Resources (ISHR)—into the chronologic narrative hitherto presented. I leave it, then, to the reader to put some of the pieces together and consider how Slater and Legg were battling one another on two fronts in two sibling organizations (ONE and ISHR).

Beginning in the autumn of 1964, Slater and Legg tried to keep their roles and occupations within each organization distinct and separate. By the spring of 1965, they were no longer able to do so, and their frustrations with each other in one arena spilled over into the other, making confrontation and separation all the more inevitable.

Rather than attempt to assess whether the division of ONE was for the better or for the worse, this chapter presents historical highlights of both organizations to illustrate the success and limitations of each. As Joseph Hansen once told me, "There have been many, many, many events that have taken us to where we are today. I think pebbles more than boulders have built this mountain, on top of which we stand."[2] This chapter presents some of those significant though largely forgotten events, the smaller battles that helped further the cause for homosexual rights in Los Angeles.

Establishing ISHR

On Independence Day, July 4, 1964, a man telephoned ONE's offices and announced that he would like to offer financial support to the organization. The caller, Reed Erickson, said that he had recently established a philanthropic organization called the Erickson Educational Foundation, a nonprofit corporation based in Baton Rouge, Louisiana. Erickson had been a Friend of ONE for several years but had never contributed on a large scale. Legg and Slater both questioned the offer, assuming it would come with strings attached. Nevertheless, Legg decided to meet with Erickson in Baton Rouge in August, and in October he flew to New York to meet with Erickson and attorney William Kraker on the occasion of the Friends of ONE's meeting at the Waldorf Astoria (as described in chapter 7).

Erickson was a female-to-male transsexual and a patient of Harry Benjamin's. Born Rita Alma Erickson in El Paso, Texas, most of Erickson's childhood was spent in Philadelphia. There Erickson went by "Eric" and began associating with lesbians as early as high school. The father moved the family to Baton Rouge, Louisiana, where he located the headquarters of his lead smelting business. In Louisiana, Erickson attended Temple University from 1936 until 1940 and then graduated from Louisiana State University in 1946, as Devor notes, the "first female graduate from LSU's school of mechanical engineering" (2002, 384). Through the help of Dr. Benjamin, Erickson began the transition in 1963 to living and identifying as a male. The sex-change procedure was completed in 1965, which set a legal precedent in Louisiana (Devor 2002, 385).

In 1964, while still in the process of transitioning, Erickson advised ONE to develop a nonprofit corporation so that he and others could reap the tax benefit from their contributions. This organization, once it secured non-profit status, could receive the donations and then channel the cash back into ONE. Also, this organization could become a research foundation dedicated to scholarship and education, and ONE could continue to publish and push toward the reformation of laws pertaining to homosexuality (Devor 2002, 387). Erickson wrote in a letter to Legg dated August 11, 1964, "I agree with the Board that a research organization would be formed first and most promptly—to liberate you and Don was our first step."

On August 17, 1964, Legg wrote to Kraker[3] asking if he had heard from Erickson regarding forming the nonprofit research foundation. Legg wrote that he had discussed the matter with ONE's Board, which had agreed that there should be three incorporators, preferably "of academic stature," and that the articles of incorporation and bylaws should be "as modest and simple as possible," as ONE's had been. "We have found this to be greatly useful here in keeping us hewed right to the line," he explained. Two days later, Legg again wrote to Kraker, telling him that they had developed the following mission statement: "To promote, assist, encourage and foster scientific research, study and investigation of male and female homosexuality and various other types of human behavior; to advance education, educational facilities and the training of persons for the aid and betterment of persons having behavioral patterns which may result in social disorientation; to this end, to gather, analyze and evaluate from a unified point of view available data from the fields of anthropology, biology, medicine, psychology, law, religion and other studies."

The founders proposed several names for the new organization: Francis Bacon Academy; Institute for Sociocultural Research; Institute of Unified Behavioral Research; Edward Carpenter Foundation; Foundation (or Bureau or Institute) for Isophyllic Research; and the one ultimately selected, Institute for the Study of Human Resources (ISHR). In order for the new organization to maintain its tax-exempt status, the founders stipulated that it would remain "educational, scientific and charitable." ISHR would apply any profits earned toward research, scholarship, and publication.

On September 21, 1964, California's Franchise Tax Board granted ISHR exemption from franchise tax. Kraker forwarded this information to Legg four days later. Legg received it on the twenty-eighth, at which time he sent a note to Erickson stating that he looked forward to "spring[ing] the organization's incorporation as a surprise announcement at the Buffet and hope[d] to get some people to shell out for it." He also said that he would meet Erickson in Manhattan on Saturday and would stay at the Taft Hotel.

Upon his return from New York, Legg wrote to Erickson on October 17 to report that he and Slater had met with Kraker twice and had accomplished several things. The address for ISHR was now 509 South Beverly Drive, Suite 1, in Beverly Hills, California (the address of Kraker's law office). They had opened a bank account in ISHR's name. Legg wrote that he had "reported in full to our Board at ONE" and that he had set a corporate meeting for October 23: "Some of the Members appear to have difficulty in visualizing how the relationship between the two bodies can function to the advantage of both. The job that night will be to spell this out clearly so that we can then proceed at once with well-defined projects. If you have any further suggestions that would help to clarify things for the doubters do send them along, although I do find that [Kraker] and I both seem to arrive independently at precisely the lines of development you and I discussed both July 4th and in New York."

Kraker sent a memo to Slater and Legg on October 31, 1964: "Get those budgets and lists together pronto." On November 7, Legg responded with a brief note to Erickson, advising him they had "not been idle." Two major projects had been put on the table. Slater proposed a "massive Bibliography operation." Second, a "legal research project [was] laid out as to design but not as to staff and budget, although we know who we would propose if funds are ever available." Legg reported trouble at ONE, Incorporated, when the printer "lowered the boom about the size of our bill with him and refused to budge for a time."

On November 13, 1964, Don Slater, as vice chairman of ISHR, and W. Dorr Legg, as secretary-treasurer, sent a formal proposal to Erickson, ISHR's president, with a copy going to Kraker.[4] The business outline consisted of two primary sections, the first relating to administration of the new organization and the second pertaining to a Human Resources Joint Study Project to be directed by Merritt M. Thompson. The human resources project would involve four subdivisions. The first would be dedicated to human behavior research, and ISHR's board had approached a psychiatrist to put together a proposal for that project. The second project involved educational research. Legg would serve as chief of this section, with Lewis Bonham as secretary. The third was divided into four data-gathering subdivisions: bureau of anthropology, bureau of biological and medical research, bureau of legal research, and religious attitudes survey project. The fourth section, which included a full outline, budget, and timetable, was a bibliography project that Slater would organize and edit.

The leaders at ONE were well aware of the great need for a bibliography on matters pertaining to homosexuality. As Slater noted in his proposal, "a bibliography is almost always a useful tool in the scientific research of any subject." Although many other fields had compiled extensive bibliographies to facilitate research, none had yet been created for this controversial topic, so it would be "the first of its kind." Slater proposed including "every discipline which may encompass homosexuality" in the work. He estimated that it would take two months to properly catalog what had been published in history and another two weeks for religion. Law would take four months, as would sociology and anthropology. Slater allocated five months for literature; medicine and psychology would require six months each. Philosophy would require four weeks.

After organizing, compiling, and indexing, Slater estimated it would take three years to complete the job. His budget called for two professional researchers and one assistant to format the bibliography. Slater would head the project with his friend John D. "Jack" Gibson, his schoolmate from USC who now had ten years of experience working for technical libraries in the United States and abroad. Slater estimated the project would cost just under $75,000. The letter and initial proposal were delayed by over a week until Slater felt he had "given the matter enough study to warrant his signing." According to a November 21, 1964, note Legg sent to Erickson, Slater worried that "too complete an outline might tend to 'freeze' into a status quo and hamper alteration that might seem desirable later on." Slater wrote to Erickson himself on November 24, 1964, stating that he felt ISHR should be "light in weight and unencumbered." He sent his own proposal, which was similar to Legg's in many ways but at odds with it in others. Similarities in both texts, however, suggest that Slater and Legg could have created one document had they been on amicable terms with one another, willing to cooperate to unify the corporate vision. Instead, they left it for Erickson to sort out.

On December 23, 1964, Legg wrote to Kraker that he had received a $10,000 grant from the EEF for the year beginning the previous October 14. Legg said that the entire amount would go toward the bibliography project. He reminded Kraker that the three-year project called for an annual budget of $25,000 but this first check at least "enabled us to start, using part-time staff and putting off for now some of the more costly parts of the project." A note to Erickson on the same day thanked him for the check and stated that Slater and Glover had been given a leave of absence from their duties at ONE, Incorporated, "in order to spend time on the bibliography project," which of numerous projects proposed was determined by Kraker to be "the simplest one for us to begin with." On February 3, 1965, Legg sent a brief note to Erickson saying that the bar on the first floor of their Venice Street office had just closed "by police order" and suggested that now "would be an ideal time to approach [the owners] with a purchase offer." Although Erickson had already become ONE's most generous benefactor, Legg continually pressed for more.

Legg, as secretary-treasurer of ISHR, sent a draft copy of the corporation's bylaws to Kraker on March 15, 1965, with copies going to the other directors, Erickson and Slater. Slater wrote to Kraker on March 18 stating that he had been unaware that they had been waiting for official adoption of ISHR's bylaws to proceed with the federal tax-exempt status. He complained that Legg's version of the bylaws created an organization very different from what Slater had envisioned: "In fact, they sound almost word-for-word like those used for ONE, Inc." Slater asked for clarification on two matters, the number of directors there would be (Slater thought three was the number they had agreed on) and whether ISHR would be a membership organization. He advised Kraker that "ONE has had, and is having, considerable trouble from this class of voters"—if not "given a voice" in the administration of the corporation "they become virtually worthless or dissatisfied." HIC's records indicate that Slater's opinions were ultimately heard and that he, consequently, was the primary author of the bylaws as they were ultimately adopted, making him the unsung father of the organization.

As we have seen, Legg immediately began a campaign against Slater after the April 18, 1965, division of ONE, and he repeatedly berated Slater to Erickson, calling him a lunatic and a thief. In consequence, Erickson promptly removed Slater from the bibliography project, and Julian "Woody" Underwood was recruited in his place. So far as ISHR was concerned, Slater had become a nobody; only the lawsuit against him endured. In effect, to many of the Friends of ONE, Slater had been reduced to a legal entity—a rogue, a criminal, and a villain. Slater's followers had been exiled from ONE Institute and its events and effectively silenced through continued legal threats and public scrutiny. Legg and his mercenary attorney Chodos tried for years to crush the "outlaw" insurgents, yet in the end Legg could only watch in growing dismay (and to Chodos's great profit) as Slater's mutineered ship sailed on. The Tangent Group and its magazine pressed ahead while the Venice Group sallied forth into the waters of education. The organizations would continue to butt heads occasionally over the next twenty years, but, for the most part, they eventually learned that each would prove more successful in its selected endeavors the more it ignored the other.

The Bibliography Project

In March 1966, Underwood submitted a report on the bibliography project to Erickson. To date, three hundred citations had been compiled, but the listing would not be published for another "four to six months." Clearly, not much had happened with the project since Slater's exodus from ISHR.

Meanwhile, Vern L. Bullough had collected eight to ten thousand index cards of material for a similar project. Bullough and his wife Bonnie had been interested in homosexual issues since the 1940s through family connections on Bonnie's side.[5] They moved to the Los Angeles area from Ohio in 1959, and Vern became head of the San Fernando Valley chapter of the American Civil Liberties Union soon after their arrival. He contacted Slater and Legg at ONE's office on Venice Boulevard to marshal the information needed to persuade the Valley chapter to adopt a policy protecting homosexuals, transvestites, and transsexuals. With the backing of ACLU executive director Eason Monroe, Bullough was ultimately successful, and in 1964 the Valley chapter adopted the policy. In 1966, the ACLU adopted a national policy very similar to the one Bullough had drafted for the Valley, making Bullough a local celebrity within the southern California homophile community.[6]

Some of Bullough's bibliographic data needed to be verified for accuracy, so in 1966 he contacted Legg for help and learned that Legg had been "getting most of his money [from the EEF] to prepare a bibliography of homosexuality." When Bullough asked to see what Legg had done, Legg produced "ten pages of typescript of a possible outline" with no books listed at all. Bullough concluded that Legg had been "getting money under false pretenses, in a sense, to do it" and believes that most of the money went to fund the lawsuit against Slater. In any case, Bullough ultimately decided to entrust his bibliography, with over 4,000 items listed, to Legg.[7] After Underwood's death in 1970, Bullough was approached to take over the project.

Soon after Bullough took the project, ISHR signed a book contract with Garland and a deal was struck. Bullough would relinquish his data provided Legg would verify and correct any questionable information. At Bullough's insistence, Jim Kepner would be hired to type up the final draft, and Barrett W. Elcano, a librarian at California State University, Northridge, would assist as well. The Erickson Educational Foundation provided additional funds to complete the project. Slater, as stated, had been dropped from the project because of his role in the division of ONE the prior year, but Bullough found him and the HIC materials to be valuable resources.

Legg had agreed to process two hundred and fifty entries a day for the bibliography, but he soon fell behind. According to Bullough,[8] the project fell into disorder. Many of the non-English citations were especially difficult to verify, with the many German citations especially problematic. Garland finally published the two-volume *Annotated Bibliography of Homosexuality* in 1976, edited by Bullough, Legg, Elcano, and Kepner. (Following debate as to whether Legg or Bullough would be listed as first editor on the volume, an alphabetic listing was finally settled upon.) All royalties and the copyright for the *Bibliography* were assigned to ISHR.

The *Bibliography* sold very well, but the published copy still contained many errors and flaws. Legg approached Erickson for funds to compile a revised edition, and Erickson approved and agreed to fund the project. There was good work done on the new volume for a full eighteen months. Then, in 1980, a dispute arose as to who would be listed as primary author. Legg had lost out to Bullough the first time around; this time, he refused to be listed second, behind relative newcomer to the project Wayne Dynes, who had been working on a bibliography of his own in New York.[9] Disillusioned from the first encounter, Bullough refused to work with Legg on the project, and Legg now refused to work with Dynes. So the project stalled halfway to completion, the "L's" having just been compiled. Whereas the second, corrected bibliography project could have been a great contribution to homosexual scholarship, that project, like so many others, fell victim to what Dynes has called "poisonous animosities."[10] Although there never was an updated version of the *Bibliography*, Dynes completed an index of his own entitled *Homosexuality: A Research Guide*, published by Garland in 1987.

The Motorcade to Protest Exclusion of Homosexuals from the U.S. Military

The first National Planning Conference of Homophile Organizations (NPCHO) convened in Kansas City, Missouri, over the weekend of February 19, 1966, with the hope of unifying the fifteen homophile organizations then working in the United States (Shilts 1993, 66). Prior to the conference, Del Martin, representing the board of trustees of the San Francisco–based Council on Religion and the Homosexual (CRH), sent a letter to participating organizations proposing that an item be added to the conference agenda. Martin recommended that the combined organizations of NPCHO coordinate a national day of protest on the upcoming Armed Forces Day, on

May 21. Martin suggested a town-hall type of meeting in each participating city that would include "speakers representing the military, the selective service board, the clergy, the legal profession and the homophile community."[11] Slater took Martin's idea and devised a slightly different scheme: a motorcade protesting the armed forces' policy of forbidding gays in the military (Shilts 1993, 65–66).

After the conference, communications continued between organizations in Kansas City, Los Angeles, New York, Philadelphia, San Francisco, and Washington D.C., but the national effort faltered and in some quarters "outright opposition to the program was voiced" (Slater 1966). Still, through the joint leadership of Slater and Hay, the Los Angeles Committee continued to push on. Beginning on March 8, 1966, Slater dedicated the Cahuenga office and entire Tangents facility to the needs of Harry Hay and the newly formed Los Angeles Committee to Fight Exclusion of Homosexuals from the Armed Forces. Hay, John Burnside, Billy Glover, filmmaker Don Schneider, Don Slater, and Jano Cybulski were the most active committee members.

Slater and Hay cochaired the biweekly planning meetings to organize the motorcade (Slater 1966). According to Randy Shilts, the committee issued a press release on February 28 announcing that the military, while "publicly paying lip service to the idea that homosexual persons are unfit for military service, has quietly instructed induction centers to make discreet 'exceptions' to the rule [in] the case of homosexuals who are not the 'obvious' types" (1993, 66). On March 18, 1966, the committee distributed the following paragraph, printed on strips of yellow paper:[12] "The pressing need for change regarding the draft status and treatment of homosexuals in the armed services is a national issue on which the homophile organizations of the U.S. have agreed to work together on a national basis by arranging simultaneous meetings in such cities as San Francisco, Seattle, Denver, Chicago, New York, Philadelphia, Washington, Miami, Boston, and Los Angeles on May 21st. To coordinate the work in the Los Angeles area the Committee to Fight Exclusion of Homosexuals from the Armed Forces was established in the local area sympathetic to the homosexual." The statement concluded with a call for assistance and action of interested parties and groups to be coordinated locally and through NPCHO.

That same day, the committee issued a formal statement in response to General Hershey's warning regarding "a dangerous shortage of eligible men to serve in the armed forces." The committee's statement complained that over seventeen million people were denied the right to join the military "simply because they are homosexual." Further, the committee complained that men who wanted to evade the draft often did so by posing as homosexuals or affecting stereotypic homosexual mannerisms, such as an occasional flick of the wrist (Shilts 1993, 67). The statement noted that "millions of homosexual men and women have served with honor as soldiers, sailors, airmen and marines in the wars of our country," but in order to do so, they had to "swear falsely before the examining boards, denying the truth about themselves under oath." Many of those (like Billy Glover) had been discharged upon suspicion or discovery of homosexual behavior. The committee urged sympathizers to write to the president and their congressional representatives "to protest this waste of needed manpower and the unjustified denial of the right of a loyal citizen to serve his country in war; and close this loophole for draft evaders." The address and phone number of the Cahuenga office concluded the statement.

Los Angles Times columnist Paul Coates interviewed Hay and published his opinion on Sunday, April 14, 1966. Hay argued that homophiles had every right to serve in the armed forces: "People are always afraid that the homophile won't be able to resist temptation in an all-male community. . . . They forget that we've had to learn control all through life." Coates asked Hay why he used the term "homophile" rather than "homosexual," and Hay replied, "Because it's a word that expresses much more. . . . It has an implication of spiritual love, while homosexual is a legal term relating to people who commit specific sexual acts." It is interesting that Hay did not use the word "gay" in this interview, suggesting that, even as late as 1966, the term had not yet taken on the political and identity-based connotations that are commonly associated with it today. It is also interesting to note how both terms, "homosexual" and "homophile," did not suit the needs of the activists nor the media. Both words began to seem cumbersome and uncomfortable as they entered into the public discourse in the mid-1960s.

Coates concluded in his commentary that the entire campaign was a waste of time. He cited Colonel M. P. Difusco, of the office of the assistant secretary of defense, who quipped, "We're responsible for a lot of young kids. If we throw them in with homosexuals, we wouldn't have an army; we'd have chaos." Coates concluded that homosexuals did have one worthy cause. "The argument for a change in the penal code that would make their deviation no crime providing it was the private act of two consenting adults, is an argument of merit. . . . But it's almost tragic that they chose to make their stand for acceptance by demanding the right to join the army. Such a totally impractical idea turns a serious social problem into material for a burlesque skit."

On Tuesday, April 26, the committee met at the Cahuenga office to decide on slogans for placards and signs. Slater presented a sheet from the Legalize Abortion Society on the proper way to carry a placard that they found useful. Slater also reported that James H. Harris, of the seventh district attorney's office, had called to offer his support and assistance "in avoiding incidents." Slater had agreed to meet with him prior to the event. Slater also reported on the ACLU conference he had attended with Legg at the Hotel del Coronado in San Diego the day before. By invitation of Vern Bullough, Slater and Legg both participated on a panel entitled "Sexual Freedom: How Free?" on the final day of a weekend-long ACLU conference at the historic hotel. (Bullough would speak again at an ACLU chapter meeting in Hollywood two days later, on April 28.) Finally, the motorcade route was planned, and the committee members agreed to begin and end near Slater's home in Echo Park and conclude by 4 p.m.

On May 1, the committee began distributing maps of the motorcade route and information regarding the protest through a leaflet campaign directed to gay bar patrons. They received little community support for the motorcade and virtually no response to their fund-raising efforts although they had distributed leaflets in selected locations from Topanga Canyon to Long Beach. The night before the motorcade, committee members created sixty picket signs and confirmed the drivers' route.

Photographers from *Time* magazine were on hand early in the day of the event. When provided the opportunity, Hay spoke out to the journalists against his fellow gays who had not assisted with the event and would probably not even participate. "With [all of] the work we've put into this thing and with the thousands of homosexuals in the area, it is fantastic to realize we will be lucky to have forty persons show up for the motorcade tomorrow— and at least twenty who do will not be gay." Sergeant Wesley Sherman of the LAPD's department of special events asked the organizers, "If you want to go into military service, why don't you just sign up?" Slater replied in an article about the motorcade, published in the May 1966 edition of *Tangents*, that a desire to go into the service was not the question. Slater pointed out, "Most other Committee members had already served and had been honorably discharged." The issue was simply that "homosexuals are asking for equal rights and benefits from their country. At the same time they recognize their equal duties and responsibilities." When the motorcade began, at 2:00 in the afternoon on Saturday, May 21, the only Los Angeles newspaper to take an interest was the *Free Press*. The city editor of the *Los Angeles Times* said that he would dispatch a reporter "only if someone was hurt."

Jim Schneider drove car six; Vern and Bonnie Bullough rode in the first car. Thirteen cars comprised the caravan, each with signs and banners bringing attention to the cause. Vern Bullough recalled surprisingly little reaction to the motorcade—most people just stared as it went by. The motorcade proceeded on without incident except that, at some point, the car that Hay drove got lost or diverted, and it and another car or two went off in a different direction. All managed to meet back up at the office on Cahuenga where they celebrated and congratulated themselves.

Although not a major event, the motorcade had symbolic significance, and some people had paid attention. Bullough described it as a complicated matter. When he and Bonnie arrived to lend their support, they had not expected to be ushered into the first car in honor of his work with the ACLU. Vern was not entirely comfortable even participating: "I was basically opposed to what we were doing because we were saying that gays could should be drafted and serve and I was opposed to the war! But I went."[13]

CBS News ran a two-minute report on the motorcade that night, and the next day Harry Hay and John Burnside appeared on the Melvin Belli show to discuss the results of the action. They later appeared on the Joe Pyne radio show to discuss the status of homosexual rights in general. Pyne interviewed Slater on the success of the protest in other parts of the country later, on May 26.

Meanwhile, the whole affair only frustrated Dorr Legg. He wrote in a letter to Erickson dated Thursday, April 21, that media hounds were regularly calling his office for information since the New York Times News Service had distributed under a Los Angeles heading "a three-column story about homosexuals and the armed forces quoting Slater from one end of the story to the other with wild talk about 'a homosexual motorcade' to drive down Wilshire Boulevard with loudspeakers." To Legg's dismay, the *New York Times* reported that *Tangents* magazine was "an outgrowth of a now defunct publication called *ONE.*" Legg further complained that the DA's office had visited the Venice office, "wondering if there are to be riots in connection with these military demonstrations! Hillel has been alerted on all these matters of course."

Sad Days for Kepner

While Slater and Legg were getting all sorts of attention in 1966, Jim Kepner felt that the time was ripe for him to take action, too. So he began an ill-fated venture that ultimately cost him his Baxter Street home. Ignoring the advice of his friends and associates, Kepner mortgaged his house to secure the capital needed to launch a new magazine to be entitled *Pursuit and Symposium.* The magazine he envisioned would serve a dual purpose. The *Pursuit* portion of the magazine would aspire to "project somewhat an image of homosexuality as a whole—if that is possible" (Kepner 1966a, 7). *Symposium* would present differing views and perspectives; in this case, the transcription of a discussion on morality featuring a philosopher, a judge, a Baptist clergyman, a psychoanalyst, and an anthropsychologist. Kepner wrote most of the *Pursuit* portion himself, crediting some of his old pen names. As Lyn Pedersen, he contributed "A Gay Camp Looks at the Camp Cult." As Robert Gregory he wrote an article on "Censorship in 1966," and as Frank Golovitz he authored a short story called "He That Loveth His Life."

In an editorial titled "Toujours Gai," Kepner uses the pronoun "we" when referring to himself in the first person, as a form of "gay editorial." In this article, Kepner wrote of his childhood and his first sexual experiences. As for the creation of *Pursuit and Symposium,* he noted that because of the recent split of ONE, Incorporated, into two factions, "where there was *ONE Magazine,* there are two. We now make it three." He added, "Many fine friends, with less intimate experience of the trying problems that tear at such small volunteer groups as One, feel this ought not to be so. We need unity, they say. Good, when possible. But don't we also value diversity? If we can't all work together in harness, we ought as least to keep working" (1966a, 23). Kepner argued that enough room existed in the field for his magazine and even others. Unfortunately, he was wrong. After two issues, Kepner went bankrupt and lost his house.

While thousands of people across the country and overseas had read Kepner's news reports and essays, Los Angelenos increasingly knew him as an archivist. He was always pleased when others expressed their interest in homosexual history, and he often invited them to peruse his personal archives of homosexual-related ephemera, which he had continued to collect since his days in San Francisco. Late in 1978, Kepner would move his vast collection from his apartment—which the Reverend Florine Fleishman[14] described to me as filled to overflowing with piles of books, newspapers, and magazines—into a storefront on Hudson Street, which some teasingly compared to a Christian Science Reading Room. Though poor to the end of his days, Kepner was content to live within this slush pile of history, and through his efforts he managed to curate one of the nation's first and perhaps greatest collections of homophile materials.

The Women

On December 16, 1967, Don Slater and HIC hosted a special event to bolster their legal defense fund. In the Embassy Auditorium at the corner of Ninth and Grand in downtown Los Angeles, they held a benefit performance of *The Women*, a comedy by Clare Boothe Luce popular within the homosexual community since its release in 1939 as an MGM blockbuster directed by George Cukor starring Joan Crawford and Rosalind Russell. According to Glover, Don Schneider (no relation to Jim Schneider) was the behind-the-scenes producer of the show, in which men in drag played *all* roles. Lyle Paige was director and Don Showman, as HIC's director of social functions, was producer. (Showman had directed the premiere of James Barr's play *Game of Fools* for the ONE Institute convention in January 1960.) The cast of fifteen included mostly professional performers with three first-timers. Lark Ballard, a dancer from the Midwest who had performed professionally in Omaha and Kansas City, played the role of Mrs. Howard Fowler. Crystal Allen was played by a professional drag queen, actually called "Chrystal," who had performed for seven years in Honolulu and then a decade longer in Hollywood. One of the performers first cross-dressed for the U.S. Air Force and had since traveled across the country performing in drag. Morris Kight promoted the event.

Jim Schneider was in the audience of about three hundred the night of the performance. He recalls some commotion coming from the entrance lobby shortly after the play began, but none of the patrons knew what took place until after the show. Six LAPD vice officers attempted to disrupt and cancel the performance, claiming that the group had not secured a permit. The officers also wanted to watch for lewd behavior. When they asked who was in charge, Slater presented himself. One officer peeked in at the audience and proclaimed, "There's nothing but fags and queers in there!" Slater rebuffed him and was cuffed and promptly taken to jail. Undaunted, Slater berated the officers all the way to the station for wasting taxpayers' money. Ultimately, the charge of not having a permit was dismissed, and Slater scored another victory when the police commission later decided to change its censorship policy regarding cross-dressing in a theatrical performance.

It is difficult to capture the cantankerous spontaneity of Slater's wit and daring at this time, but episodes such as this demonstrate why he was so admired by his cohorts at HIC. As Glover has remarked, "What is hard to put on paper that showed Don's truly remarkable character is how he constantly used the courts to make his points and try to force others to be honest." Glover recalled an incident in which he went with Slater as a witness, in case of Slater's arrest, to confront the customs office for withholding a European publication, probably either *Revolt* or *Vennen*. Slater asked to see the magazine. When the clerk complied, Slater snatched it from the man's hands and said, "Oh yes, this is ours!" He then proceeded to leave the office with the clerk behind him saying, "Mr. Slater, you can't do that . . .!" and a bemused Glover shuffling behind. Slater proceeded to the elevator with his prize, and they left.[16]

The Founding of HIC

In the spring of 1968, the Tangent Group was struggling financially. It cost $700 a month to produce *Tangents* magazine, or $8,400 per year. With an annual subscription cost of $7.00, the magazine required twelve hundred paid subscribers to "maintain the monthly publishing schedule." In a notice to subscribers in March 1968, Slater reported that during the prior year they had less than half the required subscribers to cover their expenses, and therefore they had only printed six issues for the year. Until subscriptions increased, *Tangents* would continue publishing bimonthly.

Despite *Tangent's* poor performance, HIC officially filed its articles of incorporation with the State of California on August 14, 1968. Herb Selwyn, the attorney who had helped to incorporate the Mattachine Society in 1954, acted as representing counsel. Secretary of State Frank M. Jordan formally filed the articles of incorporation on November 4, 1968. The name of the corporation became Homosexual Information Center, a General Nonprofit Corporation in the State of California. Slater selected this name so that people looking for information on homosexuality would easily find them in the phonebook. The HIC's primary purposes were "to conduct a continuing examination into the nature, circumstances and social issues of homosexuality, and to generate, gather, organize, make available and broadcast the best current thought on sexual questions generally." The property and assets of the corporation were "irrevocably dedicated to education and literary purposes," and the founding directors were Glover, Schneider, and Slater.[15] Billy Glover secured permission from the State of California for HIC to conduct transactions under the fictitious name the Tangent Group on March 6, 1969. HIC received federal tax-exempt status two years later, in 1971.

Picketing the Los Angeles Times

In October 1969, the editorial board for the *Los Angeles Times* refused to publish an advertisement for a pair of one-act plays titled *Geese*, playing at the Coronet Theatre. The play portrayed two young (and occasionally nude) male lovers vis-à-vis their parents, but the *Times* refused the ad on the grounds that it was against their policy to print the word "homosexual" (Kepner 1997). HIC had been asked to lead discussion groups after performances on Wednesday and Sunday evenings. Outraged at the newspaper's refusal, Don Slater, Joe Hansen, and Morris Kight met with the editorial board of the *Times* face to face. At 11:15 a.m. on October 29, in the office of the editor Mr. Moldanado, Paul Rothermell, administrative assistant in charge of advertising, said that the *Times* was a family paper and that the policy against using the word had been in place for a long time. So Slater and crew left to obtain a permit from a grudging judge to picket the *Times*, which they did from 10:00 a.m. until 2:00 p.m. on November 5.

Hansen's lover Wayne Placek helped to distribute a press release, issued on October 16, that read, "The *Times* by its attitude shows that it is cold and indifferent to the efforts of homosexuals to improve their legal and social position in America." As a key player of the homosexual rights movement and a legally chartered California corporation, HIC asserted that its name was hardly a put-on. "The *Times* might like to forget that there are some 200,000 homosexuals living in the Los Angeles area . . . [and] these men and women will not go away simply because the *Times* shuts them out of its advertising vocabulary." The *Times* would not so malign any other minority—"The reaction against such a restriction would be so spontaneous and so strong that even this leading paper would feel the pressure." HIC distributed announcements in gay bars the week prior to the protest, but none of the bar goers showed up. HIC's minutes regarding this lack of community involvement simply state, "This action appears to have been without result."[17]

Despite the small turnout, the protest and ensuing boycott proved very effective. Joseph and Jane Hansen created most if not all of the signs for the protest, and they marched the entire time with a dozen or so others. Representatives from *The Advocate* and the (nonhomosexual) Coalition Against Repression also joined in, and Leo E. Laurence of San Francisco's Institute for Homosexual Liberation was also there picketing. Local radio and television stations covered the protest, and Slater and Joe Hansen were both interviewed. The result was a success. As Jim Schneider put it, "Now somebody took notice at the *Times,* and I daresay Don brought about the beginning of the end for such a lily-livered policy." He added, "Yes, people today don't know what it was like back in those hectic days. Surely this was a significant victory for all homosexuals in the Los Angeles area."[18]

Introducing Morris Kight

Of all of the activists discussed so far, Morris Kight was arguably the most progressive. Boisterous and bold, Kight was a true pioneer and way ahead of his time. So far as I can tell, Kight was the first Los Angeles activist to regularly use the term "gay" in his contemporary parlance, and it is fair to say that he helped to import an ethos of gay liberation from the east. Kight claimed that he "never agreed with the basic goals or philosophies of the homophile efforts," although he did recognize that much of their work was important. He agreed with their mission of gathering and disseminating information, but he felt the homophiles were too conservative and could never "be reformed into any kind of radicalism."[19]

Kight moved to Los Angeles in 1957 at the age of thirty-eight (Picano 2002). By the time he settled into his Westlake Park neighborhood, he had years of experience as a political activist, having worked for several civil and environmental rights agencies. At some point in the 1960s, he founded an organization called Gay and Lesbian Resistance, which sought not only to further the rights of gay and lesbian people but also to work toward improving "social issues such as health care and poverty in general" (Picano 2002, 402). Kight's Gay and Lesbian Resistance began calling itself the Gay Liberation Front (GLF) soon after the Stonewall uprising and the founding of the Gay Liberation Front in Manhattan (Picano 2002).

Beans for Queens

The first organized demonstration of the GLF in Los Angeles was the protest of Barney's Beanery in February 1970. Barney's was a famous restaurant located at 8447 Santa Monica Boulevard in West Hollywood that used to display a plank inside with the words FAGOTS [*sic*] STAY OUT painted on. This sign was first posted in the 1930s in order to "ward off police pressure" (Kepner 1988, 2). Upon moving to Los Angeles, Jim Kepner refused to attend Mattachine discussion groups that were held in Barney's because he objected to sitting in the same room as that "antique" sign (Kepner 1994, 11). Sometime after the 1930s, Barney's management and clientele began to take the sign seriously. Homosexuals were vigorously excluded from dining there in the 1960s, and the West Hollywood police department encouraged this action (Kepner 1988, 2).

While some of HIC's members participated in the Barney's protest, feisty Don Slater decided to protest the protesters. On February 7, 1970, he issued a press release titled "Fagots for Staying Out of Barney's Forever, Associated." "For over 35 years Hollywood Fagots have managed to boycott Barney's Beanery," Slater reminded his readers. "Miss Barney herself, in a moment of high fagotry, was compromised into placing our slogan 'Fagots Stay Out' on the wall of her Beanery. Now a lot of do-good kai-kai sisters and trade queens are spoiling all the fun."

"Miss Barney has a right to ask us to stay out," Slater asserted. Likewise, "fagots" had every right to boycott. He continued, "So what's all the fagoty fuss? Help us keep a fagot's faith. Please don't cross the picket line. Join our efforts to boycott Barney's. Fight fagots fight! Remember the slogan: 'Fagots Stay Out.' The release was signed "Fagots for staying out of Barney's Forever, Associated," and HIC's post office box was provided.

After a solid week of picketing by Morris Kight and the others, Barney's relented and the restaurant manager handed Kight the sign. The picketers went home, victorious. The surrender was a mere feint, though, and Barney's soon put up another in its place. This second sign did not come down until 1985 (Cole 2004). In 1999, USC cinema student Andrew Colville released a documentary on Morris Kight called *Live on Tape: The Life and Times of Morris Kight: Liberator*, which the doyen Kight called a "videograph of the historical record." Although Slater may have boycotted the boycott, others at HIC apparently did participate. Colville's documentary contained footage of someone marching with a sign bearing the HIC logo, which represents the international symbol for sex and was designed by Jane Hansen.

L.A.'s First Gay Pride Parade

On May 1, 1970, Kight and the Reverend Bob Humphries contacted Troy Perry to discuss the idea of commemorating the first anniversary of the Stonewall rebellion. Perry, who had launched the Metropolitan Community Church in the fall of 1968 (see Perry 1972; Perry and Swicegood 1990), suggested a parade, and the idea immediately caught on. Knowing they would need to start an organization to launch such a crusade, they immediately came up with the name Christopher Street West. They proposed to march down Hollywood Boulevard on the last June Sunday of 1970. To begin the campaign, Kight made and distributed three thousand pink and lavender buttons that read, "GAY POWER/CHRISTOPHER STREET WEST '70" (LA Pride). The Reverend Perry helped to promote the event through a sermon delivered on Flag Day, June 14 (Perry 1972, 158–64).

Perry and Kight met with the police commission, headed by Chief Edward M. Davis, who told them that as far he was concerned, homosexuality was illegal, and therefore "granting a parade permit to a group of homosexuals to parade down Hollywood Boulevard would be the same as giving a permit to a group of thieves and robbers" (Perry 1972, 162). The commission decided to grant the permit provided the group posted two bonds totaling $1.5 million. The group was also asked to pay $1,500 "for the policemen that it will take to protect you." Unless a minimum of 3,000 people participated in the march, the celebrants would have to stay on the sidewalk.

Perry and Kight brought the case to the attention of the ACLU, which recommended they contact attorney Herb Selwyn. When Selwyn appeared with Perry before the police commission on Friday, June 19, they dropped the bond request but not the protection fee. The next Monday, June 22, Kight and Perry appeared before the California Supreme Court. The Court granted their request for the permit and instructed the police to "protect us as they would any other group" (Perry 1972, 164).

The parade commenced on Sunday, June 28, and registered groups proceeded in chronological order behind a Volkswagen Microbus blaring prerecorded marches (as there was not enough time to secure a real marching band). A group from Orange County carried a sign that read "Homosexuals for Ronald Reagan." Another said "Heterosexuals for Homosexual Freedom." One controversial float featured a man on a cross with a sign before him that read "In Memory of Those Killed by the Pigs." A campy "flock of shrieking drag queens [followed,] . . . running every which way to escape club-wielding guys dressed as cops" (Perry 1972, 165–66).

"The parade was super silly and very ragtag," said Joseph Hansen, who observed from the sidelines that day. "Nobody had any money for the floats or anything but somehow or other, they threw out a few sequins and a bit of tulle, and some paint, and got out there and did it the best we could." While ragtag, the event was spectacular in its own right, and the spirit of the event was astonishing. "Nobody knew whether we were going to have mobs dragging us down off the floats or what was going to happen," Hansen explained.

"And of course it didn't happen that way at all! Everybody just smiled and waved, if they paid any attention at all."[20]

When I asked Hansen to describe an event or occasion he had experienced working within the movement that particularly stood out in his memory, he chose to describe his feelings and experiences on this day. He had served on the planning committee as HIC's representative. He recalled that some of the people involved wanted the parade to be funny while others wanted it serious. "I did my best to mediate that and so we got a good mix—or we got a *mix*—of funny, and serious, and in between."

Hansen described the event as "*electrifying*. It really was. It startled people, but I think the most amazing thing about it was its effect on homosexuals." He recalled standing across from the Pickwick Bookshop at 6743 Hollywood Boulevard. He had worked for the Pickwick years before, and a man with whom he used to work (Lloyd, still employed there) was watching from in front of the store. When Lloyd spotted Hansen, he hollered out across the street, "JOE! Isn't this wonderful! Isn't this a *marvelous* day! Can you imagine this ever happening?" And Hansen realized the parade's great success and that it had indeed marked a change in social awareness: "The fact of the parade, the fact that nobody threw eggs or rotten tomatoes at it, and nobody jeered—people stood and smiled as it went by—was a *huge* shock and a very pleasant one to people like Lloyd, and there were thousands of them in Los Angeles at that time. I think it just showed homosexuals that being bold, being brave, and coming out was not going to have the awful results that everybody always feared. Those days were past; they were behind us. And *that* was a thrilling day. That was a *thrilling* day. . . ." Morris Kight likewise referred to his leading this parade as the happiest moment of his life (Colville 1999).

Perhaps not surprisingly, Don Slater stayed at home that day just as he had for the Barney's campaign. Slater was not a fan of the Reverend Perry, whom he thought was a gay separatist and therefore a "false prophet" (Hansen 1998, 70, 75). When I asked Hansen to describe Slater's response to the parade, he replied: "Don probably grumped and huffed and puffed and didn't think it was a good idea. Don was an integrationist, as I am. He didn't really think that anybody ought to make a spectacle of himself, you know. Don was perfectly frank about being gay, about being a homosexual. But as for making a big deal of it, as for being a bird of bright plumage, no. No, that was not for him."[21] Still, Slater agreed that HIC should play a role, and thus Joe Hansen became the organization's official emissary to Christopher Street West. Hansen also interviewed Perry after the parade for his homosexual-themed radio show, broadcast on KPFK.

The (Late) Great David Brandstetter

> Before, the detective had a dame on his arm, a whiskey on
> the bar and a revolver in his hand. Dave Brandstetter was
> just as smart, just as tough and yet he had a gay sensibility.
> That was like a bombshell for me.
> —John Morgan Wilson (as quoted in Valerie Takahama,
>   "Alive and Writing")

In 1970, Joan Kahn of Harper & Row published Joe Hansen's novel *Fadeout*. Kahn, a leading editor in mystery and suspense fiction, favored books that broke into new territory. She had also published the first novel featuring a black detective (Winn 1997, 28). Kahn's instincts paid off—*Fadeout* was a great success that remains in publication today, having been recently reprinted by Alyson Books and the University of Wisconsin Press. Solomon Hastings, in an article titled "Homosexuals in the Mystery: Victims or Victimizers?" assessed Brandstetter's acceptance by the largely heterosexual audience at the time: "Brandstetter is the most honestly portrayed gay in crime fiction: a middle-aged man—who happens to be homosexual—with mundane, everyday problems. Some of his cases involve homosexuals, others do not. He develops romantic relationships, but he does not let his personal life style interfere with his work. It merely adds richness to his character in much the way any ongoing heterosexual relationship deepens anyone else's life. Written in the dry style common to all West Coast detective and private eye stories, Hansen's work has found an audience beyond the gay community . . . with Hansen the homosexual in crime fiction finally achieves three-dimensionality" (Hastings 1997, 495).

The Brandstetter books became popular because Brandstetter was a "cool guy"—people could relate to him, partially because he was, in many ways, a typical sleuth. "My joke," Hansen told one reviewer, "was to take the true hard-boiled character in American fiction tradition and make him a homosexual. He was going to be a nice man, a good man, and he was going to do his job extraordinarily well" (Takahama 1998). Whereas male homosexuals were believed to be promiscuous and incapable of long-term romantic relationships, Hansen, whose own marriage to Jane lasted fifty-one years, portrayed Brandstetter otherwise: "While Dave's relationship with his lover has lasted twenty-two years, his father has been married nine times. . . . It's as if the only people who couldn't have relationships that lasted are homosexuals, and of course that isn't true. It's far from the truth" (Takahama 1998, 4). Hansen ushered Brandstetter through twelve volumes before retiring him permanently in 1991.

Troubles from Without and Within

After ten years of continued support, Joe and Jane Hansen resigned from HIC on June 21, 1977, prompted by a letter they had received from Glover taking them to task for "failing to contribute substantively to HIC and its activities." In his letter of resignation, addressed to Slater, Hansen voiced his many frustrations with Glover and credited him with the demise of *Tangents*. Glover had been in charge of distribution—which by the end of 1969 had become virtually nil. Since the magazine's demise, Glover had started "writing letters directed at many quarters of our society, letters he plainly believes to help right wrongs, correct erroneous positions, and generally aid the cause of homosexuals." Hansen severely criticized Glover's "ill-advised [though] numerous missives." He stated that in a recent radio address, in which he had criticized Morris Kight and Troy Perry for hurting the homosexual movement by dubbing themselves its spokesmen, he would have included Glover on that list had he not been "in the position of having to defend HIC when it was under attack." Though all agreed that Glover meant well, the Hansens believed that as a spokesperson for the corporation, "Billy has been a disaster."

They expressed their gratitude to Slater for always having considered them a boon to the organization and the movement for homosexual rights: "That sort of firm and lasting friendship is precious." But, they advised, Slater could not "have it both ways." In effect, Hansen gave Slater an ultimatum: either Glover would go or they would. Hansen answered for Slater that as chair, Slater would never do such a thing to a fellow soldier loyal to the cause for so long. The facts were clear, "We must move out and leave room for others who *can* contribute as Billy would wish."[22]

To make matters worse for Slater and HIC, Laud Humphreys, a sociologist from Pitzer College in Claremont who had worked with Legg and the Venice Group, reported in his book *Out of the Closets: The Sociology of Homosexual Liberation* (1972) that Slater's famous mutiny was a prime example of "the sort of organizational takeover that borders on larceny." Humphreys, who had never contacted anyone at the Tangent Group for their perspective on the situation, faithfully reported Legg's version of the story: "Upon arrival at the offices of ONE, Inc., one morning, a worker found the building stripped: gone were all materials pertaining to the magazine, membership and subscription lists, books, typewriters and other machines, desks, and chairs. An editor of the magazine decided that he was ONE and, taking everything with him, moved to another location to continue publishing the magazine. For a few months, there were two publications called *One*. . . . Because ONE was incorporated, the board of directors eventually won possession of the surreptitious ONE's assets—after lengthy court battles that reportedly cost ONE, Inc., in excess of $100,000. It was this financial loss that prevented the original organization from publishing the magazine for more than two years" (93–94).

Slater was dumbfounded when he discovered this passage. He wrote a complaining letter to Legg soon after reading it, but the damage was done. The success of Humphreys's prior book, *Tearoom Trade: Impersonal Sex in Public Places* (1970), ensured that this volume, too, would reach a large audience.

The Rebirth of ONE (a Phoenix Founders)

With the help of Jim Kepner, Legg, as "Richard Conger," revived *ONE Magazine* for four issues beginning in January 1972. "Conger" was listed as editor and Kepner as associate editor for these issues. They printed the magazine on high-gloss paper, eight and a half by eleven inches. While updating the design, most of the copy, headers, and line art were lifted from previous issues. The second issue, dated March/April 1972, published a detailed account of the twentieth annual meeting of ONE, Incorporated, convened in the Golden State Room of the Los Angeles Hilton. The main event was a speech by Los Angeles Councilman Robert Stevenson congratulating ONE for its "pioneer role in the battle for homophile civil rights but warned that the Gay Community must learn to stand united if it hopes to become stronger and more politically effective in the future."

Professor Legg next addressed the audience. Legg recapped some of the great moments in ONE's history, including the "founding of the first tax-exempt foundation affiliate for any homophile organization" (ISHR) and the recent "establishment by the Erickson Educational Foundation of Training Fellowships for students at Long Beach State College to be enrolled in ONE Institute Classes [1971]." Following Legg, Lisa Ben "gave a charming account of her struggles and efforts during this unique pioneer enterprise." As for other matters of business, Robert Earl resigned as ONE's president that night, and ONE announced its ninth annual European Tour, to last for three weeks beginning on September 8.

In the third issue of the new *ONE*, ISHR's address was listed as the same as ONE, Incorporated, suggesting that for all practical purposes the two organizations acted as one. Both heavily relied on the generosity of Erickson and the EEF. As the next chapter shows, this, too, was a tenuous relationship and, when the EEF's funding ceased, both ONE and ISHR would be threatened.

9

Conclusion(s)

And soon, quite soon now, in two years, in five, in forty, it will all be over, and one by one we shall all be drawn into the planet beside each other; let us then hope better of our children, and of our children's children; let us know, let us know there is cure, there is to be an end to it, whose beginnings are long begun, and in slow agonies and all deceptions clearing.
—James Agee, *Let Us Now Praise Famous Men*

AFTER YEARS OF mutual antagonism, Don Slater and W. Dorr Legg eventually buried their hatchets (after first having to remove them from each other's backs) and declared a truce between them. It is fair to wonder if their newfound respect for each other came more from having endured so many years of tenacious onslaught than from any rekindled sense of friendship. Perhaps age itself is a social lubricant. My experiences with the elders of ONE suggest that people in their later years—in this case in their seventies and eighties—no longer exasperate each other as much or spend as much time picking at each other's wounds. Although some may be too proud to instigate reconciliation, they often welcome it once the opportunity is presented. For the aging pioneers of this history, the process of compiling this book has presented a chance for a renewed friendship and understanding that has been welcomed. Through modern technological inventions such as the Internet, fax machines, and cell phones, many of these surviving elders continually communicate with one another and always feel close at hand when needed.

Passions run strong in the course of a human life. It is hardly irrelevant in a social history to speak of bonds built on love, hatred, and love renewed. In focusing only on strife, we lose the value of reconciliation, where some of the greatest lessons may be discovered. A person could view the division of ONE, Incorporated, as a process of growth—the natural and perhaps inevitable social process of corporate fission, whereby a small nonprofit corporation passed from an extended period of unity through a period of factionalism, from which two new, discrete organizations emerged. During this extended history, the participants themselves aged and their needs and desires shifted accordingly, so personally, this has also been a story of how allies turned into adversaries and then changed back into allies, through the process of what Myerhoff and Simić have called "life's career" (1978). Anthropologist Sally Falk Moore has noted that "social relationships may be accumulated over time" and, through cumulative social processes and an extended reputation and history within a particular social arena, a profound sense of love, respect, and sense of belonging can develop in old age that arises from renewed or lifelong friendships (1978, 25). I certainly witnessed this as my consultants began working with each other again after several years of isolation.

Most of the vignettes in this chapter are brief. While my purpose in this book has been primarily to relate a narrative history of ONE, Incorporated, this conclusion provides a cursory overview of what has happened to ONE and HIC between 1980 and today to give a sense of what these people were like in their later days and to present them as I have come to know them. I hope to be able to flesh out the post-Stonewall era in a subsequent book, because although the history of many of the significant events and institutions has been recorded elsewhere, the story of the rise of the gay movement in Los Angeles has yet to be compiled in one narrative whole that adequately expresses the humanity of these key players, the institutions that they formed, and the friendships that they shared. For now, let us return to the matter at hand and consider some of the significant events of these pioneers since the organizations that they founded lost their impetuous and standing within the Los Angeles movement.

HIC Closes Shop

HIC moved from its office on Cahuenga to the Outpost Building, 6715 Hollywood Boulevard, Suite 210, on November 9, 1975. Their old location had sold and the new owner intended to raise the rent considerably. The new office gave HIC a new personality. More people would walk in from off the street, but many of the traditional monthly discussion meetings HIC had hosted in the Cahuenga office, such as the Tavern Guild of San Fernando Valley, ceased. About two years later, HIC moved once again, across the street to 6758 Hollywood Boulevard, near Pickwick Books.

Jim Kepner began to call his prodigious collection the Western Gay Archives in 1975. In 1979, he incorporated as the Gay Archives: Natalie Barney/ Edward Carpenter Library and moved to a storefront location on Hudson Street in Hollywood, a few blocks away from the HIC's new office. The first directors of the Gay Archives were Kepner, Dennis Lind, and Gary Hundertmark. In 1984, Kepner would change the name of his archives once again, to the International Gay and Lesbian Archives (IGLA).

As Don Slater left the HIC's Hollywood office late one night in 1983, muggers attacked him in the dark parking lot behind the building (Lucas 1997). He managed to return into the office and called Charles Lucas for help. Lucas called fellow HIC board members Rudi Steinert and Susan Howe, who rushed to the office to find Slater drenched in blood. The thugs had taken everything—his money and briefcase, but also his clothes, shoes, and car. Lucas wrapped Slater in a blanket and managed to get him down the fire escape and into his car. Rather than go to the hospital, Slater insisted that they take him home. Sanchez arrived home early the next morning, but by then Slater had become so weak that he consented to go to the hospital (Lucas 1997, 86–87).

According to Sanchez,[1] Slater's wounds were superficial. Lucas and Howe, though, recall that Slater's face had been brutally smashed and bones had probably been fractured. Slater refused to file a police report regarding the incident. Sanchez's car eventually showed up at the local compound and, luckily, Slater recovered quickly. He easily could have been killed in the incident, which Sanchez believes was not a hate crime but a mugging with the promise of sex used as lure. The corners of Hollywood and Highland were notorious cruising grounds for hustlers at this time. It was not uncommon for one to step into the HIC office (on a slow night) and request help or proffer assistance. It was one such rogue "volunteer" who attacked Slater and took his belongings—and nearly his life. HIC subsequently closed its Hollywood office and moved its library into Slater and Sanchez's home on Calumet.

With the assistance of a Veterans' Administration (VA) loan, Slater and Sanchez purchased a second, more rustic house in southwest Colorado, near the Four Corners area. Through the 1980s, the two frequently traveled back and forth from Los Angeles to Colorado. Jennings and Glover occasionally made the twelve-hour drive as well. Slater loved the peace of his Colorado spread, but he also loved to be home in Los Angeles where the downtown spires stool like sentinels nearby as he tended to his shaded garden. He and Sanchez added a rooster named Calhoun to their extended family of urban critters that included several dogs and cats.

The Venice Group, Gentrified

Although the focus of this history has been on the history of ONE, Incorporated, and the HIC, I now turn to the history of Dorr Legg's Venice Group, ONE, Incorporated, in the 1980s through the 1990s. Reid Rasmussen, current executive treasurer of ISHR, provided much of this information, and I owe him and the other directors of ISHR a debt of gratitude for their generosity, their many years of financial support, and their endless patience as I have worked toward completing this project. Having access to the personal documents of Legg and the other directors of ISHR, as well as the many court documents surrounding the battle over an ultimate division of the Milbank estate, allows me to provide this brief overview of the fate of Legg's half of ONE, Incorporated.

Dorr Legg met David G. Cameron, a specialist in the historic preservation of buildings, during an event at the Gay Academic Union in Los Angeles in 1982. Cameron, who had never been to the Venice office, asked what the facility was like and offered to assist if they desired a new location. Legg responded that he was indeed interested, so Cameron introduced him to James E. Dunham, a real estate broker already acquainted with Reed Erickson.[2] Later that fall, Dunham advised Legg that the Milbank/McFie Estate had become available for purchase and might be an excellent home for ONE Institute, located at the corner of Country Club Drive and Arlington Avenue in the prestigious Country Club Park district of Los Angeles.

The property stretched 400 feet along Country Club Drive and 360 feet along Arlington, encompassing three-and-a-half acres. Isaac Milbank originally purchased the lot in 1913 for $70,000. Architect G. Lawrence Stimson of Pasadena designed the houses in a style reminiscent of Stimson's own residence, per Milbank's request.[3] Plans for the estate featured two main buildings with a total of twenty-seven rooms, the smaller home for Milbank's daughter and son-in-law. There was a separate greenhouse and chapel, with a chauffeur's quarters beside the garages. The estate was declared Historical Monument Number 420 by the City of Los Angeles on December 13, 1989.

After touring the site, Legg drove to Erickson's home in Ojai with photos of the estate. Erickson loved what he saw, and the prospect of purchasing it pleased him. According to court records,[4] he was smitten by the location enough to state outright: "I will buy it for you." By this time, Erickson had donated more than $187,000 to ONE (through ISHR), either personally or through the EEF. Still, the facility at Venice had decayed considerably during the past twenty years. The creaky old building showed the wear, and some had begun to call it "Dorr's Mausoleum."[5] In 1982, Erickson had promised to bequeath to ISHR $1 million worth of gold in his will. It seems that he had decided to donate the bullion now, while he was alive and there was a need.

Legg returned to Los Angeles and told Dunham to draw up an offer for the property for Erickson to sign. The property owner, Church Universal and Triumphant, Incorporated, rejected the first offer. But in January of 1983, the sellers contacted Dunham with a counteroffer, which Erickson accepted provided that the parties would evenly divide the cost of the transfer tax, and the name of the buyer would be changed from EEF to ISHR. With this agreed, the estate sold for $1,800,000.

Erickson paid for most of the property in one-and-a-half million dollars' worth of solid gold Krugerrands transported from Erickson's house in Ojai to a money exchange office in Beverly Hills on February 17. Erickson's wife, Evangeline; his secretary, Gloria Southwick; and Episcopal priest Dwain Houser, who worked for ISHR at the time, participated in and witnessed the transfer. Because the exchange office only accepted a limited number of coins each day, it took a week for the church to process the Krugerrands. By the end of the week, gold had dropped from $508 to $368 an ounce, so the church lost in the deal. Erickson later bragged that he had personally driven the price down through this transaction (Devor and Matte 2004, 195).

Zelda R. Suplee was also present to witness the gold exchange. ISHR's assistant director since October 1967, Suplee took over as ISHR's director when Erickson moved his main residence from Baton Rouge to Mazatlan, Mexico, in 1973. She moved to Los Angeles to continue working for Erickson in the spring of 1983. According to a letter she wrote to Legg on August 17, 1987, Erickson told her soon after the purchase that he intended to turn the deed to the estate over to ONE Institute by May 1, 1983. He then postponed the date to June 1, and discussion followed as to how they would publicize the event. There was no further mention of the deed, however, even though Suplee delayed the publication of the EEF newsletter by several months waiting for the official announcement. Suplee chalked it up as "just another instance of 'welshing' that I had become familiar with." Because Erickson had clearly paid for the property, uncertainty soon developed as to whom the legal owner of the estate might be.

Church Universal and Triumphant, Incorporated, presented the keys of Milbank to Legg on Sunday, March 6, 1983, and ONE and ISHR began moving in right away. On April 4, Legg wrote a letter to Erickson stating that he had received a call from attorney Herb Selwyn, who advised that the title of the estate should officially be turned over to ONE and *not* the Erickson Educational Foundation, as Erickson had apparently decided. According to Legg, if ONE were publicly associated with the EEF, it could damage their fund-raising efforts because the EEF publicly associated itself with transsexual issues whereas ONE was dedicated to the larger issue of homosexuality. "This [subject of transsexuality] brings strong emotional feelings to one part of the population while the homophile concerns touch millions of men and women." And after all, he pointed, out, transsexual concerns were "provided for in the Institute's programs through Paul Walker and the Janus Information activities." Selwyn more prudently recommended transfer of the title to ONE so that "the long-range future of ONE Institute should be insulated as much as possible from being drawn into the disposition of your estate at any time."[6] Erickson, however, held his ground. In fact, according to Legg, there were a few times in 1983 when the offices of ONE were broken into and ransacked, and materials pertaining to Erickson (such as the 1982 will and selected letters by Erickson to Legg) mysteriously disappeared. Legg, experienced in such matters, had made copies of many of these documents and kept them off-site, to emerge again during the ensuing trial.

On January 3, 1984, Erickson wrote a distraught letter to ONE, declaring his need to withdraw all support because of his "exceedingly poor health . . . destroyed by Evangelina, who never was married to me[7] and who continually drugged me, Mickey Finned me, and injected me with female hormones to lower my libido and feminize me." Erickson said ONE had two weeks to come up with funding of its own or he would be forced to sell the property. He added, "Evangelina is trying to tie up my assets and sue me for 50% of all I ever earned including Milbank. My sister and my ex, Aileen, have been blackmailing me for years, and have made problems for me with the police department in Ojai, with everyone's help."

Undaunted by Erickson's letter, Legg proceeded to hold a convocation and open house at the new facility, 3340 Country Club Drive, on Sunday, January 29, 1984. Legg convened the event while Bob Mitchell welcomed the crowd with organ music. Jesse Jacobs, president of ONE, Incorporated, gave the welcome address, and then Legg, as dean of ONE Institute, introduced Victor

J. Burner as dean of the Division of Special Programs. Legg next introduced Gene R. Touchet and Paul A. Walker as deans of the graduate school, Walker heading the San Francisco programs. Walter L. Williams was presented as dean of ONE Institute's Center for Advanced Studies, and Jim Dunham attended as director of development for ONE Institute and the community. The highlight of the event occurred when Deborah Ann Coates, Paul David Hardman, and Michael Antonio Lombardi were awarded master's of arts degrees in homophile studies.

This was not the first time ONE Institute had issued advanced degrees in homophile studies. Three years prior, in August 1981, Legg awarded ONE Institute's first (honorary) degrees in homophile studies to Reed Erickson and Christopher Isherwood during ONE's Thirtieth Anniversary Gala, held at the Los Angeles Hilton with six hundred people in attendance. According to Legg, the State of California had accredited ONE as a graduate degree–granting institution. Indeed, the official authorization to operate from the California State Department of Education Office of Private Postsecondary Education, dated August 18, 1981, designated ONE Institute Graduate School of Homophile Studies as a degree-granting institution in accordance with California Education Code section 94310(c). However, it further stated that although ONE could grant degrees, it nonetheless remained "unaccredited and unapproved, authorized by filing of public disclosure information." This document further stipulated that ONE "may not issue diplomas under this authority." This circumstance never changed.

Through the spring of 1984, Legg entertained the idea of ONE purchasing the Milbank estate from Erickson,[8] but that proved impossible because of the organization's strapped financial status. Tensions between Legg and Erickson intensified, and by summer, Erickson hired the Landsdell Protective Agency to secure the premises even though Legg remained inside. For four days, Legg was locked in. Padlocks and cables secured all five gates to the estate, and armed guards with dogs were posted all around. At one point, Legg stormed out to demand that welders stop welding the gates shut. Erickson, standing nearby, instructed one of the welders to "burn him" before scuttling off in his limousine. Although Legg was not burned, he later recalled the incident in his respondent's brief of October 16, 1991, which certainly helped his case against Erickson, whom Legg described as that "ever-eccentric, millionaire, transsexual, philanthropist."

In December 1985, Legg obtained a court injunction enjoining Erickson, his employees, or his associates "from entering . . . the garage and storage sheds located on the grounds of said Milbank estate." The same were further enjoined from "interfering and attempting to interfere with the peaceful use and enjoyment of . . . the main level of the Milbank Mansion." According to a letter from Legg to Erickson dated December 6, 1985, the deed to the property showed that the EEF, a Republic of Panama corporation, actually owned the property. "Since your Court action filed July 7, 1984, to quiet the title ownership is legally in the custody of the court until all litigation has been completed, you are NOT the owner." This referred to the EEF's action for damages and trespass it had filed against ONE and ISHR for not vacating the property as requested.

In 1986, Erickson left the United States to avoid prosecution under narcotics charges in Los Angeles and Ventura counties. The Ventura County Superior Court appointed a conservator, and the cases were consolidated and tried late in 1989, under Judge Philip M. Saeta, with no jury. Saeta found that ISHR lawfully owned the estate because of the doctrine of promissory estoppel, whereby a promisor is bound to his or her word when the promisee relies on that promise to the extent that his or her status would be significantly compromised by a breach of the agreement. Further, Judge Saeta granted Legg $10,000 in general damages and another $10,000 in punitive damages for his false imprisonment.

According to documents provided by ISHR, Erickson moved for a new trial and to vacate the judgment in June 1990, but the court denied his request. However, on July 2, he filed an appeal that successfully reversed the ruling. Legg filed a respondent's brief on October 16, 1991, written by Russell and Wynn. In January 1992, Erickson died, and his daughter Monica Erickson became executrix of his will and estate. The matter was soon returned to court, and in October of that year the parties finally agreed to a settlement, dividing the property between the Erickson estate and ISHR. The terms of this settlement were not finalized until February 1994. On July 11, 1994, the directors of ISHR voted to hire Fred Sands Realtors to sell their portion of the estate. This decision was the last formal document Legg would ever sign.

The Death of Dorr Legg

Dorr Legg died in his sleep on Tuesday, July 26, 1994. He was eighty-nine years old. According to an obituary published by ONE, Legg had been feeling weak and in ill health for several months. In his last days, he contacted several of his codirectors to request that they record his final words and life history on tape and video before it was too late. He narrated this history over a period of two hours, portions of which were quoted in his obituary.

Don Slater was distraught when he learned of Legg's death. On more than one occasion Bullough recalled to me how Slater called him late on the night of Legg's passing and said "*Lambert's dead!*" in an anguished voice and then just hung up the phone. After all Slater and Legg had experienced together and the many years of grief and frustration they heaped upon each other, the fact remained that Legg had been a committed leader of ONE and the movement for over forty-two years and, in some ways, Slater had never stopped admiring him. Slater knew that the homosexual movement had lost one of its senior elders and greatest pioneers.

Legg had helped to plan his funeral before his death. He originally wanted to be buried in his home state of Michigan but later decided that his body should remain in Los Angeles, where he had spent the last half of his life. He was buried at Forest Lawn Cemetery in the Hollywood Hills on Friday, July 29, at two in the afternoon. Nine men witnessed the interment, including Thomas Hunter Russell, president of ISHR; David Cameron, president of ONE, Incorporated; Walter L. Williams, director of ISHR; Reid Rasmussen, secretary of ISHR; and Johnny Nojima, who had been Legg's companion for thirty years and was the executor of Legg's will and estate. One month after his burial, on August 28, 1994, a memorial service was held in Legg's honor at Milbank Estate, commonly referred to as the ONE Institute Campus. This was the last public ceremony to be held at Milbank, and ONE Institute was never to hold classes again.

Qn February 27, 1995, two professors purchased the house at 1130 Arlington for $525,000, by unanimous approval of ISHR's directors. From this, $112,000 plus interest went to pay off debts that had been acquired through the term of the lawsuit. Reid Rasmussen and John Nojima were each repaid $20,000. Victor Burner and ONE, Incorporated, were each reimbursed $10,000, and Hal Call, director of the Mattachine Society in San Francisco, was to be repaid $52,000 plus interest.[9] After other fees and charges, there was little to nothing of the selling price remaining for ONE or ISHR. The smaller house, at 1214 South Van Ness, was sold to the Avatar Meher Baba Center for $380,000. ISHR's board approved this offer on November 13, 1996, and escrow closed on February 10, 1997.

Slater noted in an undated[10] letter to Jennings that former ONE president Fred Frisbie was "totally destroyed when the followers of Lambert jettisoned the ONE joint immediately upon his death" and said he would never speak to any of them again. However, when ONE Institute and Archives held its grand opening at 909 West Adams in May 2000, Frisbie attended as an honored guest. It seemed that ONE Institute would continue on, in spirit at least, in the new location, thanks largely to the efforts of Walter L. Williams, John O'Brien, Jim Schneider, and the generosity of USC.

This organization that now (in 1999) called itself ONE Institute and Archives[11] had until recently been known as ONE/IGLA, a surviving aspect of Jim Kepner's International Gay and Lesbian Archives. After Legg's death and the sale of the Milbank Estate, ONE Incorporated merged with ISHR, with ISHR being the surviving corporation and ONE, Incorporated, the merging corporation. Russell and Cameron signed the agreement of merger on December 11, 1995, as presidents of ISHR and ONE, respectively. Rasmussen signed as secretary for both organizations. Once this occurred, the organization known as ONE, Incorporated, officially ceased to exist as a separate legal entity. In 2000, ISHR gave a nod for the new organization to use the name "ONE Institute," but there is no legal corporate continuity between ONE, Incorporated, and the organization that current calls itself ONE National Gay and Lesbian Archives. Although ONE Archives continues to bill itself as the "oldest archives in the United States dedicated to LGBT issues . . . [which] began in 1953, and . . . [is now] the longest continually running gay organization in the United States" (here! Focus 2006), one need only consult the legal documents here referenced to see that this is not so. In my opinion, "ONE Archives" is best considered to be a survival of IGLA, and this is truly a heritage of which they should be proud. Legally and historically, ONE, Incorporated, more properly lives on through ISHR and HIC.

Friendships Renewed

The historical vignettes presented in the prior two chapters show that the division of ONE, Incorporated, was hardly the demise of the movement. Many significant battles had been fought and won through acts of civil disobedience that were often barely coordinated and hardly orchestrated. The movement was successful partially because, in each case, there was a clear adversary: the U.S. postmaster, the *Times*, the police commission, Miss Barney, each event a "pebble in the mountain" of the movement's history, as Joe Hansen put it. The twenty-year span between the division of ONE and its ultimate dissolution mark an era where great strides were made in the battle to secure equal rights for homosexuals. And the story is hardly over. Two of its three faces/corporations—ISHR and HIC—have managed to survive, carried as they are on battered shoulders of the surviving few, who strive to continue the process of pebble piling.

Slater and Jennings Revisited (and the Teacup of History)

Dale Jennings and Don Slater renewed their friendship after Jennings contacted Slater in 1985 in his search for employment. Between 1990 and 1995, Jennings lived a few doors west of Slater and Sanchez, in Rudi Steinert's old apartment on Calumet. During this time, their relationship became inscribed in letters and postcards, for Slater was often in Colorado, where he wrote to Jennings from his home near Durango. Although Slater insisted that others properly inscribe and date their articles and letters to him, he addressed his notes only by the day. It seems in context, though, that the sequence in which Jennings filed these letters reflects the order he received them.

The letters reveal a mutual love for nature and travel. Slater often wrote of the mountainous scenery and wildlife around the Durango area. In the early winter of 1995, he wrote excitedly to Jennings that he had seen a small herd of elk in a nearby field and watched them for nearly twenty minutes. He wrote occasionally of death, reflecting that Chuck Rowland was in the hospital and in bad health. "Things become precious when we lose them. Life, for instance. I was reminded of this yesterday when I saw a snowflake fall. Wonderfully intricate, the minute it came to earth it began to die. I've perked up today. . . . There is no time to be moody."

In the autumn of 1994, John O'Brien, a New York expatriate and Stonewall "veteran" who now was president of ONE/IGLA, contacted Don Slater with a proposal. O'Brien had joined the Young Socialists Alliance, a youth division of the Marxist Socialist Workers Party in New York, but as with Jennings, Hay, and Kepner, the Communist Party had cast him out because of his sexuality (Carter 2004, 120). O'Brien was as intelligent as he was belligerent, a brash and muscular man who grew up in Spanish Harlem. He had been actively protesting for civil rights since he was a teenager, when he sojourned to Alabama to participate in a civil rights protest for blacks. O'Brien had participated in the Stonewall Rebellion and had since dedicated his life to gay causes. Even after years of living in Los Angeles, he was New York to the core; when I met him, he frequently spoke of how much he missed his Manhattan home.

When he contacted Slater, he was working with Walter Williams in Los Angeles to help ONE/IGLA move into a new facility offered by USC. Slater had been leery but intrigued by ONE/IGLA's offer. In one of his Durango letters to Jennings, Slater wrote that he was not interested in hearing about what HIC's role in the new organization might be so much as he wanted "clarification about them and their arrangements with the university." What relationship existed, for instance, between ONE and IGLA? Slater asked to see their articles of incorporation and the legal documents that bound them. He requested that O'Brien provide in writing "the names of all those involved in the project—including those on the staff of the university—and their position and place in the scheme." Only after such fact finding could they decide if they wanted to participate at the "new USC complex" and, if so, what role they would play.

One afternoon in January 1995, Jennings, as HIC's secretary, met with O'Brien to discuss the future of the extensive collection of books and records on the homosexual movement housed the past several years in Slater's home. O'Brien was not getting the warm reception from Jennings that he expected. O'Brien pointed out that the addition of HIC's materials to the ONE/IGLA collection would mean that ONE would have amassed not only the largest holdings of gay and lesbian archival materials in the nation but would be among the nation's most historically viable as well. O'Brien aimed to continue to form and direct what would eventually be heralded as the Nation's LGBT Attic, a veritable gay Smithsonian. There was some confusion, though, regarding O'Brien's position and credibility; Jennings reported to the HIC that he was "head of the Queer Studies department at USC," whereas, in fact, O'Brien had no official ties with USC at all.

Walter Williams, USC professor of anthropology and board member of ONE/IGLA, soon joined them at the archives. Williams had brokered the arrangement between ONE and USC whereby ONE could move its holdings and operations into an evacuated fraternity house near campus for a number of years. Jennings remained suspicious of O'Brien and of ONE's motivations in general but noted in his report back to the HIC that he was "more attracted to Williams' mind." He noted that, in arguing that the collections should be unified, Williams seemed totally convinced that gay and lesbian scholars had passed the point in history where gays lived in any legitimate danger. As Jennings saw it, Williams believed that an era of tolerance had arrived and there was no threat of conservative regression, backlash, or fallout against the improving civil attitudes and court victories the movement had accrued over the past forty-five years. A lifelong student of history and a well-traveled veteran of World War II, Jennings found "such self-assurance alarmingly immature." He added, "It didn't strike them that their wealth, success and political power are irrelevant. No political power is permanent."

Besides this, Williams and O'Brien had an awkward sense of urgency about them, and Jennings felt pressed for an immediate answer and commitment. He began to suspect that ONE intended a one-sided donation rather than the more balanced agreement that HIC certainly deserved and could bargain for. Jennings pressed O'Brien for details: Would he ensure HIC an autonomous space within ONE, secure with locks, control of the keys, and their own computer and phone line? Would HIC receive representation on ONE's board? HIC had, after all, been a successful, functioning, and autonomous organization dedicated to the rights of homosexuals since their split with ONE in 1965. Since then, HIC's achievements had been every bit as prestigious as ONE's—in some ways more successful—yet the operational philosophies of the two organizations remained distinct.

In his report back to HIC, Jennings reminded his fellow directors that ONE had a long history of antagonism toward HIC's views. Even if one of HIC's directors were allowed to sit on ONE's board, this would not ensure that HIC would be guaranteed a lasting vote. "Once on the Board, you could be eliminated quickly," he warned.[12] HIC responded to ONE/IGLA's offer prudently. They agreed to become an autonomous special collection within ONE/IGLA, provided that ONE/IGLA's board put its terms in writing. This was never done.

One other issue troubled Jennings and the other directors of HIC. They knew from their long-standing involvement within the homophile movement that "history" as they had lived it and the history they read in books and articles were often out of sync and occasionally even at odds. Would ONE Institute accurately present HIC's history to the public? Would it honor O'Brien's pact of autonomy and the board's offer to support HIC's president, Jim Schneider, in a position of leadership?

Jennings had attempted to illustrate this point to O'Brien through allegory by relating a story regarding a trend that developed within the elite class of sixteenth-century Holland. The affluent Dutch learned that they could order Chinese porcelain in designs "duplicated to the last detail," and to do so had become fashionable. Jennings related this conversation in his report to HIC's board. One lady was fond of a particular set of Dutch scenes in blue on white. Sending a damaged cup which she no longer wanted, she asked that the pattern be copied. In due time her set arrived, copied exactly down to the smallest detail including an identical nick in each cup.

"But isn't that what she wanted?" O'Brien replied, clearly missing the point. Jennings attempted to clarify by stating that he was still "miffed" that Timmons had inscribed his mother upon history "as a commie cell leader" (1990, 144). O'Brien astonished Jennings by responding, "That's your opinion. She might have been a cell leader without you ever guessing."

Clearly this meeting between two prominent homosexual rights activists had not gone well. Jennings's subsequent report to his fellow directors would prove prophetic and foreboding: "I feel that USC's basic motive in wanting [HIC's collection] (and they really want them badly) is for the purpose of enhancing their prestige and promoting more money. I'm fairly sure that once they got their hands on the HIC collection, they'd wash their hands of us." The directors decided to wait for O'Brien to put an offer in writing, but despite his reassurance that one was pending, no document ever came, and the HIC archives remained stacked, piled, and boxed haphazardly throughout Slater's aging but stately Victorian home on Calumet.

The Death of Don Slater

Don Slater died of heart failure on February 14, 1997. That evening, Schneider had driven Sanchez to the Veterans Hospital in west Los Angeles only to find that Slater had died thirty minutes earlier. Sanchez broke down when he found that the man he had loved for more than fifty years had passed on in solitude, and Schneider did his best to comfort him. The next day, Schneider took Sanchez to Armstrong Mortuary downtown, to arrange for Slater's cremation.

This was an awful time for Sanchez, to say the least. Not only had he lost his lover of fifty-two years but the flurry of activity that suddenly surrounded him was emotionally intense and financially overwhelming. As soon as news of Slater's death spread, several people began pressuring Sanchez to leave the house on Calumet. Fred Frisbie told him that he and Slater had agreed that if anything happened to Slater, Sanchez should settle in with him. Slater's cousin, who lived nearby, told Sanchez that there had been a lot of seismic damage to the structure of the house and pointed out that the stone foundation was crumbling away. As Sanchez was aware, the steep roof was again beginning to leak. To make matters worse, Slater had purchased the Durango house through a VA loan; because Sanchez did not qualify as surviving partner or spouse, the balance of the mortgage came due immediately. Fortunately, Slater and Sanchez owned everything else in joint tenancy; otherwise, Sanchez would have lost much more than the right to carry the mortgage. Sanchez amazed everyone when he sold the Calumet property for the first offer, and he used the money to pay off the house in Colorado. He moved there as fast as he could to settle in with the one person he felt had been a good friend to him, a neighbor named Hazel, who remains his closest friend to this day.

Sanchez brusquely departed for several reasons. For one, many of his "friends" were no longer in the black: "Sugar Daddies and Sugar Mommas were getting hard to come by," he told me in a bemoaned voice during one telephone conversation. Some of his old Hollywood friends, having fallen on hard times themselves, began calling him to request that he return the gifts they had given him in better days. Others were no longer around, many having died from AIDS-related illnesses. Suddenly, the old Calumet Victorian seemed haunted, saturated with memories and brimming with death. With friends looming like vultures, Sanchez at one point began recklessly throwing things in the trash, to later be salvaged by O'Brien and Schneider.

Sanchez still resides in the Colorado home that he and Slater purchased more than thirty-five years ago. He still dances or exercises every day: "I am active for *life*," he says proudly. Sanchez owns the house now and has a trailer on-site, to host his mother or anyone else who visits. He travels the Four Corners area in a large Ford pickup and works as a bilingual Latin entertainer specializing in country-western music. He can perform clog, Spanish, and Flamenco dances, and his repertoire includes dozens of folk and popular songs in four different languages.

Although somewhat lonely as a widower, Sanchez manages to keep himself active and happy. He currently studies acrylics and oil painting with an artist from Santa Fe and recently donated one of his paintings to a fund-raiser for a new library in Durango. He has been single for nearly nine years now. He wishes he could find another male companion to share the rest of his life with, but he realizes that his living in a remote country home makes that possibility unlikely. He has no Internet access but frequently travels the Four Corners region in his pickup, a traveling bard with hundreds of songs to sing and some amazing stories to tell. (Unfortunately, he cannot relate many of them.) Remembering Slater's attack outside the Hollywood office, Sanchez began to fear for his own safety as an elderly gay man. After he moved to Colorado and became more comfortable in his solitude, he began to hear stories of homosexual murders, most notoriously that of Matthew Shepard, bludgeoned to death on October 7, 1998 (see esp. Loffreda 2001).

Sanchez is the only consultant who requested that I protect his identity by using a pseudonym. He has become all too aware of his own vulnerability, and thoughts of renewed publicity scare him. Although he answered my questions patiently and engaged my attention through many stories of the people he knew and worked with, he confided to me once that he had been so scared after my first contact with him, and my telling him about my research and the Web site, that he had motion sensor lights installed on his house. That was certainly not the response I had anticipated! I immediately removed a photo of him in his twenties from the Web site and altered it to disguise somewhat his identity. Many of his HIC colleagues have expressed their annoyance and even anger at this request, calling it an act of a coward. After visiting him, however, and seeing the gun he keeps by his entry door, I understand how an aging man living in solitude can feel vulnerable and scared.

I should note that I hesitated to contact Sanchez for a very long time. When Billy Glover provided me with Sanchez's phone number and address, I immediately phoned him to introduce myself and to tell him that HIC continued to care for his archives and that the most valuable materials likely would join with the Vern and Bonnie Bullough Collection on human sexuality at California State University, Northridge. He was pleased that HIC continued to function and that it had developed such a prestigious association. I found Sanchez to be receptive and engaging—and very alone. Immediately he sent me a special (belated) birthday card, and then another for Christmas. In May 2006, I traveled to his mountain home thanks to a grant from ISHR, and we spent a memorable day together touring Mesa Verde. I could tell that it hurt for him to discuss his past with Slater; although he answered my questions and allowed me to tape his answers, he frequently changed the topic to happier times. Sanchez is clearly not one to dwell on the past. He and I now speak frequently, and I look forward to my next visit to Durango this summer, this time with my partner. And this time, I'll try my best not ask him to dredge through those memories.

Promises Made, Promises Broken

Before Sanchez left for Durango in 1997, two men approached HIC's directors, Schneider and Glover, and offered to help protect the materials in their charge. The first was Vern Bullough, who wanted HIC's collection to join with his archives, the Vern and Bonnie Bullough Collection on Sex and Gender at California State University, Northridge (CSUN). HIC's officers immediately allowed Bullough to take several duplicate books to CSUN and promised more than once that the remaining materials had been properly sorted. The other man to approach, not surprisingly, was O'Brien, executive director of ONE/IGLA.

O'Brien again invited the board of HIC to the USC facility, a few days after Slater's death. He assured Schneider, Sanchez, Glover, and Jennings that if they would agree to house their collection within ONE's new facility, HIC would remain autonomous, and ONE would not simply "merge" its files and archives into the general collection (although HIC's books might be intermingled within ONE's stacks). The two-story brick structure showed promise, but it lacked climate control and adequate office space. It had been severely vandalized by the exiting fraternity and was in need of total refurbishing, inside and out. O'Brien predicted that ONE would complete the renovation within a year, and HIC could then move into its own space, a large area that had formerly been the kitchen and had its own entrance.

This offer appealed to Schneider, Glover, and Sanchez, partially because Slater had been a USC alumnus, and Jennings had studied cinema there for two years. Jennings, though, remained leery of the deal. He and Slater had argued before that if it wanted the collection so badly, ONE should at least offer HIC a permanent position on ONE's board. ONE's board of directors agreed to this and asked HIC to nominate one of its members. HIC elected Schneider to the post and decided to move its office and its collection to ONE/IGLA.

As president of HIC, Schneider retained custody of the materials until O'Brien completed the renovations. With Glover in Louisiana and Sanchez in Colorado, he took responsibility for the entire HIC archives. Schneider purchased ten large black filing cabinets for the clippings, correspondence, and newsletters, which he stowed in his company's warehouse, and two other cabinets for HIC's collection of hundreds of old ONE and Tangents magazines. Schneider stored the remaining 276 boxes in a separate facility, which he began to pay for from his personal funds. ONE's board expressed its gratitude by voting Schneider back onto the board in the fall of 1997, thirty-two years after his dismissal by Legg. The occasion meant a lot to him. He felt that he had made the right choice, and his recently deceased cohort could rest a little easier because of it.

John O'Brien sent a letter to Billy Glover on April 2, 1997. He began by discussing arrangements for Slater's memorial service, which Albert Brecht, cochair of USC's Lambda Alumni Association, was helping to coordinate. O'Brien noted that USC had committed $50,000 to the "architectural needs" of the West Adams building, which would be disbursed by July 1, 1997. An additional $140,000 would be given after that date to complete the job, not including "other moneys set aside for roof, security and structural foundation work." O'Brien stated that work on the building should be completed and the facility open by the spring of 1998. He invited HIC to participate in the grand opening as a "special invited guest." He suggested that HIC might want to have its own opening at some point, "which we would of course honor and try to be helpful in providing space and staff support." He added, "Several of our special collections have their own activities. We just try to coordinate them, to not conflict if possible in dates and times."

O'Brien predicted that it would take two years to process the HIC materials, and he offered his assistance to complete the job. He suggested that they work together toward organizing HIC's collection to make it accessible to researchers. He wanted to assess what materials and computer databases would be needed and to set up a budget to carry out the work. He asked HIC to "develop close working ties with ONE to help assist in having the building open and the HIC Collection functioning." He pledged that ONE Institute was "committed to working with HIC to organize and save this important collection. . . . I can assure you that I will do my most to have this history-making alliance between us grown and produce an effort we will be proud of."

The five-page executive director's report to the directors of ONE Institute, though, dated the following day, April 3, struck a different tone. At least three of those pages detailed his "rescue" and "preservation" of HIC's archives. His report described "harsh and unhealthy conditions," and he complained of working long hours—over ten days—with little or no help from others. He did mention other ONE, Incorporated, assistants, such as Ernie Potvin and Bill Kaiser, and noted that Kepner had been there for a brief while, too. O'Brien complained, "The only members of HIC to do work were Tony Sanchez and Don Schneider.[13] Mr. Schneider helped considerably during the weekends when not at his work in both physical moving and providing boxes, purchasing file cabinets, and providing storage of the file cabinets in his offices."

According to Schneider's records, 276 boxes held the HIC's collection and historical records after Slater died. Most of them, 253 boxes, went to Iron Mountain storage facility, which cost Schneider $70 per month to store them. O'Brien took the remaining twenty-three boxes, as overflow, to be stored with the ONE Institute materials with the understanding that they would be returned to HIC once the materials were situated at the West Adams facility. According to Schneider, these twenty-three boxes were never returned.

Compared to the concern and generosity expressed in his letter to Glover, O'Brien's address to ONE's board seems harsh and exaggerated. "These were very labor-intensive and unhealthy work conditions and long exhaustive hours," he complained. "I sat for many hours with a mask on mainly to dust the ONE files and other rarities to box for saving. . . . It was the worst conditions that I have experienced in many years, reminding me of the old IGLA storage areas on Lexington before I joined the board." He claimed to have found "the original ONE Inc. organizational files and correspondence hidden in the bottom of assorted boxes in no order, throughout the basement and garage." He explained the significance of this discovery: "Don was always worried that someone would steal back these files and thus he hid them. No one had seen them since April 1965. These files contain original papers and many photographs on a Who's Who of our Movement from 1952 to 1965. . . . In addition to all the original ONE Inc. materials and library, we obtained all the papers and books from the HIC that they had acquired since 1965. This included (ironically given the conditions at HIC's archives) the collections of other groups and individuals, that were sent them for safe keeping."

O'Brien next made a surprising admission: "I decided not to box the original ONE Inc. files and correspondence to be placed in storage with the rest of the HIC collection. It needed immediate attention and it was really not theirs. On Saturday March 29 Bill Kaiser and I placed them in alphabetical order in file cabinets. We will, over the next couple of Saturdays, transfer these folders to better ones. We will then turn them over to be catalogued and filed under ONE Inc., at our Werle building location [in West Hollywood]."

His report concludes, "No one has known or seen what these files have contained, for over thirty years. The HIC board members never saw the materials (even Don who kept them in grocery boxes all these years never reviewed them!)." This, of course, was patently untrue; the materials had been available to the public for years. O'Brien also noted that many of the materials seemed well cared for, and some parts of the collection were well organized. He even noted that Legg had a key to the Cahuenga offices at some point in the 1970s, which should have suggested that there had been reconciliation between HIC and ONE. Yet his conclusion to ONE/IGLA was that had it not been for his heroic acts, "the HIC collection (and some of the best of ONE Inc.) would all have been lost."

O'Brien did not know that multiple copies of all of those documents existed and were on file with ISHR. In 2004, those records were duplicated, bound, and made public by ISHR's executive secretary, Reid Rasmussen, with copies going to ONE Archives, HIC, and CSUN. The files that O'Brien coveted and claimed to have confiscated were HIC's legitimate historical records and archives.

O'Brien estimated it would take up to two years of extensive effort to properly process and archive the HIC materials, and funds and a staff would be needed to accomplish this. He told the directors at ONE/IGLA that he planned to meet with HIC's board by the end of the month, in order "to proceed with these problems." (This never happened.) In the meantime, he pledged to seek financial and volunteer assistance to start the work and also to help arrange a memorial for Slater at USC:

> This is all part of our setting up a positive working relationship with HIC members and the easy transfer of their materials to the new USC building.

I hope to have a written agreement of the understanding between HIC and ourselves signed at the end of this month. Once the building is finished the HIC collection will be transferred to this building for processing.

And so it was settled. ONE/IGLA, with HIC on board as an autonomous special collection, was scheduled to open within the year, with the HIC installed in the area that had been the fraternity's kitchen, on the first floor. This was great space, it had plenty of room for the collection, bookcases, and file cabinets—and ONE would provide it rent free, as well. It was an incredible offer. Again, it was never put it into writing.

In October 1998, Schneider expressed his frustration during a board meeting at ONE's West Hollywood office that O'Brien was not moving fast enough on the project and had perhaps muddied the waters with USC. The other directors agreed, and ultimately accepted O'Brien's resignation as president of ONE/IGLA. Schneider became the head of the Building Committee: through his hard work and dedication to the project (and his bringing to the project the talented carpenter Gus Sanchez), ONE Institute and Archives held its first public event, a memorial service for Dale Jennings, on June 25, 2000.

In the fall of 2000, the HIC collection at last moved into the Adams Boulevard facility. While Walter Williams focused on raising more money to complete the renovations and worked to develop the museum exhibits, Schneider oversaw the actual construction. After much intensive labor, ONE Institute's volunteers began to unpack the collection as the work neared completion. The official grand opening of the archives followed in May 2001. All board members pulled together to host a gala ceremony with hundreds of attendees, the likes of which the homosexual public of Los Angeles had not seen since Kepner's memorial service in 1998 and would not see again until Morris Kight's service two years later.

Soon after this, however, the HIC materials spawned new controversy as some of ONE's librarians sought to merge the books and magazines into the general collection without ever having produced a written agreement nor having provided the basic elements of the promises made by O'Brien. In order to protect its assets, HIC's directors, Schneider, Hansen, and Glover,[14] decided to move their collection out of ONE Institute and into the Vern and Bonnie Bullough Collection on human sexuality at California State University, Northridge, where the library's staff had agreed to help inventory, receive, and properly archive the materials while working with HIC to ensure its survival as a viable nonprofit corporation, maintaining control over most of its assets. The HIC collection was removed from ONE Institute in December 2001 and put into storage until the materials could be properly inventoried and transitioned to CSUN. In May of 2002, however, HIC received a surprising letter from Tony Gardner, head of special collections at Oviatt Library. Gardner wrote that he had received a letter from the directors of ONE Institute and Archives in which they claimed to be the legal and legitimate owners of all the HIC materials. It has since cost the HIC thousands of dollars in attorney's fees (and storage) to counter the spurious claims of ONE Archives. But at last CSUN determined it was safe to accept the HIC materials, and a deal was finalized in the spring of 2007.

The Death of Jim Kepner

On Friday, November 14, 1997, Jim Kepner complained of a severe stomach-ache to his friends Walter Williams, John O'Brien, and the Reverend Florine Fleishman. He was taken to Midway Hospital, where doctors discovered a perforated intestine. Reparative surgery on Saturday, November 15, failed, and seventy-five-year-old Kepner did not survive the procedure. When Williams went to collect Kepner's personal belongings, the officials asked if he was family. Williams replied affirmatively. Later, Williams thought badly about this, but upon reflection he realized that they had become a family, of sorts. Because they had worked together toward common goals and the advancement of ONE Institute, O'Brien, Williams, and Fleishman—no matter what others might say—had indeed become Kepner's family.[15]

At his passing, hundreds of his friends remembered Kepner as one of the true, first, and greatest pioneer journalists of the homophile movement. His memorial service was held on May 22, 1998, at the Samuel Goldwyn Theater of the Academy of Motion Picture Arts and Sciences in Beverly Hills. It was an extravagant affair: hundreds of prominent gay and lesbian activists attended, and the list of speakers included Urvashi Vaid, Malcolm Boyd, Mark Thompson, Lisa Ben, Hal Call, Del Martin, Phyllis Lyon, Jose Sarria, and Harry Hay. I drove in from my home in Las Vegas to assist Williams in distributing information on ONE/IGLA to the attendees. I was introduced to Jim Schneider, who was distributing Joe Hansen's biography of Don Slater, *A Few Doors West of Hope*, in the foyer. Shoulder to shoulder with Schneider, I greeted hundreds of other gay and lesbian pilgrims, many who had traveled great distances to celebrate the life and accomplishments of Jim Kepner. I was at once humbled and invigorated by the experience, which Paul Cain has rightly called "the most illustrious assemblage ever of gay movement leaders" (2002, 26). Despite the sadness of the occasion, I cannot imagine a finer inauguration or welcoming into the rank and file of the homosexual rights movement than the one I experienced that night.

The Death of Dale Jennings

In the summer of 1998, Jennings moved from his apartment on Calumet to Schneider's house in Commerce as he could no longer care for himself alone. At first, Schneider enjoyed Jennings's company, but within weeks of his arrival, Schneider realized that Jennings had difficulty remembering basic things, like closing the door behind him and turning off the stove. Concerned, he took Jennings to the VA Hospital for testing, where he was diagnosed with vascular dementia, a harbinger of Alzheimer's. The hospital advised Schneider that Jennings would require around-the-clock supervision with a professional nursing staff. So, with Schneider's assistance, Jennings entered the Del Rio Convalescent Center near Schneider's house. Schneider was able to secure Jennings the only private room on the premises. Jennings volunteered for a study for a promising new drug under development but, ultimately, these efforts proved futile. Jennings was to end his days as his sister had, suffering from senile dementia and brain degeneration.

Jennings died of respiratory failure on May 11, 2000. Schneider stood bedside as he perished. This event profoundly affected Schneider, who has described Jennings's last, laborious breath many times to those who would listen.

The day following Jennings's death, Schneider and Williams drafted an obituary, announcing the death of this all-but-forgotten pioneer. I was recruited to help distribute the release, which I published on the ONE/IGLA Web site I had managed since Ernie Potvin died, and we faxed it to newspapers all over the country. A few gay newspapers, such as the Las Vegas *Bugle*, picked up the story. *The Los Angeles Times* published a cursory obituary on Friday, May 19 (which erroneously referred to me as a "friend of Jennings"). The *New York Times* published an extended and detailed obituary on Monday, May 22, by Dudley Clendinen, reprinting a passport photo of young Dale Jennings that Schneider provided.

Schneider arranged to have Jennings cremated, as he had done for Slater three years before. He sent the ashes to Jennings's nephew, Patrick Dale Porter, who resided in northern California. Porter received the ashes on May 26 and wrote to Schneider that they would be scattered offshore near Trinidad, California, where Jennings resided in the 1970s after the success of *The Cowboys*. After years of strife, frustration, anxiety, and poverty, Dale Jennings could finally rest.

With Jennings gone and most of the HIC materials stored with Iron Mountain, the organization's future rested with Schneider. With Glover in Louisiana, Hansen in Laguna Beach, and Sanchez in Colorado, he felt alone for the first time in decades. Schneider could only pay the bills and keep the organization intact, while keeping an eye out for those who might help. HIC was down, but it was not out. In time, Schneider hoped, the materials would be safe in the facility at USC, and HIC would have an office from which to regroup and press on. In the meantime, there was a lot of work to be done.

Further Loss

Two other deaths should be noted. On November 24, 2004, Joseph Hansen died alone in his Laguna Beach home. According to the housekeeper who found him, he had been sitting on the side of his bed, trying to catch his breath—this time to no avail. Hansen had been living on the edge for quite some time; when I first met him in 2001, he answered his door with a lit Marlboro in one hand and oxygen mask in the other. By the time he died I was used to writing obituaries and distributing press releases, but Hansen's death was different. Hansen had become a friend to me, though I feared his sharp tongue. Though he could be frustrating to work with—a curmudgeon incarnate—I had learned a lot from him, looked forward to our occasional visits, and developed a fondness for him that can only be called love.

This was a new experience for me. As ethnographer and historian, I stepped to the plate and helped to notify the public of his passing, as I had done for Jennings. But in so doing, I felt that I was somehow denied the time and privacy for my own mourning. And I felt an emotion that was new to me as a researcher: guilt. I felt guilty for having not called him more often or treated him to more burgers at Ruby's, his favorite diner. I felt guilty for the time it took me more than an hour to get from my home in San Fernando Valley to Laguna Beach, to find him standing in his open doorway fuming mad. For Hansen, as with Jennings, old age meant poverty. One time I arrived for a winter visit to find him bundled up like a Canadian lumberjack, breath vapor curling about his head. His heater had stopped working, he explained, and he didn't want to impose on his landlord to have it fixed. When I realized how poor Hansen was, I raised funds to purchase the exclusive rights to some of his short stories to post on HIC's Web site, but perhaps I could have done more. For about a year prior to his passing, Jim Schneider had provided him with $300 a month to live on.

The second death to be noted is the passing of Vern L. Bullough. Bullough had become my primary mentor through this project, a fellow academic with a simple desire to understand people, their motivations, and their institutions. As the only survivor of this history available to me who had known and worked with both Slater and Legg equally, he became one of my most objective and knowledgeable resources.

Prior to his death of cancer on June 21, 2006, Bullough was arguably the greatest living sexologist in the United States. He and his wife Bonnie had identified as sexologists since the early 1960s, when they joined the Society for the Scientific Study of Sex. His most significant contribution to the field—his "magnum opus," as he called it—was *Sexual Variance in Society and History*, published in 1976 and funded through a grant from the EEF. Subsequent publications include *Homosexuality: A History* (1979) and, with Bonnie, *Cross Dressing, Sex, and Gender* (1993). Through his career, Bullough wrote, edited, or coauthored over fifty books and 150 professional articles on subjects ranging from prostitution to homosexuality to the history of medicine and nursing. A constant activist and ally to lesbians and gays, Bullough often appeared in court as an expert witness in support of lesbian and gay parents, and he felt that the fight for gay marriage was the next great battle that the movement should undertake.

Bullough's death brought me a different emotion than guilt. Underlying my sorrow was a deep sense of loss. Bullough had become a touchstone for me. His unwavering confidence in my work with the HIC carried me through some very difficult periods, both financially and emotionally. Bullough was the only one of my mentors to be with me throughout this long process, from start to finish. Standing up to ONE National Archives the past few years has been a brave thing to do, and scary at times. Without Bullough's confidence and reassurance that I was on the right track and doing the right thing, I'm not sure I could have succeeded. As it is, I am proud to have helped HIC to partner with the special collections of Oviatt Library, CSUN, where the materials will be available to the public through the Vern and Bonnie Bullough Collection on Sex and Gender. I am pleased that ISHR has continued to support my research and has recently funded the new design of the HIC Web site. (Bullough was a member of ISHR's board and continually promoted my cause to his fellow directors.) And I was honored to speak on behalf of the homosexual community at his memorial celebration, held at the Center for Inquiry in Hollywood on September 30, 2006 (see White 2007).

There are obligations that come with fieldwork that are seldom addressed in graduate school. Traditionally, ethnographers enter into a remote and exotic field site, stay for an extended term, and then return home to begin processing their data. Through distance and time, ties, while not severed, become attenuated. But for those of us who work in our own neighborhoods, our consultants become our colleagues and, perhaps, our friends; thus, it becomes increasingly difficult to separate our personal lives from our profession. Although every situation is different, perhaps today's ethnographers should be taught a new set of fundamental tools.

What is an ethnographer to do when threatened with a lawsuit? When an aged consultant dies? When one discovers an unethical, immoral, or even illegal happening? Do ethnographers have the same sort of protections as journalists? How are our obligations different from those of journalists? Historians? I had to find my own way through a maze of such unexpected questions and problems. Some of these issues became more poignant through a project I was working on at the same time as this, dealing with a transsexual consultant who lived on parole on skid row, in downtown Los Angeles, and was assigned to a parole agent who clearly did not like her.[16] In the United States, urban anthropology cannot be disentangled from legal anthropology, medical anthropology, and applied anthropology (let alone social/cultural linguistics, economics, religious studies, and life history). But, to turn an argument by ethnographer Sherry B. Ortner on its head, (1991, 186), if we don't do it, who will? What other discipline is broad enough to even attempt such comprehensive reconstructions and analysis while delicately balancing the personal against the political?

Rather than shrink from the task of documenting and "ethnographizing" American cultural history, limiting our discipline only to the "mission of understanding other cultures" (Ortner 1991), contemporary cultural anthropologists would do well to take a fresh look about them. If we fail to turn our analytical eye onto ourselves, then ethnographers will continue to be criticized as only being concerned with the exotic, while histories of our own institutions and the individuals that drive them will be lost or inadequately recorded. Our comprehensive (social) science is the broadest yet devised. As we can embrace both ethnography and ethnology, certainly we can embrace both "self" and "other."

Finis

This book has delineated the social history of the homosexual rights movement, as it originated and has been continued in Los Angeles, California. It has attempted to relate the history of several organizations over the period of over fifty years, as constructed through participant observation and life history interviews from several of the surviving elder pioneers of that movement.

To use Jennings's metaphor, this has been an attempt to repair the chip in the teacup of gay history by using methods I had learned as a cultural anthropologist in order to cross-check and verify "facts" as I found them. In researching the fifteen-year history prior to the infamous April 27, 1965, split, I found that although the corporation sprang from a few common needs—most notably the repeal of the sodomy laws and equal rights for homosexuals—the individuals involved banded together to form not only a corporate network but also established bonds of friendship so strong that they became a virtual family to one another, a fictive kinship system that often transcended bonds of blood. As these pioneers grew old together, they began to realize that they needed each other in ways they had not anticipated. The history of the movement since the split stands as testament to the durability of these bonds, as when Jim Schneider invited Jennings into his home when he was diagnosed with Alzheimer's and when he attempted to comfort Sanchez after the death of his lover of over fifty years.

Two patterns have emerged as I have compiled this history that deserve mention. First, most of the activists, with the exception of Slater, moved to Los Angeles from other places, especially the Midwest. Like Jim Schneider, many of them brought a heartland ethic of hard work and family devotion when they migrated to Los Angeles. Once here, they wanted to reach out to homosexuals who remained "back home," and they did this through publishing ONE. This could explain the emphasis these people placed on publishing and disseminating information and history on homosexuality to those not in the urban centers.

A second pattern of note is that a great majority of these activists enjoyed long-term relationships. Even Billy Glover, the corporate playboy when he first joined with ONE, settled down for a long-term relationship once he met Melvin Cain in 1963. The stability provided them not only an emotional bulwark against the corporate strife and politics that plagued the organizations, but these partnerships also provided financial security. Bullough often reminded me that without Sanchez's work supporting Slater, Nojima's backing of Legg, and Jane Hansen's providing for Joe in lean times, these pioneer activists would not have been able to have the luxury of time to conduct their work (especially before the substantial subventions of Erickson). With the exception of Erickson, the contributions of life partners in the early days of the movement provided far more support than those of wealthy philanthropists or foundations. It seems that good lovers often make good activists. Those who are able to dedicate themselves to an organization for a long duration are also likely to form equally enduring personal relationships.

One of the things that has haunted my consultants in their later years is their fear that they had been forgotten by the movement that they helped to launch, and in many ways, their fear has come to pass. While some, such as Joseph Hansen, are occasionally remembered in the gay press, none (except perhaps for Bullough) have the notoriety or the income that they had enjoyed in their salad years. Hansen himself often said that he felt in his later days that he was "living at the bottom of the food chain," and while too proud to impose on his friends, their assistance helped him to survive. When Hansen died in November 2004, his HIC cohorts distributed the press release and helped his transgendered son, Jamie, get through the difficult times. As these pioneers have moved toward the inevitable end, they have rekindled their affection for each other and come together as family. Although I did not intend to conclude this book with a discussion of gay kindred, the experience of these pioneers show that these are pressing issues for gays as they grow older, especially after the death of a life mate or long-term partner.

If "gay" is not community, it is nothing. As society often turns its back on us, let us not turn our backs on each other. If there are any lessons to be learned from this history, it is that we need each other. I hope that through reading about this history, LGBT individuals will realize that we are often our own worst enemies. Those of us who integrate into our communities, moving to the suburbs and living a quiet (though not closeted) existence, can still participate in and contribute to the movement. Anyone with e-mail, a fax machine, telephone, or mail service is a potential activist. And those of us who live in the gay enclaves—West Hollywood, the Castro, Greenwich Village, Montrose, or Dupont Circle, to name a few—should not write off those in the suburbs as "assimilationists" in denial of their essential gayness. If we are to move forward on issues such as homosexuals/gays in the military or same-sex/gay marriage, then we need to put our differences aside long enough to recognize our common goals, our common adversaries, and our common needs as human beings.

Appendix A
Significant Locations

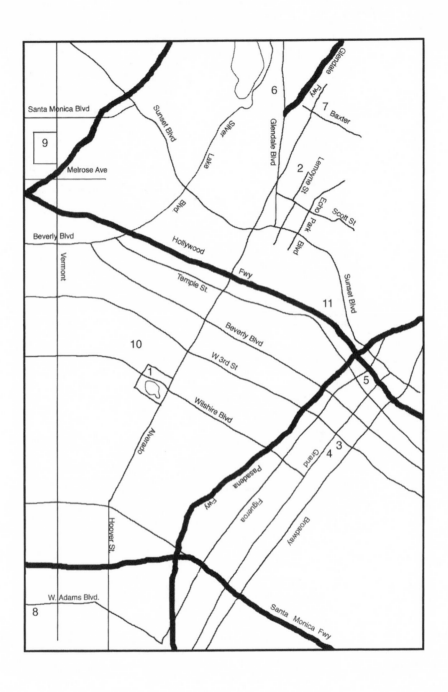

Map and Legend

Significant locations in the homosexual rights movement in the Silver Lake and Echo Park areas, 1950–55.

Legend

1. Westlake Park (now MacArthur Park).
2. Residence of Dale Jennings, 1933 Lemoyne.
3. Office of ONE, Incorporated, 232 South Hill Street.
4. Pershing Square, Fifth and Olive.
5. First residence of Don Slater and Antonio Sanchez, 221 South Bunker Hill Avenue.
6. Residence of Harry Hay, 2328 Cove Avenue.
7. Residence of Jim Kepner, 2141 Baxter Street.
8. Residence of Bill Lambert, Twenty-seventh and Dalton.
9. Los Angeles City College.
10. Residence of Chuck Rowland, 417 South Coronado.
11. Later residence of Don Slater and Antonio Sanchez, 1354 Calumet. Rudi Steinert (and later Dale Jennings) lived nearby at 1411 Calumet.

Appendix B
Pseudonyms

Pseudonyms

Real Name	Pseudonym(s)
Roy Berquist	Rolf Berlinson
Merton L. Bird	M. Byrd
Monwell Boyfrank	Manuel Boy Frank
Joan Corbin	Eve Elloree
Gregory Coron	Gregory Carr
Fred Frisbie	George Mortenson
Jack Gibson	Leslie Colfax
Billy Glover	W. E. G. McIntire
Barbara Grier	Gene Damon
Joseph Hansen	James Colton
Jane Hansen	Jane Race
Henry (Harry) Hay	Eann MacDonald
Ann Holmquist	Ann Bannon
Ross Ingersoll	Marcel Martin
Dale Jennings	Hieronymous K., Elizabeth Lalo, R. Noone, Jeff Winters
Jim Kepner	John or Jane Arnold, Dal McIntyre, Lyn Pedersen, Frank Golovitz
William Lambert/Dorr Legg	Hollister Barnes, Marvin Cutler, Richard Conger, Alison Hunter, Wendy Lane
"Mac" McNeal	K. O. Neal
Robert "Bob" Newton	Robert Earl

Betty Perdue	Geraldine Jackson
Arthur A. Peters	Fritz Peters
Chuck Rowland	David L. Freeman, Don Fry
Stella Rush	Sten Russell
Edward Sagarin	Donald Webster Cory
Chuck "Chet" Sampson	Chuck Thompson
Helen Sandoz	Helen Sanders, Ben Cat
Donald Slater	Leslie Colfax, Gregory James, Dal McIntire
Rudolph "Rudi" Steinert	Rudy H. Stewart
Merritt M. Thompson	Thomas M. Merritt
D. B. Vest	Gerald Heard
Joe Weaver	Joe Aaron
Bailey Whitaker	Guy Rousseau
Irma "Corky" Wolf	Ann Carll Reid

Corporate Pseudonyms

Cal, Del, Hal, Sal, or Val McIntire (ONE, Incorporated, after 1960)
Robert Gregory (first used by Julian "Woody" Underwood)
Ursula Enters Copely (HIC)

Appendix C
Dramatis Personae

Martin Block. Owner of Studio Bookshop on Hollywood Boulevard in the 1950s. An original founder of ONE, Incorporated, and editor of *ONE Magazine*.

Monwell Boyfrank. Joined ONE at the urging of his friend Henry Gerber. Replaced Morgan Farley as a board member in 1963. Sided with Legg after the 1965 division.

Vern Bullough. Worked with Slater and Legg to have the southern California ACLU defend homosexuals in 1965.

John Burnside. Long-term companion to Harry Hay. Elected to ONE's board and resigned on the same night.

Melvin Cain. Met Billy Glover on November 22, 1963, and began to volunteer for ONE, Incorporated.

Joan Corbin. As "Eve Elloree," primary artist for *ONE Magazine*.

Reed Erickson. Founder of ISHR, he served as its president for fifteen years. Purchaser of the Milbank Estate.

Morgan Farley. Helped ONE to find and secure the Venice Street office in 1962.

Fred Frisbie. Early member of Mattachine and long-term supporter of ONE, Incorporated. In 1961, replaced Kepner as president of ONE.

John D. "Jack" Gibson. As "Leslie Colfax," worked with Don Slater to invent the library system used to catalog ONE's archives.

Billy Glover. Began volunteering for ONE, Incorporated, after moving to Los Angeles in 1962. Currently vice president of HIC.

Joseph Hansen. Began writing for *ONE Magazine* in 1961. With his wife, Jane, helped to found HIC in 1968 and to produce and edit *Tangents* magazine. Helped to organize the first gay pride parade in June 1970 as HIC's representative to Christopher Street West. A director of HIC until his death in November 2004.

Harry Hay. Founder of Mattachine in Silver Lake in 1950. Helped to organize the 1966 motorcade protesting the exclusion of homosexuals in the military. Hay is largely considered the father of the contemporary gay rights movement.

Ross Ingersoll. Editor of *ONE Magazine* after Jim Kepner's resignation in 1961. Continued to work with Slater after the 1965 split of ONE, Incorporated, and subsequent transition from *ONE Magazine* to *Tangents*.

Dale Jennings. Among the first five founders of Mattachine and first editor of *ONE Magazine*. First secretary-treasurer of ONE, Incorporated. Resigned from ONE for reasons unknown on March 22, 1954.

Eric Julber. Attorney who helped to incorporate ONE in 1953. Fought for the right to distribute *ONE Magazine* through the mail, landing a significant Supreme Court victory in 1958.

Jim Kepner. An editor of *ONE Magazine* from the resignation of Jennings in March 1953 until 1960.

Morris Kight. Chairman and founder of Christopher Street West and organizer of the first gay pride parade in Los Angeles, June 1970.

William Lambert/Dorr Legg: As William Lambert, among the first officers of ONE, Incorporated. As Dorr Legg, one of the founders and key administrators of ONE's education division, ONE Institute of Homophile Studies.

Chuck Rowland. One of the first five founders of Mattachine. Believed with Hay that homosexuals comprised a cultural minority.

Stella Rush. Director of ONE, Incorporated, from 1955 until resigning in 1960. Served on the editorial board for eighteen months prior to her resignation.

Chet Sampson. Owned a travel agency. Coordinated the second trip to Europe in 1965.

Jim Schneider. Volunteer for ONE, Incorporated, since 1962. Current president of HIC.

Herb Selwyn. Attorney who incorporated Mattachine Society in 1954 and signed the articles of incorporation for HIC. One of the few attorneys in Los Angeles willing to represent people accused of homosexual acts during the 1950s.

Donald Slater. A founding editor of *ONE Magazine* and first vice president of ONE, Inc.

Rudi Steinert. One of the first students of ONE Institute in the fall of 1956. Longtime friend and neighbor to Slater and Sanchez on Calumet. Conducted ONE's first European tour in 1965.

Merritt M. Thompson. Professor of education at USC. Dean of ONE Institute since its inception in 1956.

Bailey Whitaker. African American schoolteacher who helped create *ONE* magazine and proposed the name "ONE" after a line from a poem by Thomas Carlyle.

Irma "Corky" Wolf. As "Ann Carll Reid," editor of *ONE Magazine* after Jennings's resignation in 1954.

Notes

Introduction

1. Legg, in *Homosexuals Today*, noted that Lisa Ben had previously achieved some notoriety through writing science fiction (1956, 90). However, Ben later told historian Paul D. Cain that she "was not a minor star of science fiction" and asked that he help debunk that myth (Cain 2002, 13).

2. Personal interview, September 6, 2004.

3. Personal communication via e-mail, November 28, 2006.

4. Personal interview, September 23, 2004.

Chapter 1: Mattachine (1948–52)

1. Comments made in *Symposium on Outing*, at the HIC office in the spring of 1990. The exact date was not recorded and has yet to be ascertained.

2. Ibid.

3. George Mortensen, personal communication, February 3, 2001.

4. On the berdache, see Lang (1998), Roscoe (1991), and Williams (1986). On two-spirit people, see Gilley (2006) and Jacobs, Thomas, and Lang (1997).

5. It should be noted that during his years as a Communist, Hay had married his wife, Anita, in September 1938, and they adopted a daughter, Hannah, in 1943. During this time, he continued having affairs with men and cruising Pershing Square. He and Anita divorced in September 1951, about the time of his first anniversary with Gernreich. Hay (1996) and Slade (2001) cover the details of their unhappy relationship.

6. A copy of "Preliminary Concepts" is reprinted in Hay 1996, 63–75.

7. Paul Cain interview with Jim Kepner, January 8, 1994.

8. Ibid.

9. According to an October 1990 letter to Dale Jennings.

10. Ibid.

11. Ibid.

12. Ibid.

13. HIC *Newsletter* #42, undated (probably 1990).

14. According to Jennings's birth certificate.

15. Undated fan letter.

16. Letter to "Lee," June 7, 1983.

17. Letter from Jennings's nephew, Patrick Dale Porter, to Jim Schneider, dated May 11, 2000.

18. Ibid.

19. Jim Schneider, personal communication.

20. These photos can be seen at the HIC Web site under Jennings's personal profile.

21. Letter to Jennings from Don Slater, November 27, 1990. Also letter to Jim Schneider from Patrick Dale Porter, May 11, 2000.

22. Antonio Sanchez, personal communication, January 16, 2004.

23. According to Porter's letter to Schneider, Tuck's real name was Esther Mayer, and she had been an actress in Jennings's theater company in the 1940s.

24. Letter from Patrick Dale Porter to Jim Schneider, dated May 11, 2000.

25. Screen Actors' Guild.

26. According to ONE's attorney Herb Selwyn, in the 1950s Section 288a involved oral copulation, a crime that was punishable with up to fourteen years in prison. Although the law could theoretically be applied to heterosexuals as well as homosexuals, it was seldom applied to heterosexuals (Marcus 2002, 38).

Chapter 2: *The Launch of ONE (1952–53)*

1. Personal communication, letter from Fred Frisbie dated February 3, 2001.

2. Ibid.

3. Called "Dale Martin" in a copy of the original minutes on file in the HIC archives.

4. Identified as Johnny Button by Martin Block (Marcus 2002, 39).

5. July 1995 newsletter.

6. Lambert was his mother's maiden name.

7. Interview with Paul Cain, March 12, 1994.

8. Personal communication, e-mail from Wayne Dynes, November 28, 2006.

9. Also known as Knights of the Clocks, an acronym for Cloistered Order of Conclaved Knights of Sophistry (Faderman and Timmons 2006, 112).

10. Although Legg claimed Knights was founded as early as 1947, Kepner found on perusing the secretary/treasurer records that it started later. Interview with Paul Cain, January 8, 1994.

11. According to Martin Block, this meeting was held at Johnny Button's West Hollywood home. Also according to Block, Button first proposed the idea of the magazine (Marcus 2002, 39). With this known, Legg probably referred to Button when he reported that the host of that week's Mattachine discussion group came up with the idea for the magazine, then "thought better of the idea the next day, and quickly resigned" (Cain 2002, 5).

12. A pseudonym.

13. Now the location of the Walt Disney Concert Hall (111 South Grand Avenue).

14. Listed as "M. Snider" in Slater's minutes of January 9, 1953.

15. Slater and Sanchez resided at 221 South Bunker Hill Avenue at the time.

16. Kepner has pointed out that the name evoked a "ubiquitous World War II joke about an army sergeant teaching a group of rookies to count off." According to the joke, the sergeant came up to the first recruit, who had refused to speak out, and barked: "'Hey! You! Ain't you one?' 'Yes,' lisped the recruit, 'Are you one too?'" Kepner added that because of the famous joke, "'He's one' was common Gay jargon" (1998, 3).

17. According to later corporate records, the first issue garnered $76.50 in prepublication donations, their entire pre-1953 income.

18. Letter to Jim Schneider from Patrick Dale Porter dated May 11, 2000.

19. Personal communication with Fred Frisbie, June 22, 2000.

20. According to Bullough (1976). Bullough's primary source of these pseudonyms was Dorr Legg.

21. Writing as David L. Freeman.

22. Jennings used this word to describe Rowland, Hay, and Lambert in his 1990s correspondence with Don Slater.

Chapter 3: Cleaning House (1953–54)

1. Document provided by ISHR. Although the letter is dated February 24, 1953, the attorneys did not stamp it as received until November 5, 1953.

2. The dramatic twist of this final sentence might be considered Jennings's signature, although I have not been able to verify his having used the Saunders pseudonym.

3. For the full articles and bylaws of ONE, Incorporated, see the history section of HIC's Web site: http://www.tangentgroup.org.

4. A letter from Jennings to the board dated October 27, 1953, refutes this, stating that the bylaws had indeed been adopted during this October 18 meeting. It seems that the bylaws that were adopted on October 16 were never properly ratified by the directors.

5. I discovered Jennings's acceptance speech in his personal files in the HIC archives and have since posted it on the HIC Web site.

6. Kepner (1998, 5) seems to attribute the "sharper layout and delightful artwork" of this issue to Jennings's resignation, but Jennings was very much a part of this issue and did not resign from ONE, Incorporated, until March 1954.

7. I was unable to ascertain if Eric Julber or Herb Selwyn contributed this statement. Both attorneys were working for ONE and/or Mattachine at this time. Selwyn composed wallet-sized cards titled "Know Your Legal Rights" that were distributed by Mattachine in the late 1950s (Marcus 1992, 58), but he could not recall having contributed this earlier statement.

8. On the Stonewall uprisings, see esp. Duberman (1994) and Carter (2004).

9. This is the first revelation of everyone's real name in the corporation's minutes.

Chapter 4: The Establishment of ONE Institute (1955–60)

1. Slater was officially elected secretary-treasurer during a special meeting of the board of directors on April 1, 1954, with Lambert and Wolf present.

2. Personal communication with Vern Bullough.

3. Reported as August in Marcus (1992, 43).

4. Written by John O'Brien, Walter L. Williams, and Ernie Potvin.

5. Interview with Paul Cain, January 8, 1994.

6. Kepner has described his coming out experience in an article titled "*Toujours Gai*," published in the first issue of *Pursuit and Symposium* (1966).

7. Several of these are in the Vern and Bonnie Bullough Collection on Sex and Gender at Oviatt Library, CSUN.

8. Interview with Paul Cain, January 8, 1994.

9. Ibid.

10. Ibid.

11. Ibid.

12. Ibid.

13. Ibid.

14. As Ann Carll Reid.

15. Reprinted in Legg 1994, 347–51.

16. 1958 annual report for ONE, Incorporated.

17. Legg continued to be known as Lambert when listed in *ONE Magazine*, but for his new role as professor and director of ONE Institute, the name W. Dorr Legg better suited him.

18. The complete text of this brief has been posted on the HIC Web site: www.tangentgroup.org.

19. 1958 annual report for ONE, Incorporated, p. 3.

20. A newsletter for the Friends of ONE launched in 1956.

21. *ONE Confidential*, Fall 1958, p. 2.

22. Ibid.

23. Ibid.

24. Ibid.

25. Although these volumes never materialized, portions from Kepner's work "Introduction to Homophile Studies" and Legg's "Homosexuality in History" were later printed in the fall 1958 issue of the *One Institute Quarterly*.

26. Julber filed the writ in person and paid his own travel expenses (Hansen 1998, 37).

27. Dated October 21, 1957.

28. It is exceedingly rare for corporate minutes to refer to officers by their "real" first names. The only other minutes I have found that listed members by their real first names were those of Jennings's resignation on March 22, 1954.

29. The name "Jim" was scratched out as women's editor and "Nancy" written in.

30. *ONE Confidential*, Winter 1958, p. 1.

31. Ibid., p. 2.

32. Annual report, 1958, p. 6.

33. Ibid., p. 12.

34. Ibid.

35. Ibid., p. 14.

36. Ibid.

37. Probably either Jack Gibson or Slater himself.

38. According to the minutes, this election actually occurred during a board meeting on February 2, 1960.

39. Legg continued to tell people that ONE had been unable to achieve tax-exempt status because it made a profit through its selling of *ONE Magazine*. Legg related this, for instance, to Evelyn Hooker in a letter dated February 8, 1968 (document provided by ISHR).

40. Personal communication, e-mail, February 13, 2007.

Chapter 5: Separation (1960–62)

1. Annual report, 1960, p. 17.

2. Ibid., p. 5.

3. Ibid., p. 6.

4. According to Bullough et al. (1976), Marilyn Moon and Nancy Cowan were the real women behind the pseudonym of Alison Hunter, although Slater sometime used the name, too. In the 1967 agreement of settlement, Legg's faction claimed the exclusive right to the pseudonym.

5. Annual report, 1960, p. 17.

6. Letter to Don Slater, June 21, 1977.

7. Proposed Baker Foundation report dated August 16, 1962.

8. Ibid.

Chapter 6: Division (1963–65)

1. Boyfrank's minutes are erroneously dated 1962.
2. Boyfrank's minutes seem to be erroneously dated Sunday, March 3.
3. Lambert first invited Winn to join ONE in April 1963.
4. In Slater's notes and deposition from the pending trial. For a full copy, see the HIC Web site at www.tangentgroup.org.
5. Sanchez's proxy request, on file in the Slater collection at the HIC, is dated January 27, 1964, and authorizes Don Slater "to act as my proxy in all considerations pertaining to the 1963 Business Meeting held at ONE's offices 2256 Venice Blvd., Los Angeles, January 27, 1964." However, this is not the correct date for the business meeting.
6. Legg's reply to Ed Raiden's interrogatories, January 26, 1966.
7. Ibid.
8. Letter from Don Slater to Ed Raiden, August 15, 1965.
9. Such introspection on Slater's part is suggested in his notes for the pending court case, as I discuss in the next chapter.
10. Legg's reply to Ed Raiden's interrogatories, January 26, 1966.
11. As "R. H. Stuart."
12. Vol. 9, no. 11.
13. Ibid., p. 3.
14. Ibid., p. 4.
15. Faderman and Timmons (2006, 116) list Nojima as a founding member of ONE, Incorporated, but this is not true. According to Dynes (2002, 102), Legg and Nojima did not become partners until about the time of this meeting, in the mid-1960s.
16. Boyfrank later penned in his minutes "to fill out the term of Joe Aaron, resigned," although Weaver (as "Aaron") had not resigned as this point.
17. Here, Ingersoll's recollection may be incorrect. According to Hansen and others, Slater was not present at this meeting.
18. Although many have referred to the event described as "the Heist"—a phrase Slater himself often used—I have decided on the term "mutiny" at the request of my consultants.

Chapter 7: Two Years of War (1965–67)

1. Although technically true, it should be noted that while not an officer, Slater remained a director; also, the reason he had been removed from ONE's payroll was because he was being paid through ISHR.
2. Legg, Slater, Sanchez, Boyfrank, Bonham, Newton, Coron, Dyer, Weaver, Steinert, Winn, and Sampson.
3. Letter to "Those Concerned with the internal affairs of ONE, Incorporated," dated May 8, 1965.

4. A blank name commonly used in lawsuits at this time, as in John or Jane Doe. A real name might be added later should the name of a person become known to the plaintiff.

5. As for the mention of "Does One through Twenty-Five," the claim stated that they did not know who or what comprised this group but asked to provide their names in future court filings.

6. The defendants had to purchase a bond themselves, valued at $20,000, from Northwestern National Insurance Company, for the amount of $200. They did this on July 22, 1965.

7. Billy Glover, personal communication, summer 2003.

8. Glover and Sanchez, personal communication, February 28, 2007. Glover, Sanchez, and Schneider recall the bond having been for a larger amount, perhaps $50,000, and the person who loaned Slater the money was Katina Barinos.

9. Aaron actually resigned on April 23, less than a week after the split.

10. Legg reported that a meeting of members occurred later that Sunday, April 18, 1965, at 5:00 p.m., but I have been unable to find copies of the minutes of that meeting (although they were supposedly admitted as Exhibit F).

11. From appellant's opening brief, appeal from Superior Court of Los Angeles County, Hon. Richard L. Wells, Judge.

12. Ibid.

13. Ibid.

14. According to Reid Rasmussen, part of the delay was that Legg refused to take the oath.

15. The full transcripts of this interrogatory can readily be accessed through the history section of the HIC Web site (www.tangentgroup.org). Most of the quotes in this fictionalized vignette are taken verbatim from the transcript and therefore mirror the capitalization and punctuation style of that document.

16. Other previous directors Slater named were Robert J. Underwood, Ronald Longworth, Clarence Harrison, John Lawson, Don Plagmann, and Dale Jennings.

17. Answers of plaintiff to interrogatories propounded by defendant Bank of America, June 15, 1966.

18. ISHR provided this document.

19. From a letter to Chodos from Lewis Bonham, March 6, 1967. ISHR provided this letter.

20. ISHR provided this letter.

21. Early drafts were titled "Agreement of Compromise," but the parties changed it to "Agreement of Settlement" by the final version.

22. The original printed date was 1965, but on signed copies the year was changed to 1967.

23. According to Joseph Hansen, Legg already had a copy of the mailing list that he had made illicitly prior to the mutiny. When Slater and others wondered how Legg could continue to distribute the magazine, he told them that he had committed

the list to memory (see Dynes 2002, 100). Legg also asserted that Slater had never returned a draft of his master's thesis on the sociology of homosexuality (Dynes 2002), but I have not found such a document in the HIC archives and seriously doubt such document ever existed.

24. Drafts of this letter indicate Legg originally intended to sign the document, rather than Bonham.

Chapter 8: The Founding of ISHR, HIC, and Christopher Street West (1965–70)

1. ONE Institute provided a copy of this document via fax on July 8, 2002.

2. Interview with Joseph Hansen, September 2, 2004.

3. In correspondences with Erickson and Slater, Legg referred to him as "Bill Crocker" or "Bill C."

4. In later drafts of this proposal, Robert G. Winn is listed as vice president in place of Don Slater.

5. See Gallo (2006), 47–48.

6. Interview with Vern Bullough, September 23, 2004.

7. Ibid.

8. Interview with Vern Bullough, February 19, 2002.

9. Ibid; also telephone interview with Wayne Dynes, June 21, 2004.

10. Personal communication, e-mail with Wayne Dynes, June 22, 2004.

11. Document in the HIC archives (date-stamped—erroneously?—March 4, 1966).

12. Found in the HIC collection.

13. Interview with Vern Bullough, September 24, 2004.

14. Interview with the Reverend Florine Fleishman, October 20, 1999.

15. A copy of the official bylaws is available in PDF format on the HIC Web site at www.tangentgroup.org.

16. Billy Glover, personal communication, February 14, 2004.

17. Dated November 14, 1969.

18. Letter from Jim Schneider to Walter L. Williams, March 21, 2001.

19. Paul D. Cain interview with Morris Kight, March 13, 1994.

20. Personal interview with Joseph Hansen, September 2, 2004.

21. Ibid.

22. Hansen continued to support the HIC, though, and after Slater's death in 1997, he regained his role on HIC's board in order to help steward the organization.

Chapter 9: Conclusion(s)

1. Antonio Sanchez, personal communication, February 11, 2004.

2. David Cameron, interview by Holly Devor, May 14, 1996. Interview notes provided by ISHR.

3. From an unpublished draft manuscript, "A History of the Milbank/McFie Estate," by David G. Cameron, provided by ISHR.

4. *Reed Erickson et al. v. W. Dorr Legg et al.* "Appeal: Respondent's Brief," by Thomas Hunter Russell and Robert A. Wynn. Filed on October 16, 1991. Document provided by ISHR.

5. Wayne Dynes, personal communication, e-mail, February 13, 2007.

6. ISHR provided a copy of this document.

7. According to Holly Devor, Erickson and Evangelina Trujillo Armendariz were married in Baton Rouge in 1967, Erickson's third marriage (2002, 385).

8. Letter to Erickson from Legg, dated April 2, 1984.

9. Walter Williams persuaded Hal Call to donate this money back to ISHR to establish a scholarship.

10. Fall/Winter 1994(?).

11. Now the ONE National Gay and Lesbian Archives.

12. Letter dated January 30, 1995.

13. Should have been Jim Schneider.

14. Hansen was not aware of the situation until afterward, but he supported the move and has been supportive of the association with CSUN.

15. Walter Williams, personal communication, November 16, 1997.

16. This is the same consultant I wrote about before (White 1998).

References

Agee, James, and Walker Evans. [1939] 2001. *Let Us Now Praise Famous Men*. Boston: Houghton Mifflin.

Alwood, Edward. 1996. *Straight News: Gays, Lesbians, and the News Media*. New York: Columbia University Press.

Archer, Bert. 2002. *The End of Gay (and the Death of Heterosexuality)*. New York: Thunder's Mouth Press.

Bailey, F. G. 1983. *Tactical Uses of Passion: An Essay on Power, Reason, and Reality*. Ithaca, N.Y.: Cornell University Press.

———. 2001. *Stratagems and Spoils: A Social Anthropology of Politics*. Cambridge, Mass.: Westview Press.

Barr, James. 1950. *Quatrefoil*. New York: Greenberg.

———. 1951. *Derricks*. New York: Greenberg.

———. 1955. *Game of Fools*. Los Angeles: ONE, Incorporated.

Benedict, Ruth. 1934. *Patterns of Culture*. New York: Houghton Mifflin.

Benjamin, Harry. 1952. "Review of *The Homosexual in America: A Subjective Approach* by Donald Webster Cory." *American Journal of Psychotherapy* 6 (April): 356–59.

Bérubé, Allan. 1990. *Coming Out Under Fire: The History of Gay Men and Women in World War Two*. New York: Free Press.

Boas, Franz. 1920. "The Methods of Anthropology." *American Anthropologist* 22, no. 4: 311–21.

Briggs, Arthur A. 1952. *Walt Whitman, Thinker and Artist*. New York: Philosophical Library.

Bruner, Jerome. 2002. *Making Stories: Law, Literature, Life*. Cambridge Mass.: Harvard University Press.

Bullough, Vern L. 1976. *Sexual Variance in Society and History*. New York: Wiley Interscience.

———. 1979. *Homosexuality: A History.* New York: Garland.

———. 2002a. *Before Stonewall: Activists for Gay and Lesbian Rights in Historical Context.* Binghamton, N.Y.: Harrington Park Press.

———. 2002b. "Harry Hay." In Bullough 2002a, 73–82.

———. 2002c. "William Edward (Billy) Glover." In Bullough 2002a, 121–23.

———, and Bonnie Bullough. 1993. *Cross Dressing, Sex, and Gender.* Philadelphia: University of Pennsylvania Press.

———, W. Dorr Legg, Barrett W. Elcano, and Jim Kepner. 1976. *An Annotated Bibliography of Homosexuality.* 2 vols. New York: Garland.

Cain, Paul D. 2002. *Leading the Parade: Conversations with America's Most Influential Lesbians and Gay Men.* Lanham, Md.: Scarecrow Press.

Calverton, V. F. 1931. *The Making of Man: An Outline of Anthropology.* New York: Modern Library.

Carter, David. 2004. *Stonewall.* New York: St. Martin's Press.

Center for Preservation Education and Planning. 2000. *Gay and Lesbian L.A. History Map.* Los Angeles: Los Angeles Gay and Lesbian History Research Project.

Cole, Rob. 2004. "Remembering Morris." www.lapride.org/MorrisKight.htm. Accessed May 24, 2004.

Colville, Andrew. 1999. *Live on Tape: The Life and Times of Morris Kight: Liberator.*

Cory, Donald Webster [Edward Sagarin]. 1951. *The Homosexual in America: A Subjective Approach.* New York: Greenberg.

———. 1953. An Address to the International Committee for Sex Equality. *ONE* 1, no. 2 (February): 2–11.

D'Emilio, John. 1983. *Sexual Politics, Sexual Communities: The Making of a Homosexual Minority in the United States, 1940–1970.* Chicago: University of Chicago Press.

Devor, Aaron H., and Nicholas Matte. 2004. "ONE Inc. and Reed Erickson: The Uneasy Collaboration of Gay and Trans Activism, 1964–2003." *Gay and Lesbian Quarterly* 10, no. 2: 179–209.

Devor, Holly. 2002. "Reed Erickson: How One Transsexed Man Supported ONE." In Bullough 2002a, 383–92.

Duberman, Martin. 1994. *Stonewall.* New York: Plume.

Dynes, Wayne R. 1985. *Homolexis: A Historical and Cultural Lexicon of Homosexuality.* New York: Gai Saber Monograph No. 4.

———. 1987. *Homosexuality: A Research Guide.* New York: Garland.

———. 2002. "W. Dorr Legg." In Bullough 2002a, 94–102.

Faderman, Lillian, and Stuart Timmons. 2006. *Gay L.A.: A History of Sexual Outlaws, Power Politics, and Lipstick Lesbians.* New York: Basic Books.

Ford, Clellen S., and Frank A. Beach. 1951. *Patterns of Sexual Behavior.* New York: Harper & Brothers.

Frisbie, Fred [George Henry Mortenson]. 2000. "Random Notes about Pioneering Movement of Gay Rights." HIC collection. Unpublished essay dated June 22, 2000.

———. 2001. Letter dated Feb. 3, 2001

Gaddis, John Lewis. 2002. *The Landscape of History*. Oxford: Oxford University Press.

Gallo, Marcia M. 2006. *Different Daughters: A History of the Daughters of Bilitis and the Rise of the Lesbian Rights Movement*. New York: Carroll & Graf.

Gambone, Philip. 1997. *Something Inside: Conversations with Gay Fiction Writers*. Madison: University of Wisconsin Press.

Gannett, Lewis, and William A. Percy III. 2002. "Jim Kepner." In Bullough 2002a, 124–34.

Gerber, Henry. 1962. "The Society for Human Rights." *ONE Magazine* 10, no. 9 (September): 5–10.

Gilley, Joseph. 2006. *Becoming Two-Spirit: Gay Identity and Social Acceptance in Indian Country*. Lincoln: University of Nebraska Press.

Glover, William Edward. 1997. "Soldiering On." In Homosexual Information Center, Inc. 1997, 29–30.

Hansen, Joseph. 1970. *Fadeout*. New York: Harper & Row.

———. 1992. "Autobiography." In *The Gay and Lesbian Literary Companion*, ed. Sharon Malinowski and Christa Brelin, 231–52. Detroit: Visible Ink Press.

———. 1997. "Forward." In Homosexual Information Center, Inc. 1997, 3–5.

———. 1998. *A Few Doors West of Hope: The Life and Times of Dauntless Don Slater*. Universal City, Calif.: Homosexual Information Center.

———. 2002. "Don Slater." In Bullough 2002a, 103–14.

Hastings, Solomon. 1997. "Homosexuals in the Mystery: Victims or Victimizers?" In Winn 1997, 494–96.

Hay, Harry. 1996. *Radically Gay: Gay Liberation in the Words of Its Founder*, ed. Will Roscoe. Boston: Beacon Press.

here! Focus. 2006. *The One Archives*. Video Web broadcast on YouTube (www.youtube .com). Accessed January 15, 2007.

Homosexual Information Center, Inc. 1997. *Don Slater: A Gay Rights Pioneer Remembered by His Friends*. Los Angeles: Homosexual Information Center.

Hooker, Evelyn. 1965. "Male Homosexuals and Their Worlds." In *Sexual Inversion*, ed. Judd Marmor, 83–107. New York: Basic Books.

Hoskins, Janet. 1993. *The Play of Time: Kodi Perspectives on Calendars, History, and Exchange*. Berkeley: University of California Press.

———. 1998. *Biographical Objects: How Things Tell the Stories of People's Lives*. New York: Routledge.

Humphreys, Laud. 1970. *Tearoom Trade: Impersonal Sex in Public Places*. Chicago: Aldine.

———. 1972. *Out of the Closets: The Sociology of Homosexual Liberation*. Englewood Cliffs, N.J.: Prentice-Hall.

Ingersoll, Ross. 1997. "The Great Divide." In Homosexual Information Center, Inc. 1997, 11–13.

Jacobs, Sue Ellen, Wesley Thomas, and Sabine Lang. 1997. *Two-Spirit People: Native*

American Gender Identity, Sexuality, and Spirituality. Champaign: University of Illinois Press.

Jennings, Dale. 1953a. "To Be Accused, Is to Be Guilty." *ONE Magazine* (January): 10–13.

—— [Hieronymous K.]. 1953b. "The Mattachine." *ONE Magazine* (January): 18–19.

—— [Jeff Winters]. 1953c. "As for Me…" *ONE Magazine* (February): 11–13.

—— [Jeff Winters]. 1953d. "Homosexuals Are Not People." *ONE Magazine* (March): 2–6.

—— [Jeff Winters]. 1954. "Can Homosexuals Organize?" *ONE Magazine* 2, no. 1 (January): 4–8.

——. 1968. *The Ronin.* Rutland, Vt., and Tokyo: Charles E. Tuttle.

——. 1971. *The Cowboys.* New York: Stein and Day.

——. 1990. "The Trouble with Fairies." Unpublished manuscript. HIC collection.

——. 1991. "Angels on the Head of a Pin." Unpublished manuscript dated August 24. HIC collection.

——. 1992. "A Boy Named Jack." Unpublished manuscript dated April 14. HIC collection.

—— [Jeff Winters]. 1998. "Jim Kepner." *ONE/IGLA Bulletin* (Winter): 1, 6–7.

Kaiser, Charles. 1997. *The Gay Metropolis: 1940–1996.* New York: Orion Books.

Katz, Jonathan Ned. [1976] 1992. *Gay American History: Lesbians and Gay Men in the U.S.A.: A Documentary.* Rev. ed. New York: Meridian.

Kepner, James. 1966a. "Toujours Gai." *Pursuit and Symposium* 1, no. 1 (March–April): 3–7, 23.

—— [Lyn Pedersen]. 1966b. "A Gay Camp Looks at the Camp Cult." *Pursuit and Symposium* 1, no. 1 (March–April): 17–18.

——. 1971. *The House That Found a Home.* Los Angeles: Rancho SouthEast Press.

——. 1988. *Gay Los Angeles: The Early Days.* Los Angeles: International Gay and Lesbian Archives.

——. 1989. *Our Movement Before Stonewall.* Los Angeles: International Gay and Lesbian Archives.

——. 1994. "Goals, Progress and Shortcomings of America's Gay Movement." Self-published lecture, July (originally published 1993).

——. 1997. "A Pioneer Passes." In Homosexual Information Center, Inc. 1997, 6–7.

——. 1998. *Rough News, Daring Views: 1950's Pioneer Press Journalism.* New York: Harrington Park Press.

——. n.d. "The Women of ONE." http://www.lib.usc.edu/~retter/onewomen.html.

——, and Stephen O. Murray. 2002. "Henry Gerber (1895–1972): Grandfather of the American Gay Movement." In Bullough 2002a, 24–34.

Kinsey, Alfred C., Wardell B. Pomeroy, and Clyde E. Martin. 1948. *Sexual Behavior in the Human Male.* Philadelphia: W. B. Saunders.

Kinsey, Alfred C., Wardell B. Pomeroy, Clyde E. Martin, and Paul H. Gebhard. 1949. *Concepts of Normality and Abnormality in Sexual Behavior.* New York: Grune and Stratton. Reprint from *Psychosexual Development in Health and Disease.*

LA Pride. "CSW History." http://www.lapride.org. Accessed March 15, 2007.

Lait, Jack, and Lee Mortimer. 1951. *Washington Confidential.* New York: Crown.

Lang, Sabine. 1998. *Men as Women, Women as Men.* Austin: University of Texas Press.

Legg, W. Dorr [Marvin Cutler], editor. 1956. *Homosexuals Today: A Handbook of Organizations and Publications.* Los Angeles: ONE, Incorporated.

——, editor. 1994. *Homophile Studies in Theory and Practice.* San Francisco: GLB Publishers.

Licata, Salvatore J. 1978. *Gay Power: A History of the American Gay Movement, 1908–1974.* Ph.D. diss., University of Southern California.

——. 1981. "The Homosexual Rights Movement in the United States: A Traditionally Overlooked Area of American History." *Journal of Homosexuality,* 6, nos. 1–2: 161–89.

Loffreda, Beth. 2001. *Losing Matt Shepard: Life and Politics in the Aftermath of Anti-Gay Murder.* New York: Columbia University Press.

Lucas, Charles. 1997. "The Happy Warriors." In Homosexual Information Center, Inc. 1997, 14–16.

Marcus, Eric. 1992. *Making History: The Struggle for Gay and Lesbian Equal Rights, 1945–1990: An Oral History.* New York: HarperCollins.

——. 2002. *Making Gay History: The Half-Century Fight for Lesbian and Gay Equal Rights.* New York: New York: HarperCollins.

Martin, Del, and Phyllis Lyon. [1972] 1991. *Lesbian/Woman.* Volcano, Calif.: Volcano Press.

Masters, R. E. L. 1962. *The Homosexual Revolution: A Challenging Exposé of the Social and Political Directions of a Minority Group.* New York: Julian Press.

Maxey, Dr. Wallace de Ortega (editor). 1958. *Sex and Censorship.* Vol. 1, no. 1. San Francisco: Mid-Tower.

Moore, G. Alexander. 1998. *Cultural Anthropology: The Field Study of Human Beings.* San Diego: Collegiate Press.

Moore, Sally Falk. 1978. "Old Age in a Life-Term Social Arena: Some Chagga of Kilimanjaro in 1974." In Myerhoff and Simic 1978, 23–76.

Murdoch, Joyce, and Deb Price. 2001. *Courting Justice: Gay and Lesbian Americans vs. the Supreme Court.* New York: Basic Books.

Murray, Stephen O. 2002. "Donald Webster Cory." In Bullough 2002a, 83–93.

Myerhoff, Barbara G. 1979. *Number Our Days.* New York: E. P. Dutton.

——, and Andrei Simic, editors. 1978. *Life's Career—Aging.* Thousand Oaks, Calif.: Sage.

Ortner, Sherry B. 1991. "Reading America." In *Recapturing Anthropology: Working in the Present,* ed. Richard G. Fox. Santa Fe, N.M.: School of American Research Press.

Perry, Troy. 1972. *The Lord Is My Shepherd and He Knows I'm Gay: The Autobiography of the Reverend Troy D. Perry*. Los Angeles: Universal Fellowship Press.

———, and Thomas L. P. Swicegood. 1990. *Don't Be Afraid Anymore: The Story of Reverend Troy Perry and the Metropolitan Community Churches*. New York: St. Martin's Press.

Picano, Felice. 2002. "Morris Kight (1919–): Community Activist." In Bullough 2002a, 399–405.

Potvin, Ernie. 1997. "Jim Kepner 1923–1997." *ONE/IGLA Bulletin* 4 (Winter): 1, 6–7.

———. 1998. "Kepner Remembered: Pioneer Gay Journalist, Historian and Archives Founder Departs at 74." *ONE/IGLA Bulletin* 5 (Summer): 1, 6–13.

Praunheim, Rosa von. 1979. *Army of Lovers*. London: Gay Men's Press.

Pronzini, Bill, and Marcia Muller. 1986. *1001 Midnights: The Aficionado's Guide to Mystery and Detective Fiction*. New York: Arbor House.

Rodgers, Bruce. 1972. *The Queen's Vernacular: A Gay Lexicon*. San Francisco: Straight Arrow Books. (Reprinted in 1979 as *Gay Talk: A Sometimes Outrageous Dictionary of Gay Slang*.)

Roscoe, Will. 1991. *The Zuni Man-Woman*. Albuquerque: University of New Mexico Press.

———. 1996a. "Gay Liberation: The Birth of an Idea." In Hay 1996, 3–14.

———. 1996b. "Mattachine, 1948–1953." In Hay 1996, 37–59.

Rush, Stella. 2002. "Helen Sandoz a.k.a. Helen Sanders a.k.a. Ben Cat (1920–1987)." In Bullough 2002a, 145–47.

Sagarin, Edward. 1966. *Structure and Ideology in an Association of Deviants*. Ph.D. diss., New York University.

———. 1969. *Odd Man In: Societies of Deviants in America*. Chicago: Quadrangle Books.

Saunders, Judith M. 2002. "Stella Rush a.k.a Sten Russell (1925–). In Bullough 2002a, 135–44.

Sears, James T. 2006. *Behind the Mask of the Mattachine: The Hal Call Chronicles and the Early Movement for Homosexual Emancipation*. Binghamton, N.Y.: Harrington Park Press.

Shilts, Randy. 1993. *Conduct Unbecoming: Gays and Lesbians in the U.S. Military*. New York: St. Martin's Press.

Slade, Eric. 2001. *Hope along the Wind: The Life of Harry Hay*. Portland, Oreg.: Eric Slade Productions. Eric Slade, director; Eric Slade and Jack Walsh, producers. First broadcast on WGBH-TV in Boston on June 17, 2002, and KQED-TV in San Francisco on June 28, 2002.

Slater, Don. 1966. "Protest on Wheels." *Tangents* 1, no. 8 (May): 4–8.

———. 1970. "You've Come a Long Way from Being Gay, Baby." *Tangents* (January–March): 2, 30.

Soule, Thomas. 2006. "Look Us in the Eye." *Orange County and Long Beach Blade*. October, pp. 14–20.

Strait and Associates. 1964. *The Lavender Lexicon: Dictionary of Gay Words and Phrases*. San Francisco: Strait and Associates.

Streitmatter, Rodger. 1995. *Unspeakable: The Rise of the Gay and Lesbian Press in America*. Boston: Faber and Faber.

Takahama, Valerie. 1998. "Alive and Writing." *Orange County Register*. Show Monday section. August 19, p. 4.

Thompson, Mark. 1987. "Harry Hay: A Voice from the Past, a Vision for the Future." In *Gay Spirit: Myth and Meaning*, ed. Mark Thompson, 182–99. New York: St. Martin's Press.

Thompson, Merritt M. [Thomas M. Merritt, Ph.D.]. 1933. *The History of Education*. New York: Barnes & Noble.

——. 1969. Reminiscence of a Friend of ONE. *ONE letter* 14, no. 10 (October).

Timmons, Stuart. 1986. "The Future of the Past: Who Controls Gay History?" *The Advocate* (May 27): 30–33.

——. 1990. *The Trouble with Harry Hay: Founder of the Modern Gay Movement*. Los Angeles: Alyson Publications.

——. 2000. Personal Communication: "Eulogy for Dale Jennings." Los Angeles: ONE Institute and Archives.

Turner, Victor. 1969. *The Ritual Process: Structure and Anti-Structure*. Chicago: Aldine.

——. 1974. *Dramas, Fields, and Metaphors: Symbolic Action in Human Society*. Ithaca, N.Y.: Cornell University Press.

Weston, Kath. 1991. *Families We Choose: Lesbians, Gays, and Kinship*. New York: Columbia University Press.

White, C. Todd. 1998. "On the Pragmatics of an Androgynous Style of Speaking (from a Transsexual's Perspective)." *World Englishes* 17, no. 2 (July): 215–23.

——. 2002a. "Dale Jennings: ONE's Outspoken Advocate." In Bullough 2002a, 83–93.

——. 2002b. "Jim Schneider: ONE's Guardian Angel." In Bullough 2002a, 115–20.

——. 2007. "Vern as an Activist in the Gay, Lesbian, Bisexual, and Transgender Community." *Memorial Celebration for the Life of Vern L Bullough 1928–2006*. Amherst, N.Y.: Center for Inquiry.

Williams, Walter L. 1986. *The Sprit and the Flesh: Sexual Diversity in American Indian Tradition*. Boston: Beacon Press.

Winn, Dilys. 1997. *Murder Ink: The Mystery Reader's Companion*. New York: Workman.

Index

C. Todd White is visiting assistant professor in the Department of Anthropology at James Madison University. White received his Ph.D. in anthropology from the University of California in May 2005. He is the editor of *San Dieguito and La Jolla: Collected Papers of Claude N. Warren on the Archaeology of Southern California* and coeditor of *Before Stonewall: Activists for Gay and Lesbian Rights in Historic Contexts.*

The University of Illinois Press
is a founding member of the
Association of American University Presses.

Composed in 10.5/13 Adobe Minion Pro
with Memphis and Latin display
by Jim Proefrock
at the University of Illinois Press
Designed by Dennis Roberts
Manufactured by Sheridan Books, Inc.

University of Illinois Press
1325 South Oak Street
Champaign, IL 61820-6903
www.press.uillinois.edu